The South Asia File

A Colonial Paradigm of Indian History
Altering the Mindset of the Indic People

Narrated by

Kosla Vepa

An abbreviated version of this essay was presented on January 27th, 2006 at Milpitas, CA

Originals

Delhi 110052

Published by
Originals
A-6, Nimri Commercial Centre,
Ashok Vihar Phase-IV,
Delhi-110052
Phone: 011-27302453
e-mail: info@Lppindia.com
www.Lppindia.com

Indic Studies Foundation,
948 Happy Valley Rd.,
Pleasanton, Ca 94566, USA
Email:webmaster@indicstudies.us
http://www.indicstudies.us

ISBN 978-8454-085-7

Printed in India

In India I found a race of mortals living upon the Earth, but not adhering to it, inhabiting cities, but not being fixed to them, possessing everything but possessed by nothing.- Apollonius Tyanaeus, Greek Thinker and Traveler, 1st Century AD

This work is dedicated to the revitalization of the Sarasvati River valleys and the guardian deity of knowledge, the Goddess Sarasvati who protects us all from the state of Avidya or lack of knowledge.

Territory ruled by the British East India Company experienced the first Bengal famine of 1770. An estimated 10 million people died.

Throughout the entire course of recorded European history, from the remote times of which the Homeric poems preserve the dim tradition down to the present moment, there has occurred no calamity at once so sudden and of such appalling magnitude as the famine which in the spring and summer of 1770 nearly exterminated the ancient civilization of Bengal. It presents that aspect of preternatural vastness which characterizes the continent of Asia and all that concerns it. The Black Death of the fourteenth century was, perhaps, the most fearful visitation which has ever afflicted the Western world. But in the concentrated misery which it occasioned the Bengal famine surpassed it, even as the Himalayas dwarf by comparison the highest peaks of Switzerland. It is, moreover, the key to the history of Bengal during the next forty years; and as such, merits, from an economical point of view, closer attention than it has hitherto received. Lower Bengal gathers in three harvests each year; in the spring, in the early autumn, and in December, the last being the great rice-crop, the harvest on which the sustenance of the people depends. Through the year 1769 there was great scarcity, owing to the partial failure of the crops of 1768, but the spring rains appeared to promise relief, and in spite of the warning appeals of provincial officers, the government was slow to take alarm, and continued rigorously to enforce the land-tax. But in September the rains suddenly ceased. Throughout the autumn there ruled a parching drought; and the rice-fields, according to the description of a native superintendent of Bishenpore" "became like fields of dried straw." "Nevertheless, the government at Calcutta made with one lamentable exception, hereafter to be noticed" no legislative attempt to meet the consequences of this dangerous condition of things. "All through the stifling summer of 1770 the people went on dying. The husbandmen sold their cattle; they sold their implements of agriculture; they devoured their seed-grain; they sold their sons and daughters, till at length no buyer of children could be found; they ate the leaves of trees and the grass of the field; and in June, 1770, the Resident at the Durbar affirmed that the living were feeding on the dead. Day and night a torrent of famished and disease-stricken wretches poured into the great cities. At an early period of the year pestilence had broken out. In March we find small-pox at Moorshedabad, where it glided through the vice-regal mutes, and cut off the Prince Syfut in his palace. The streets were blocked up with promiscuous heaps of the dying and dead. Interment could not do its work quickly enough; even the dogs and jackals, the public scavengers of the East, became unable to accomplish their revolting work, and the multitude of mangled and festering corpses at length threatened the existence of the citizens.....

John Fiske, American philosopher in The Unseen World, Chapter IX, THE FAMINE OF 1770 IN BENGAL. see also The Annals of Rural Bengal. By W. W. Hunter. Vol. I. The Ethnical Frontier of Lower Bengal, with the Ancient Principalities of Beerbhoom and Bishenpore, second Edition. New York: Leypoldt and Holt. 1868. 8vo., pp. xvi., 475.

Contents

List of Plates

Foreword

At a time when politics is overriding on history, it is refreshing to find the beginning of a welcome politics-exposing and scientific-data-emphasizing new trend in Indian historiography. This trend is being set up by an emerging group of scientists and technologists who want to correct, and guard against, the politically polluted Indian historical writings. The author of the present book, Dr. Kosla Vepa, is a distinguished member of this new trendsetting group.

Dr. Vepa and other members of this group happen to have an advantage over professional historians. In a situation of paradigm shift, necessitated by discovery of basically new kind of data and evidence, the professional historians (the writer of these lines included), find it arduous in coming out of the mould in which they have been cast. Since unlearning is a task ever more difficult than learning, it is irksome for them to unlearn much what their gurus had taught them. As against it, Dr. Vepa and his batch of 'unburdened historians' are more open to new ideas and alternative thinking. Furthermore, being science-oriented, they are intrinsically more objective and exact in their approach to historical problems and issues.

To be sure, they are not trespassers in the discipline of history, as some think. We need to remember that in the past too several non-professional historians like K. P. Jayaswal and D. D. Kosambi, coming from various fields as law and mathematics and sharing different paradigms of history, have made significant contributions to Indian history. What is new is that it is for the first time that we have before us such a rich harvest of historical literature from the pen of non-professional historians grounded in science and technology.

Dr. Vepa is genuinely sensitive to the severe damage that the colonial paradigm of Indian history has done to Indic psyche. Much of it is beyond restitution, no doubt. Nevertheless, he is right in thinking that exposing the politics behind the emergence and dominance of the colonial paradigm of Indian history will go a long way in removing the distortions that a false history has created in socio-political mindset of Indic people.

Frankly speaking, the colonial paradigm of Indian history is not a paradigm in the real sense of the term, for it did not have a natural inception. Paradigms in history, or in any other discipline, change after long intervals in a natural course. A paradigm comes under crisis when it fails to provide satisfactory solutions to some of the most fundamental problems in the field. If the crisis intensifies, it gives rise to a new paradigm. This is how paradigms change. It is worth noting that the traditional paradigm of Indian history, which the colonial paradigm tried to replace, never came under any such crisis. In fact, it exists even today. The colonial paradigm is clearly an artificial creation of the British not to 'judge' history impartially (as was the tradition in the traditional paradigm), but to 'plead' it to foster colonial interests.

As Dr. Vepa rightly observes, Britain was terribly terrified and alarmed when it had a glimpse of Indian national solidarity during the tumultuous days of the uprising of 1857. This led her to realize that the only way to maintain its hold on India was to change the very mindset of the Indic people. She adopted several measures to do it. Rewriting of Indian history was a major step in this direction. Efforts were made to show: that Indic civilization was ever poor and fragmented; that Indic people were inherently passive, always needing foreign stimulus (mostly in the form of invasions) to arouse them; that both, the Sanskrit language as well as the Vedic culture, were foreign imports; and, that India was a dark hole of ignorance till all worthwhile knowledge reached here from the West. The kind of colonial paradigm of Indian history that emerged in this process is best commented on by Dr. Sarvepalli Radhakrishnan. "The West tried its best", writes he (*Indian Philosophy* 2:779), "to persuade India that its philosophy is absurd, its art puerile, its poetry uninspired, its religion grotesque and its ethics barbarous."

Besides describing in detail the various aspects of the paradigm of Indian history that the British invented and perpetuated, Dr. Vepa deals also with the other means that the colonial overlord adopted to pollute the psyche of Indic people. He refers, in this connection, to acts such as encouraging the formation of a Sunni Islamic power which would gradually spread its influence all over the country, reinventing social hierarchy, institutionalizing a vastly expanded Caste system, refashioning of Indian legal system, etc. His book contains as many as eleven highly informative relevant appendices making it by far the most comprehensive work on the subject published till date. His style of narrating relevant developments is unique. It makes things vivid and crystal-clear to even a layman.

Dr. Vepa refrains from being pedantic. In fact, his aim is to convey his message to a far larger audience than the one constituted by professional and non-professional historians alone.

I have great pleasure in recommending the perusal of this nice book to everyone interested in changing fortunes of Indic people and Indian history.

Shivaji,

Prof. Shivaji Singh, Ph.D.,

National President, ABISY

Gorakhpur, U.P., India

July 15, 2008.

Preface

It is by now widely recognized that the 200 years of Colonial rule coupled with almost 600 years of domination by Islamic sultans and Padshahs, prior to the arrival of the British, has had a profoundly adverse impact on the material well being of the Indic populace and has altered the political map of the Indian subcontinent. A sustained holocaust of enormous numbers of people in the tens of millions, the eventual impoverishment of the populace and the creation of a Sunni Islamic center of power in the subcontinent were the most visible or well known aspects of this period.

What is less well appreciated is the equally profound impact this had on the mind of the Indic. The colonial overlord changed the way the Indic looked at himself in myriad different ways. He rewrote the history of India, refashioned the legal system, reinvented the social hierarchy, institutionalized a vastly expanded Caste system, and divorced him from the language of his ancestors, all this in the space of less than 200 years. This presentation is a narrative of some of these efforts both during the colonial period as well as the years after independence It is a singularly fascinating story, albeit not as well publicized, of how the shaping of the Indic mind and the Indic society has gone on for the last 2 centuries to the point where it touches the lives of most Indics today. I am confident that this narrative will be as fascinating to others as it was to me, when I first became aware of it. This is the textual depiction of the power point presentation made on January 27, 2006 at the Swagat Restaurant, Milpitas, CA under the aegis of India Research Foundation. This essays is broadly divided into three phases. Primarily a British Endeavor.

Phase I Pre Independence (till 1947),

Phase II Post Independence (till 1998),

Primarily orchestrated by Britain during the 50's and 60's with USA playing an increasingly dominant role especially after 1971.

Phase III Recent initiatives

Essentially a development initiated by ABV's 'natural allies' speech at UN. His predecessors Rajiv, P V Narasimha Rao and even Gandhi, tried but were unsuccessful in overcoming hostility of entrenched foreign policy mandarins in the US State Department.

I acknowledge with heartfelt thanks the immense amount of work that went into the presentation by many associates in IRF including but not restricted to Arun Sharma, Ratnendra Pandey, Durvasula Ramana Murty, Dinesh Neelavar, Shyam Pelleti, and Shyam Prakash. The original deas for this monograph stemmed from conversations with Dinesh Neelavar spread over an extended period of time.

1. The Colonial Paradigm of Indian History

The Steel Frame

It is a tribute to the persistence and tenacity of the colonial overlords, hailing from what was then, a nondescript island of the northwest coast of the vast Eurasian landmass, that the prevailing paradigm on the origins and chronology of the Indic civilization is largely constructed by them. This is all the more astonishing, when we ponder on the fact that their domination of the subcontinent, which had a tradition going back several millennia lasted less than 2 centuries. Such a paradigm which we shall define as the Colonial Paradigm, while substantially erroneous, is posited on certain assumptions.

> The key assumption is that the Indic[1] civilization that remains extant has been brought into the area by migrating races such as the Aryans, and in fact some would argue, that such a statement holds also for the so called Dravidians of India[2].
>
> The second assumption implicit in all the assertions made by Occidentals about India is that no date for any significant scientific advance should be attributed to the Indics prior to the Golden age of Greece beginning in 600 BCE.

According to such a narrative everything that was worth preserving has been handed down to us over the centuries by migrations, within the last 3 1/2 millennia, into the subcontinent, from somewhere else. It is also true that the history that is taught the children of India today

---

1. We will define the adjective Indic (as in Indic civilization) to be inclusive of all the people who derived their civilization from the Dhaarmic traditions of the Indian subcontinent.. For the most part we will restrict ourselves to the subset of those residing in the subcontinent most of the present day Afghanistan and some eastern regions of present day Iran.

2. See Appendix K.

is vastly at variance with the puranic accounts handed down to us over several millennia. It is to state it without any embellishments, a revised history that is completely at odds with the traditional history of India. Even so great an effort as *the History and Culture of the Indian people* edited by RC Majumdar, the most famous of Indian historians at the time of Independence accepts the basic framework of the History of India as revised by the British colonialists. Fifty years after independence the narrative has not changed and the banner of the colonial version of history is now borne by the Indian left including the Communists and the rump of the Congress party left behind after successive defections from its fold and whose only common ideology is the adulation of the descendants of Jawaharlal Nehru, who share neither his scholarship nor his reverence for the land and its people.

A substantial percentage of Indians now feel they have a stake in the preservation of this false history and when confronted with the reality of their acquiescence to a false and revised history of their own land by a very recent arrival on the scene, react with irrelevant responses, such as why blame the British. The issue is not one of blame, for after all we are in great admiration of the British for the extraordinary sagacity they displayed in prolonging their rule by every artifice imaginable and in any event it is not about the British at all. One possible reason for such a stance by the Indic in our view is the so called Societal Stockholm Syndrome, which we have elaborated upon elsewhere. Another possible explanation is that long centuries of servitude as a Dhimmi in Dar ul Islam have robbed the majority of the Indic of the capability to think and reason for himself, with the result that he has internalized the notion that what others say about his history has to be more accurate than the narrative contained in the epics and the Puranas from which we derive our values and culture. We have also dealt with the systematic approach that the British used to remake the weltanschuung of the Indic and to create an international image of the Indic that is much at variance with reality, and the success they achieved in the resulting internalization of these views by the Indic himself in our essay titled the South Asia File. This monograph is an elaboration of that essay.

In a related study, we document the motivations of 2 classes of individuals. One category belonged to individuals who made it a lifelong passion to study the Indic people and their achievements in sciences and the arts and in the process undertook a dangerous and long journey in order to satisfy their curiosity. The other category belongs to those who were influenced considerably by the work of the

Indic ancients. The study is startling in that the current disdain with which the Indic is held in the post colonial era is a development that occurred mainly in the last 200 years and that for most of our recorded history the Indic has been held in high esteem by the denizens of the globe. It appears the British had no small part in assiduously cultivating such a picture of the Indic. We say this because substantial numbers of scholars from Britain have expressed their disdain for the contributions of the Indics in unequivocal terms. But the pattern of spending a lifetime studying the Indics for a lifetime and imbibing their knowledge and then subsequently belittling their achievements that was first exhibited by the Afghan scholar Al Biruni (a very rare instance of such behavior in the ancient and medieval world) is more prevalent in recent times. To the extent that the contributions of the ancient Indics are held in high esteem by the occidentals, after the advent of colonial conquest, it is because it was understood that these were contributions made by the so called Aryans immediately after arrival in the subcontinent and that such a creative and inventive spark was extinguished shortly thereafter. Exemplifying such a viewpoint, we quote W W Rouse Ball, the historian of mathematics.[3]

> 'The Arabs had considerable commerce with India, and a knowledge of one or both of the two great Hindoo works on algebra had been obtained in the Caliphate of Al-Mansur (754-775 AD) though it was not until fifty or seventy years later that they attracted much attention. The algebra and arithmetic of the Arabs were largely founded on these treatises, and I therefore devote this section to the consideration of Hindoo mathematics. The Hindoos like the Chinese have pretended that they are the most ancient people on the face of the earth, and that to them all sciences owe their creation. But it is probable that these pretensions have no foundation; and in fact no science or useful art (except a rather fantastic architecture and sculpture) can be definitely traced back to the inhabitants of the Indian peninsula prior to the Aryan invasion. This seems to have taken place at some time in the fifth century or in the sixth century when a tribe of Aryans entered India by the North West part of their country. Their descendants, wherever they have kept their blood pure, may still be recognized by their superiority over the races they originally conquered; but as is the case with the modern Europeans, they found the climate trying and gradually degenerated.'

3. W.W. Rouse Ball in '*A Short account of the History of Mathematics*' Dover Publications, 1960, (Originally appeared in 1908, page, 146.

We remind our readers that such an unabashedly racist sentiment was expressed as late as the beginning of the 20th century, after the Renaissance and the Enlightenment. But it is possible that the Occidental does not judge the impact of these major historical periods in terms of the resulting boorishness of their behavior towards peoples other than their own faith or their ethnic origin.

We begin our story by turning our attention to the question of why India has been a subject of such intense interest at least over the prolonged period of over 2 millennia.

Why was India such a subject of intense study for over a period of 2 millennia?

That India has been a subject of exhaustive study and ubiquitous interest to a wide variety of peoples from all corners of the ancient and the modern world throughout the millennia is certainly not in dispute. To begin with we like to understand the various motives behind this intense interest. Was it merely intellectual curiosity? Was it really the intention to study these subjects in order that they may be critiqued extensively and then rubbished as inconsequential to the progress of humankind? Was it a curiosity into the origins of the European languages and history, given that the oldest and most prolific literature of antiquity was in Sanskrit and Pali? We feel the answers were unique to each individual. But certain patterns are emerging among indologists particularly of British and German origin.

There are many reasons for this intense and sustained interest, not least among them being the considerable prowess of the ancient Indic in matters of scholarship, relating to the exact sciences. The Indian university system of the ancient era was world renowned and attracted students from a wide variety of countries. They were strung across the northern Indo Gangetic plain starting from Takshashila on the western end to the famed universities of Nalanda, Odantipura and Vikramshila in present day Bihar.

Indology is a name given by Indologists to the academic study of the history, languages, the sciences and cultures of the Indian subcontinent. Strictly speaking it encompasses the study of the languages, scripts of all of Asia that was influenced by Indic culture. As one can imagine this encompasses almost all of present day Asia except perhaps the very northernmost reaches of Siberia. Indology as viewed by its practitioners in Europe and America is analogous to Entomology, the science of insects, in more ways than one. In both instances the subjects of the study have little say in the matter and the scope of the study. The study is always carried out to be of benefit to the people who undertake the study and there is little or no benefit to the subject of the study who may end up sacrificing his life for the 'cause'. Indological studies or the study of the Indic people in a scholarly and serious manner can be broken up into 6 major categories in some cases with overlapping time periods.

Regions of the world where interest in Indic studies was predominant

1. **Babylonian and Greek (2500 BCE to 150 BCE).** The Semitic and Mediterranean world had ubiquitous contacts with the Indic. We are in the long drawn out process of researching this phase of Indology. Our knowledge of the facts, are meager at the moment. But the more we learn about the Greeks who for the most part hailed from Asia Minor, like the Trojans of Homer, the more it is apparent that they learned a lot of their sciences from the Indian subcontinent.

This came to a virtual stop during the heyday of the Roman Empire when it became the paramount Mediterranean power after the fall of Carthage. Rome remained a major trading partner of India but ceased to be interested in Indic scholarship. The Byzantines or the Eastern Empire centered in Constantinople, even though it has sufficient contacts ceased to evince interest after the advent of the adoption of Christianity, as India came to be associated increasingly with the Pagan practices that they were trying hard to extinguish in Europe.

2. **China and the Sinic Civilization. (2500 BCE - 1200 CE)** The interaction between the Indic and Sinic civilizations has been one of long standing, reaching back to the ancient era, and it has been a two way street, contrary to popular misconceptions. The interaction has been ubiquitous and consistent. India has borrowed much from the Sinic civilization ranging from the mundane to the sublime and vice versa. There is much work yet to be done to study the extent of this interaction, an area that was merely of tertiary interest to the European.

3. **Arab and Non Arab Islamic studies of India** (most of the Islamic savants who studied India did not speak Arabic as their native tongue, but were descended from converted central Asian and Indic civilizations (700 CE to 1200 CE). In fact it can safely be said that the Arab savants had enormous respect for the capabilities of the Indics as did the Greeks like Pythagoras and Apollonius of Tyanneous before them. The glaring exception to this statement is the cognitive dissonance

exhibited by Al Biruni, the most well known amongst the Islamic indologists, who spent a considerable portion of his life in India while expressing scathing contempt and stereotyping of Hindus in his remarks about Indians in general. That there is a contradiction between spending a great portion of one life learning from a people and then trashing them unequivocally does not seem to bother AlBiruni. Furthermore , Al Biruni even though a native of Khorasan (Khwaresm), was raised in Ghazni and spoke a dialect of Farsi known as Dari, which is spoken even today in Afghanistan. These areas of Afghanistan were in fact freshly Islamized after the last of the Hindu Shahi Kingdoms were defeated not very much earlier. The point being Al Biruni was no stranger to Hindu scholarship or culture prior to coming to India. Such an attitude of studied indifference and condescension even after a lifetime of imbibing Indic knowledge, became more and more prevalent after the advent of the colonial era and the norm rather than the exception.

The scholarly exchanges with the Khilafat came to a halt after the sack of Baghdad and Damascus by Hulagu, the grandson of the Mongol Great Khan Chinghiz, the most victorious conqueror of all time. It was also severely impacted when vast numbers of Indics were taken in slavery, especially able bodied men and women, and those with skills in the arts and sciences and equally large numbers were killed at the rate of 100,000 a day during and after a battle. So great were the numbers of Indian slaves who flooded the slave markets of Damascus that the price of slaves dropped dramatically and would seriously impact the economics of slavery as a profitable activity. Some have estimated the sustained decimation of the Indic population over the 5 centuries of Islamic domination of the subcontinent to be in the neighborhood of over 70 million people and for the first time India, always a highly densely populated country in relative terms to the rest of the globe, suffered a drop in population. The scholars retreated farther and farther to the south until they reached Kerala, which is where the Kerala School of astronomy and mathematics flourished for at least 300 years, producing such stalwarts as Nilakanta Somayaji, till the 1700's.

4. **Pre- British colonial Catholic Church dominated study of India** It may be surprising to learn that one of the first pioneers in European Indology was the 12th Century Pope, Honorius IV. Then as now, the primary focus of the study was not the scientific acquisition of knowledge but to arm themselves with enough facts to be able to convert the Indic population to Christianity.

5. **British colonial Indology (1780 CE - 2000 CE)** which was in reality dominated by German scholars. Interest in Indology only took shape and concrete direction after the British came to India, with the advent of the discovery of Sanskrit by Sir William Jones in the 1770's. Other names for Indology are Indic studies or Indian studies or South Asian studies.

The extraordinary level of interest by German scholars in Indic matters is a very interesting narrative in its own right and we need to reflect upon the highlights of this phenomenon. The German speaking people experienced a vast increase in intellectual activity at about the same time that Britain colonized India. We do not understand the specific factors that came into play during this time, other than to remark on the tremendous intellectual ferment that was running concurrently during the French revolution, and the keen interest that Napoleon showed in matters scientific including the contributions of the orient. Clearly the remarks that Sir William made about Sanskrit as well as the high-level of interest that he provoked in the Sanskrit language, contributed to the overall sense of excitement. But why was it Germany and not Britain as the center of research on the Oriental contributions. The answer lies in the intense search for nationhood that was under way in Germany during that period. When Sanskrit was discovered, and it dawned on the Germans that the antiquity of Sanskrit was very great, and that Sanskrit and German were somehow related, the Germans suddenly had an answer to the question of their own ethnic and linguistic origins. Sir Henry Maine an influential Anglo Indian scholar and former Vice Chancellor of Calcutta university, who was also on the Viceroys council, pronounced a view that many Englishman shared about the unification of Germany.

"A nation has been born out of Sanskrit"

From the beginning, the great interest that Germany showed in Sanskrit had to do with their own obsessions and questions regarding their ethnic and linguistic origins. It had very little or at least far less to do with the origin of the ancient Indic, about whom they had considerably less interest. And yet, that does not stop the proponents of the AIT in India, whose knowledge of European history appears to be rudimentary at best, from asserting that AIT is an obsession of nationalistic Hindus. Such is the fate and the perversion of history that conquered nations can aspire to Different aspects of this fascinating chapter, on the postulation of an Aryan race and its corollaries the Indo European, Indo German are described for instance by various authors Trautmann[4], Rajaram[5] and Arvidsson[6] and very recently by Prodosh Aich.[7] The interesting but curious aspect of this phenomena is that while the concept of the Aryan race has been well nigh discarded by most of the modern generation of the European world, it lingers on in the narrative of Indian History, a relic of the heyday of Europe's dominance on the world scene, when racist theories were abundant to explain this dominance as being a consequence of their heritage as an Aryan people.

In contrast to the Germans and the French, whose interest in matters Indic was catalyzed by their observance of the ubiquitous presence of the Indic civilization in South East Asia, the British had a particular reluctance to study the nature and extent of the Indic civilization. First and foremost amongst their reasons for this neglect was the reluctance to admit that a subject people had any worthwhile civilization to speak of, let alone one that was of far greater antiquity than their own. Britain was the last of the 3 major powers in Europe to have a chair in Sanskrit, and it was almost 50 years after the death of Sir William that England got around to establishing a chair at Oxford, the famous Boden chair.

> One of the criticisms leveled at the new breed of Indian historians who wish to uncover the authentic history of India after the morass of inconsistencies to which it has sunk is that they are motivated by political considerations and the further charge is made that they are 'nationalistic'. Apart from the question of any violation of ethics by being nationalistic not being apparent to me, this is to us a perplexing charge to make, since it is apparent that political motivations have been always dominant in the pursuit of Indological studies during the colonial era, right from the outset since the time of Sir William Jones, when he discovered the existence of Sanskrit. One such political motivation was the need for the European to define his identity outside the framework of Semitic traditions which dominated the religious life of Europe. The notion that the North European Viking owed much of his civilization to the Mediterranean

---

4. Trautmann, Thomas, '*Aryans and British India*', 1997, University of California Press.

5. Rajaram, Navaratna, '*The Politics of History*', Voice of India, 1995.

6. Stefan Arvidsson, 2006:38 *Aryan Idols*.

7. Prodosh Aich, *Lies wirth Long Legs*, 2006, Samskrti, New Delhi.

Semite was not palatable to most of the elite among the countries of Northern lands of Europe for reasons which we do not have the time to go into now. So, the discovery of Sanskrit was accompanied by a big sigh of relief that the languages of Europe did not after all derive from Hebrew but from an ancestor language which was initially assumed to be Sanskrit. In the immediate aftermath of the discovery of Sanskrit by Sir William Jones, there was a great gush of admiration and worship of the sublime nature of the Sanskrit texts such as Sakuntala. But as the European realized that the present day practitioners of Sanskrit were not blonde and blue-eyed (remember ideas of racial superiority were dominant in 18th century Europe despite the advent of the enlightenment and the renaissance) this was found to be equally unpalatable.

The European indologist therefore came upon the ingenious explanation that the Sanskritic culture of the subcontinent was not native to the subcontinent but was impregnated by a small band of nomadic Viking like marauders who then proceeded to transform themselves within the short space of 200 years into the intellectual class of India. This hypothesis (because that is what it was) had of course no basis in fact, but it served the purpose and killed several birds with one stone. It denied India the autocthonous legacy of the dominant culture of the subcontinent, and helped create a schism in the Indian body politic, and further implied that the native Indics were incapable of original thought and certainly was not capable of producing a language like Sanskrit. It filled the obsessive need during those decades that the European had for an ancestor that was not Semitic in origin. Lo and behold the ancestor did not come from India but from a long lost Shangrila of whom there were no survivors (so that their hypothesis could never be contradicted). Thus was born the mythical Aryan, whose only qualification was that he should hail from a land that was anywhere but India, preferably from a region not very densely inhabited or conscious of their antiquity. Further it gave the excuse for the British to claim that they were indeed the later day version of the Aryans destined to lord it over lesser, more unfortunate people by reason of the fact that they were Aryans. See for instance (Trautmann (1997) or Chakrabarti (1997)..

In short, the study of India, during the colonial era has always been accompanied by a healthy dose of imperialist dogma and by disdain for a people who they felt could so easily be vanquished in battle by handful of Englishmen. This is in addition to the normal human tendency to exhibit a degree of the 'Not Invented Here' syndrome or the propensity to devalue the acquisition of knowledge by people and civilizations other than their own. This is a train of thought that needs to be explored further, but we do not wish to be sidetracked from the main topic. We hasten to add that the fundamental scholarly impulse and intellectual curiosity that drives most scholars still motivates a substantial section of the indologists, regardless of nationality, despite much pressure from European academia to toe the line and not to stray from the conventional wisdom. But this stream of objective scholars died out pretty soon after and became almost extinct in the nineteenth century, and in general, with a few exceptions amongst the French, the European Indologists toed the party line that Indic contributions were shallow and insubstantial.

In fact the British presence in India was steadily increasing long before the Battle of Plassey in 1757 CE, but so great was the insularity of the colonial overlord that it took almost three hundred years for a relatively well educated scholar like Sir William Jones to show up in India after Vasco da Gama landed of the coast of Goa in 1492 CE, and notice the similarities between Sanskrit and the European languages. Prodosh Aich has done extensive research into primary sources and has come to the conclusion that the vaunted linguistic scholarship of Sir William was to put it mildly much exaggerated. We shall examine the background of Sir William especially his early years to see wherein lay the truth.

But the discovery of Sanskrit by Sir William and the coming of the British had a terminally fatal effect on the conduct of scientific studies in India. It cut off the Indic from his own native source of traditional learning and replaced it with the traditions of a land far away with which he had no physical contact, and could not relate; with the result that literacy fell to 6% at the turn of the 20th century. Education was tightly controlled by the government and all support to schools that did not teach English was summarily stopped, except in states that were ruled by a local Maharajah such as Travancore Cochin, Baroda and Mysore. India was turned into a vast Gulag where no ideas other than those of the British were allowed to penetrate and the Indian was effectively barred from traveling to foreign lands, except on a one way trip to a distant land as indentured labor, lest they return with the subversive notions of freedom and democracy which as Churchill remarked on more than one occasion were not applicable to the subject populations of their Colonies. So great was the travel restriction that the Indic internalized this consequence of the rule of the Colonial

Overlord, to be a characteristic of the assumed native propensity to aversion of adventure and exploration. There was no money allocated for research and no encouragement of savants, who had little opportunity to pursue further research. So the steady supply of Indic scientists which lasted till about 1780 CE finally died out and Indic science was almost extinguished from the land.

This is not to say that there have been no benefits accrued from the change in the medium of instruction to English. Due to the fortuitous circumstance that a substantial part of the new world now spoke English, placed Indic youngsters at an advantageous situation when it came to getting admission to graduate studies in North America. This coupled with the investment in higher education made by Jawaharlal Nehru India's first Prime Minister catapulted India into the leadership ranks of countries who were players in the new Information Technology. But the negatives remain. The vast majority of the Indian population is not a participant in this new bounty, because they do not have the access to the expensive schools that purvey access to such an education.

The most telling impact of the newly coined endeavor called philology, that was the result of this unwanted gush of attention engendered ever since the discovery of Sanskrit, was the manner in which the Indic was viewed by the rest of the world and even more importantly the internalization of the British and European view of India, by the average literate English educated Indic. Till then the Indic was widely respected throughout the world and his geographical origin was synonymous with scholarship. Today, it is commonplace in India to deride somebody who expresses pride in his tradition and his civilization as being jingoistic. The Colonial overlord went to extraordinary lengths to undermine the Civilizational commonalities amongst the people of India by various and diverse means. Anything that had a negative impact was played to the hilt. The antiquity of Indian history was systematically whittled away and the new dates had to conform to the notion that India did not contribute anything of value to civilization and that all she knew in the area of science and mathematics, was learned from the Greeks. The Indian was uniformly characterized as a shiftless indolent individual with very few redeeming qualities.

So great was the change and so lasting in its effect that today vast numbers of Indian youth have almost the same opinion of India and Indic traditions that the Colonial overlords had, of India in the eighteenth and nineteenth century. There has been a massive change in the psyche of the Indic, much of it for the worse, a fact that was brought out in vivid portrayals by V S Naipaul when he coined the phrase 'the wounded civilization' in his references to the subcontinent.

Examples of the internalization of the European views of India abound in India today. Even eminent Indian historians like RC Majumdar have expressed some of these views in writing without substantiating how they arrived at such conclusions. We give below a sample. It is ironic that these viewpoints are usually expressed by Indics rather than non Indics.

Table 1 The General British view of the Indic during the Colonial Era
The Caricaturization of the Indic
There is a strong undercurrent in the Occident that it Is the religious beliefs of the Indic that are the root cause of his misfortunes.
The Indic is inherently incapable of adventurous behavior and will not venture beyond the confines of the Indian subcontinent (Kaalapaani syndrome).
The Indic is incapable of original, rational and creative ideas. The Indic is incapable of independent thinking and is unquestioning in his adherence to authoritarian diktats such as those in the Vedic texts and is only capable of rote learning (presuming it is conceded that the Indic is capable of learning at all).
The caste system is an artifact of the Indic religious belief system, and that the Indic is inherently opposed to egalitarian ideas and is wedded to the racial and ethnic stratification of his own society.
The Indic is especially unique and egregious in the manner in which he exploits his fellow Indics.
The Indic is fundamentally not tuned to making progress and advancing in the modern world, and is lost in an ancient mind set.
Everything good and worthwhile in the Indian subcontinent has been imported by the invaders, and the only indigenous characteristics are those like caste that are inherent to the Indic civilization.
The Indic is fatalistic and will not make an effort to change his destiny which is written in stone the moment he is born.

The Indic is lazy and indolent
The Indic has no sense of history and is even poorer at keeping records of his historical past
As a consequence of the above the Indic is socially backward, possibly morally corrupt and perennially hence dependent upon Westernization to reform the current problems in Indian society.

From such a viewpoint it was indeed a short step to assume as Karl Marx did, that the Indic was destined to be ruled by others. The germ of such a vast change in psyche was the goal of Thomas Babington Macaulay and he would have been rather pleased to see the consequences of his minute on education where he proposed changing the medium of instruction to English in the 1830's in order to produce a class of Brown Englishman who would occupy positions intermediate between those of the Colonial overlords and the unwashed masses of the subcontinent. In the same vein, HH Wilson, the first occupant of the Boden Chair in Sanskrit, wrote as follows,

"From the survey which has been submitted to you, you will perceive that the practical religion of the Hindus is by no means a concentrated and compact system, but a heterogeneous compound made up of various and not infrequently incompatible ingredients, and that to a few ancient fragments it has made large and unauthorized additions, most of which are of an exceedingly mischievous and disgraceful nature. It is, however, of little avail yet to attempt to undeceive the multitude; their superstition is based upon ignorance, and until the foundation is taken away, the superstructure, however crazy and rotten, will hold together."

Power over a vast area like India does strange things to people, one of which is the loss of 'common sense', not to mention the loss of humility, and one can see the process of creating the mythological Indian has already begun as early as 1833, the process of remaking the Indic mindset had commenced in earnest. There is an immense irony in this state of affairs and that is that India is well on its way to becoming the largest English speaking nation in the planet. If present trends continue the number of English speaking people residing in India will exceed that of the Unites States within 20 years[8]. The

8. I mention this important artifact not in glee or in adulation of Lord Maccaulay, nor even in alarm, but merely to reflect on the consequences. Our preference would have been the gradual introduction of English and certainly not as a mandatory requirement, which resulted as we shall see shortly in dire consequences.

implications are enormous. For instance, India will become the largest producer of English books in the planet, a state of affairs that may already be true because of the huge market of South and South East Asia.

6. **Indic studies by native Indics when the Indic tradition miraculously resurrected itself shortly after the beginning of the twentieth century from an almost comatose condition (1900 CE to the present)**

So we come to the sixth and current period of Indological studies. The European, with few exceptions continues to study the Indic past as if the present day practitioners did not exist. In this the indologists tried to emulate Egyptology and the study of Meso American civilizations. In both these instances, the Europeans could say anything they liked without being challenged by survivors of the tradition and get away with it, because there were no survivors after the routine scourging of native populations using the well entrenched twin techniques - first with the sword and then the Holy book to erase all prior traditions, as well as inflicting upon them diseases which effectively decimated their populations. They studied India in the same vein, making untenable assumptions and hypotheses and then indulged in circular arguments that anything that does not fit the assumption that they made, is invalid.

But the Hindu is a strange creature, imbued with the genetic longevity of the cockroach and the intellectual hardiness that comes from millennia of tradition devoted to scholarship. Indics were the first to codify the principle of acquisition of knowledge known now by the name of Epistemology and they resisted the imposition of a history and a narrative that was substantially at variance from their Puranic traditions. These principles of acquisition of knowledge are alluded to in my booklet on Dhaarmik traditions and include Perception and Observation (Pratyaksha), Anumaana (inference), Comparison and Analogy (Upamaana), shabda (acceptance, though not necessarily uncritical acceptance, of the Word as manifested in the ancient scriptures, Arthapaati (implication) and anupalabdi (non apprehension and skepticism in the face of non-apprehension).

The systematic approach, combined with the methodology of learning recommended by the Upanishads namely, the triune method of *shravana*, *manana* and *nididhyasana* forms the core of the approach to all kinds of knowledge, whether It be Paara Vidya or Apaara Vidya (see Glossary). The term *Shravana* refers basically to hearing, but also includes reading, discussions and the like. *Manana* is contemplation of what has been studied or heard. *Nididhyasana* is concentration on the subject to the exclusion of everything else. It may not always be possible or advisable to practice multitasking, which has become de rigueur in this age of rapid technological change. Usually, the initial knowledge about anything has to be acquired through a guru, because he is the dependable authority on the subject. *Manana* and *Nididhyasana* depend on one's own effort, with some guidance from the guru. The role of the teacher is only as a guidepost. The journey has to be undertaken by us with our own efforts.

It is this comprehensive approach to the acquisition of knowledge that has given the edge to the Hindu Vis a Vis other civilizations over the millennia and is catalyzing the reclamation of the high ground in the field of Indic studies. This is not to say that the Modern Indic should ignore the work done by others in this field, but it does mean the converse that indologists outside India, can no longer ignore the legitimate claims to scholarship of Indic savants in the study of their own History. Let us hope that as we go from here that he, the Western Indologist will abandon the politically motivated approach that he has taken till hitherto and will accord the discerning Indic savant the same consideration and apply objective criteria to the studies undertaken by those who are not of a European background. Certainly it means that he should eschew the use of the convenient and stereotypical characterization of anything that he does not like as being a product or a conspiracy of the Hindutva or a Hindu nationalist.

In reality, there is a basic contradiction in the western characterization of the Hindu and the pejorative use of the word Hindu nationalist. The Hindu faith or Sanaatana Dharma has often been characterized in my view with adequate justification, as being too eclectic and all encompassing. In fact in the quote above Hyman Wilson characterizes it as being 'heterogeneous and contradictory'. And yet, there is the constant and ubiquitous drumbeat in the use of the word Hindu nationalist, which implies an exclusionary stance and narrow mindedness. To the followers of Plato and Socrates in the Occidental world, I ask, well, which is it, eclectic and all encompassing weltanschuung, or exclusionist and narrow minded.

Eurocentrism and Mathematics

For some, their Eurocentrism (or Greco-centrism) is so deeply entrenched that they cannot bring themselves to face the idea of independent developments in early Indian mathematics, even as a remote possibility.

The geographical location of India was a key factor in the exchanges which India had with various regions of the world. This enabled her from the very beginning to play an important role in the transmission and diffusion of ideas. The traffic was often two-way, with Indian ideas and achievements traveling abroad as easily as those from outside entering her own consciousness. Some sources even credit Pythagoras with having traveled as far as India in search of knowledge, which may explain some of the close parallels between Indian and Pythagorean philosophy and religion. These parallels include:

A belief in the transmigration of souls;

The theory of four elements constituting matter;

The structure of the religio-philosophical character of the Pythagorean fraternity, which resembled Buddhist monastic orders; and

The contents of the mystical speculations of the Pythagorean schools, which bear a striking resemblance of the Hindu Upanishads.

According to Greek tradition, Pythagoras, Thales, Empedocles, Anaxagoras, Democritus and others undertook journey to the East to study philosophy and science. By the time Ptolemaic Egypt and Rome's Eastern empire had established themselves just before the beginning of the Common era, Indian civilization was already well developed, having founded three great religions ş Hinduism, Buddhism and Jainism ş and expressed in writing the massive literature (of the Veda, the Brahmanas, the Upanishads, the Purana), as well as fundamental theories in science and medicine. There are scattered references to Indian science in the literary sources from countries to the west of India after the time of Alexander.

Transmittal of Knowledge—Was there theft of Intellectual Property

There is another point to be made about the direction in which knowledge was transmitted. Many have been the individuals from other parts of the world who studied at Indian universities like Nalanda, Takshashila, Vikramshila, and Odantipura till the 12th century. It was a rare instance where they would go back and denigrate the knowledge they had so acquired or the land they acquired it from, and in fact went out of their way to eulogize the education they received at these locations which were studded all along the Gangetic valley, but particularly so in Vihara (Bihar). However all this changed during the16th century when the Society of Jesus (Jesuits) sent highly educated (for those days) individuals, the number sometimes exceeding 70 or 80 at times at any given point in time, whose sole purpose was to extract as much information from the people who practiced such skills, like Jyotish Pandits and engage in intellectual property theft. What defines such activity as theft? If the recipient does not acknowledge the source of his teaching then it is fair to call it theft.

Differing standards for Claims for transmission of knowledge

In fact no study of this kind would be complete without a reference to the differing standards by which Occidentalists have concluded whether a particular discipline was imported or exported out of the Occident. We quote C K Raju[9]

> "However, we have also seen that the standard of evidence is not uniform, but varies with the claim being made. The standard of evidence required for an acceptable claim of transmission of knowledge from East to West, is different from the standards of evidence required for a similar claim of transmission of knowledge from West to East. Thus there is always the possibility that similar things could have been discovered independently, and that western historians are still arguing about this. even in so obvious a case as that of Copernicus. Finally we have seen that this racist double standard of evidence is not an incidental error, but is backed by centuries of racist tradition, religious exhortations by Popes, and by legal interpretations authoritatively handed down by, say the US Supreme Court."

Priority and the possibility of contact always establish a socially acceptable case for transmission from west to East, but priority and definite contact never seems to establish an acceptable case for transmission from East to West, for there is always the possibility, that similar things could have been discovered independently.

"Hence to establish transmission we propose to adopt a legal standard of evidence, good enough to hang a person for murder. Briefly we propose that the case for any must be established on the grounds of

1. Motivation,
2. opportunity,
3. Circumstantial evidence and
4. Documentary evidence.

---

9. C K Raju '*Cultural Foundations of Mathematics*', Centre for Studies in Civilizations (PHISPC), Pearson Education, 2007, p. 313.

The importance of epistemological continuity has been repeatedly stressed above; any such claim must also take into account epistemological issues"

Examples abound, especially when it comes to areas such as Mathematics, Astronomy and Linguistics and the discovery of the origin of scripts. In particular we cite the instance of David Pingree's PhD thesis titled 'Materials for the Transmission of Greek astrology to India'. Notice he does not ask whether such a transmittal ever happened. That is a given, a hypothesis that needs not be proven. This is another example of a circular argument. Assume the answer in your initial hypotheses and then claim that it is an incontrovertible fact.

The inconsistencies in the Occidentalist Paradigm of Indian history

What are the major contentions and the resulting contradictions in the Occidentalist (an Occidental who studies the civilizations and the linguistics of the languages of the orient) chronology of India.

Table The inconsistencies in the current narrative of Indian history
The inherent contradictions of the Aryan Invasion Theory by the mythic and yet to be identified Aryan race.
The insistence on clinging to a racial terminology even when it is widely discredited and abandoned elsewhere
The insistence that Indic astronomy, geometry and mathematics was not autochthonous to India but was borrowed from the Greek or the Babylonians
The origin of the Brahmi script becomes a victim of the 'anywhere but India' syndrome
Devaluation and denigration of the extent of the ancient Indic contribution to Mathematics and Astronomy
Dating of the Mahabharata
Dating of the Satapatha Brahmana
Dating of the Veda
Dating of the Vedanga Jyotisha
Dating of the Sulva sutras

The beginning of the Vikrama era
The dating of the Buddha
The dating of the Arthashastra
The dating of Chandragupta Maurya
The dating of Panini's Ashtadhyayi and consequentially the dating of Panini himself
The dating of Aryabhata
There are resulting inconsistencies in the chronology of the Indic historical narrative, which is now horribly mangled to fit the straightjacket of British assumptions

In discussing the individuals, one is struck by the generally, high intellectual caliber of the scholars who form the bulk of the Indologists. And yet a very high percentage were loathe to discard the prevalent racist dogma of the day, that the Indics were incapable of a high level of intellectual effort and that therefore the only explanation (of the high level of civilization in the Indian subcontinent relative to the rest of the ancient world) was that such a circumstance could only have been possible if an alien civilization had transplanted it from somewhere else, The Occidental was unable to free himself from the bondage and blindness resulting from the prejudice that the Indic was incompetent to make these discoveries.

It is also becoming increasingly clear that the initial assumptions regarding the competence and scholarship of such well known people as Sir William, Max Mýller, Franz Bopp, and many others have to be reevaluated and that the vast majority of the so called Sanskrit scholars were indifferent to mediocre scholars in the Sanskrit language and were rather presumptuous in their pronouncements on the nature, antiquity and significance of the literature that was now available to them. The extensive forensic investigation that Prodosh Aich has carried out and reported in his book called "Lies with long Legs¿, on the competency of these scholars yields some shocking facts including misrepresentation of their earned degrees and consigns most of these individuals to the category of mediocre imposters.

My objective in this monograph is not to recite a litany of grievances against the Occidental (rhymes with oriental) but to understand the great lengths that the Occidental went to in order to distort the history of India. We hope thereby to unearth the philosophical underpinning to the long and steady evolution of the

Indic civilization it breadth and what is indeed remarkable its staying power. The other great civilizations have either altered significantly or been driven extinct. There is very little left of the Greek civilization (although the west fancies itself the successor to the Greco Roman civilization. The ancient Greeks would be considered Pagans by the established churches today, and hardly any of their life style remains. It is also important to remember that most of the Greek savants were natives of Asia Minor and their life style was more akin to that of Persia than that of France or England, neither of which were pretty far along the Civilizational curve, in any event, during that period of history.

Importance of Chronology

The Indic civilization is for all intents and purposes the only one, amongst the ancients, surviving virtually intact. The Gayatri mantra and the invoking of Savitur are at least 7000 years old. It already asks for enlightenment and not for bread, because they had mastered agriculture and had no problem with adequate food. People (west of the Urals) wonder what happened to the Indus Valley civilization. Nothing dramatic happened they just moved on and their descendants became the Gujaratis, Maharashtrians and other residents of modern India. It is this unbroken continuity that rankles with the Occidental, because he is all too conscious that his own history is replete with wars (e.g. the hundred year's war between England and France), extinct civilizations, and gratuitous destruction. Hence his obsession to endow India with a similar heritage.

A false chronology leads to false conclusions about who we are as a people in very fundamental ways.. For example the Aryan Invasion Theory seeks to bestow on us a heritage which is far removed from the Vedic heritage in very significant ways and constrains our History with a timeline that is totally artificial, ignores our whole puranic history and devalues the unique nature of the culture and ethos of the subcontinent.

We who are of Indic heritage realize only too well that a mere claim of antiquity will not gain us the respect of the world. We are fully cognizant that antiquity is not even necessary to achieve dignity and respect, but it is indeed remarkable to see the great lengths that some amongst the occidentals today will go to deny us the antiquity which we feel is the right one. If indeed the occidental regards antiquity as merely incidental to his heritage or to his weltanschauung, his actions bespeak otherwise. The ferocity with which he argues against our historical heritage is only matched by the tenacity with which he would deny us a place at the table with other major powers, and that is another story unto itself.

Methodology

One of the goals of our series of seminars is to arrive at a robust methodology and associated axioms that Indic narrative of our past should adhere to. In every case we should examine the implied and explicit assumptions we make and the validity of the resulting inferences. We regard all approaches as fair game (including numismatics, deciphering the inscriptions in the sky using astronomical software that can be employed for back calculating events of the past, epigraphy where available etc. The caveat is that it must adhere to and not violate a consistent episteme or pramana. It is my firm conviction that the current history, as revised by the colonial overlord, and taught to our children worldwide does not meet the minimum standards of any episteme. I do not know of any civilization or nation that lets its history be hijacked by those who have a minimum accountability to ensure its veracity and in fact has an agenda that is very cavalier and nonchalant, if not hostile to our traditional heritage. Till the advent of independence we had an excuse that we were held on a short leash by the colonial overlord, but what is the excuse today?

We hold as canonical, the axiom that an accurate history and chronology is an essential adjunct of any civilization as it evolves into different paradigms in the future. Put simply, if we do not know our past (or have merely a vague notion of and a nonchalant interest in our past), we would be severely handicapped in evaluating the decisions we make for the future. I was always under the impression that to repeat or emphasize this tautology would be akin to preaching to the choir. I was astonished to learn that there are significant numbers who do not subscribe to this notion.

We will focus on methodologies and principles to follow, conscious as we are that in the space of 7 hours, it would amount to hubris, to attempt to rewrite the history of this multifaceted but unique heritage of the subcontinent.

A question that often occurs to most of us, and I am certain we are not unique in this respect, is to ask why the Indic civilization which had reached such lofty levels several millennia ago, has sunk to such depressed levels today. I am sure the answers to this question are manifold, but we have attempted to peel the layers of the onion to understand why we are where we are today. If we come across as placing the responsibility for such a transformation on others such as the British and the Islamic invaders, who marauded the land for over 7 centuries, that certainly is not the intent. The responsibility for being at the current state of affairs clearly lies with the people of the subcontinent, but we feel it is an obligation even a duty to seek the causes of this transformation and let the chips fall where they may. Civilization is a precious good, in the words of Will Durant, and its fragile structure and delicate fabric can easily be disturbed leading to extinction of cultures as we have seen repeatedly throughout History. The Indic civilization may have survived one onslaught but may not prove to be resistant to future such onslaughts should they occur. It behooves us therefore to seek to understand the nature of the threat(s) that the civilization faces as she enters a new millennium.

Explanatory notes

The dates associated with most of the gentlemen we will identify, especially in our sequel to this essay on the Indologists, should be regarded only as approximate at least to the nearest decade, as there were no accurate birth records prior to the 18th century. Unlike in ancient India where a birth was sometimes recorded with the appropriate Nakshatra, Tithi, Masa and Samvatsara, such access to a calendar was not easily available to the ordinary folk in Europe till well into the enlightenment and in fact the Gregorian calendar was defective till 1540 CE. As such the birthdates of most European individuals other than royalty, prior to the nineteenth century, must be regarded with circumspection and merely as an approximation.

One final comment before we begin. It is estimated that the total manuscript wealth available in India today is in the order of 5 million according to the National Mission for Manuscripts was established in February 2003, by the Ministry of Tourism and Culture, Government of India. A unique project in its program and mandate, the Mission seeks to unearth, preserve, catalog, index and make available for research the vast manuscript wealth of India.

These manuscripts cover a variety of themes, textures and aesthetics, scripts, languages, calligraphies, illuminations and illustrations. Together, they constitute the 'memory' and the DNA, of India's history, heritage and thought. These manuscripts lie scattered across the country and beyond, in numerous institutions as well as private collections, often unattended and undocumented. The National Mission for Manuscripts aims to locate, document, preserve and render these accessibletto connect India's past with its future, its memory with its aspirations. The electronic catalogue or database contains data on about three hundred thousand (300,000) manuscripts, and the database is steadily increasing day by day.

This is the case despite heavy losses due to wars, destruction and natural decay. Out of this staggering number about 1 million have been catalogued in India and perhaps another 200,000 abroad in various libraries such as the Bodleian Library in Oxford. This is by far the largest extant literature from the ancient world for any civilization. There is nothing even remotely comparable anywhere else. In one field alone, namely astronomy, the late David Pingree found so many manuscripts that he called the resulting effort at cataloguing a Census, a Census which took several volumes to compile

And yet we are told repeatedly that the ancient Indics were deficient in historical record keeping. Our riposte is the query 'relative to whom were they deficient?' Where else in the world do we find a literature going back to 4000 BCE? It is no wonder that scholars have found the study of India to be such a fertile field and continue to find it so even today.

An example of a manuscript on palm-leaf, Bihar or Nepal, 11th c., 32 ff., 5x31 cm, 2 columns, (3x27 cm), 5 lines in an early Bhujimol script, borders marked with double lines with orange pigmentation between lines, 1 miniature in text. Binding: Nepal, 11th c., carved wooden covers, decorated with 10 miniatures, poti with hole for the binding cord. Provenance: 1. Monastery in Nepal (ca. 11th c.-); 2. Sam Fogg cat. 17 (1996):40.

The immense importance of India to Britain's Empire, and to its greatness and its prosperity.

Lord Curzon, before he went out to India as Viceroy, laid great and repeated emphasis, two or three times, upon the fact of this importance of India to Britain."

India, " "he said," was the pivot of our Empire. (Hear, hear.) If this Empire lost any other part of its dominion we could survive, but if we lost India, the sun of our Empire would be set" (Times, 3/12/1898).

Lord Roberts, after retiring for good from India, said to the London Chamber of Commerce : "I rejoice to learn that you recognise how indissolubly the prosperity of the United Kingdom is bound up with the retention of that vast Eastern Empire." (Times, 25/5/1893).

He repeated "that the retention of our Eastern Empire is essential to the greatness and prosperity of the United Kingdom." (Times, 29/7/1893)

And with still more emphasis he pointed out upon what essential condition such retention of the Indian Empire depended not upon brute force ; but

however, "he said," efficient and well-equipped the army of India may be, were it indeed absolute perfection, and were its numbers considerably more than they are at present, our greatest strength must ever rest on the firm base of a united and contented India.

Quoted in "Dadabhai Naoroji: *Poverty and un-British rule in India* (1901)"

http://www.archive.org/details/povertyunbritish00naoruoft

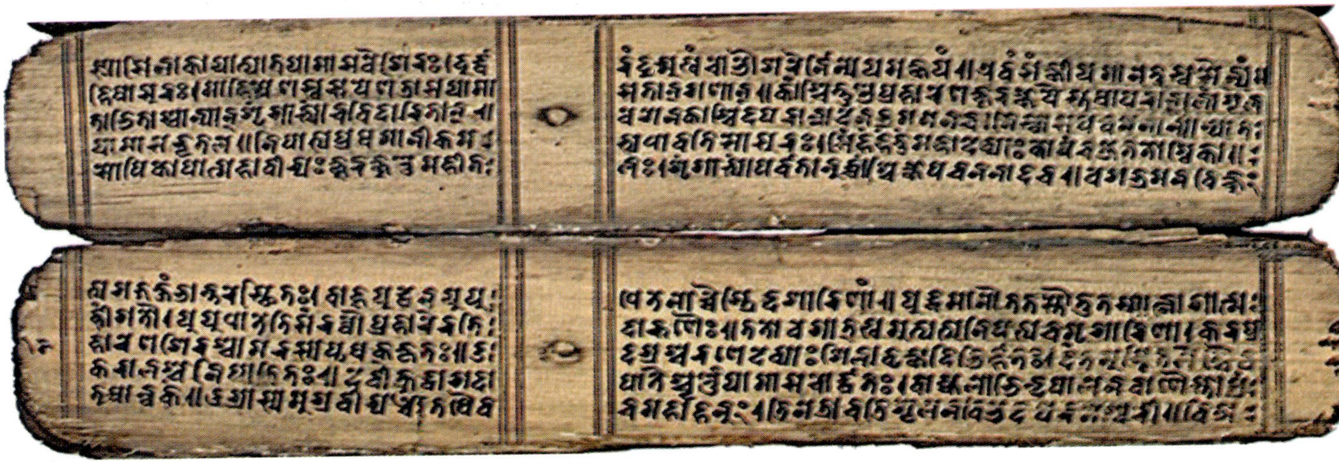

Plate 1: The Devi Mahatmya MS in Sanskrit *(facing pg. 22)*

2. The Indic Civilization and the Colonial Power

India regards herself as a Civilizational power. Such a viewpoint is not new. Many Historians including Arnold Toynbee[10], Fernand Braudel[11], Will Durant[12], and Samuel Huntington[13] have remarked on the Civilizational power of India. It is a common thread running through the early writings of Nehru continuing on to the viewpoint of Jaswant Singh, the erstwhile Minister of External Affairs[14]. What does it mean to be a Civilizational power? Simply, it means that for a large part of its history spanning several millennia and except for an interregnum of 8 centuries of foreign domination, India has exerted considerable influence on the cultures and civilizations of most of Asia. To those who infer such an influence to be mostly a historical curiosity with no relevance to the present, I would draw attention to the equally widespread acceptance of Indian movies (this industry is commonly referred to in the subcontinent as Bollywood) throughout the world. In addition, a new phenomenon which has arisen in the world is the ubiquitous presence of highly skilled and even more highly educated Indian technologists, engineers, doctors, software engineers and the increasing dependency of the West, in particular the US, on Indian technological manpower. Truly few would have anticipated, even as late as 2 decades ago, the extent to which the Indian Diaspora has spread to the four corners of the globe.

---

10. Arnold Toynbee *A Study of History.*

11. Fernand Braudel *A History of Civilizations.*

12. Will Durant *The Story of Civilization.*

13. Samuell Huntington *The Clash of Civilization.*

14. Jaswant Singh *National Security*, Lancer Publications.

It is clear that India occupies a unique position in this planet both in a geographical sense as well as in a Civilizational sense. It has been our observation that the uniqueness of the Indian civilization and history is also accompanied by a unique set of threats to her security. It is our contention which we plan to develop in this essay, that these threats to her development as a viable and powerful nation state are very real and that indeed her very survival as a nation state and a civilization is in question if not in jeopardy, if she chooses not to address these threats in a coherent manner.

While developing the thesis as set forth above, it is the purpose of this essay to review the history and civilization of India with particular relevance to those issues which impinge on the security of the civilization and the state, and to analyze the nature of the threats that the modern federal republic of India faces during the coming decades.

At the core of the opposition to India amongst many quarters in the world is the notion that Indian nationhood is a nebulous entity. Churchill is reported to have remarked with his characteristic contempt for anything Indian that India is merely a geographical expression and that it is no more a country than the Equator. Be that as it may, foremost in this cacophony of naysayers is of course Pakistan which makes no secret of the fact that it considers the Indian nation an anomaly and would dearly love to see it broken up, even if in the process it endangers its own survival as a nation.

If that were the only opposition to Indian nationhood, life would be relatively simple for those in India who are entrusted with the responsibility for framing Indian foreign policy. Alas, such is not the case. There is a whole gaggle of disparate entities keen to see India dismantled. Not least amongst these is the powerful anti Indian lobby in the US State department and the US Senate who make no secret of their distaste for a strong India. More pernicious is the left secular lobby in India that barely hides its extraterritorial leanings towards Chinese and other ideological moorings and would not mind sacrificing the notion of the nation state called India in order to achieve power in the remnants of the subcontinent.

There are many reasons why this topic is of significant interest not only to residents of the subcontinent and the Indian Diaspora but also to the very influential and diverse set of India watchers throughout the world. These are also the reasons why certain state and non-state entities have gone to great lengths to devalue the durability and robustness of the Indian Republic and continue to attempt to prevent it from assuming its logical place in the family nations.

First among these reasons is that India is an extraordinarily free and open society. It can be asserted with reasonable certainty, that few countries can boast of such freedom of action and thought as there is in India. India has a vociferous, argumentative, and cacophonous free press, very much like that in the US and arguably acts in a far more unfettered manner than the established press in leading capitals such as Washington and London. Such freedom of the press offers opportunities not only for the unhindered expression of views, but also to plant seeds of misinformation among the millions of Indian residents.

Second, India is a large country not only because the size of its population but also because of its geographic location. The Indian sphere of influence could potentially encompass a vast area between the straits of Hormuz and the straits of Malacca. There is a certain amount of fear as well as envy that one day; one of the most poverty-stricken nations in the world will transform herself into a powerful economic nation. It is rare to find acknowledgement, in the Western press or even in the English language press in India, that such a transformation is indeed under way, barring the unavoidable reference to the growing economic clout of the Indian Union.

Third, India is a new kid on the block. It is a natural human tendency to limit the membership of an individual when he or she seeks membership in a particular group and prevent the expansion of an existing club. As an example there is great reluctance on the part of the UN Security Council Permanent five to expand the club of those who possess the veto power, a veto power that puts these countries beyond the reach of international condemnation. Any number of reasons have been given until fairly recently to prevent the entry of India into these exclusive clubs, but it is clear that the main reason for exclusion of the nation with the world's second largest population is primarily based on considerations of exclusivity and 'why should we upset the cozy apple cart' where we and we alone (the UNSC P5) will decide what is good for the rest of the world.

Fourth, as far as the West is concerned, India does not fall easily into the category of a friendly subservient nation. For starters, the majority of her population do not subscribe to an Abrahamic faith (Christianity, Islam and Judaism). The West understandably has always felt more comfortable with nations that 'look and feel' like themselves; this, in spite of the fact that hitherto the major conflicts of the world have almost always taken place between protagonists of the same religion and culture. Notwithstanding the fact that the majority of terrorist acts against the US are committed by persons almost none of whom are Hindu, there is an undercurrent of hostility to the Hindu faith which is assiduously fanned by various church groups and which is far in excess of the animosity felt against Muslims even after 9/11/2001.

Fifth, even when individuals adopt what is clearly a practice derived from Hindu traditional texts such as Hatha Yoga, there is a special attempt made to divorce such practices from their native origins. Increasingly, the reference to its Indian origins is omitted when discussing a subject such as Yoga. In fact few in the west are aware that the decimal place number system in universal use today was developed in India and that it was only in the 14th century that Europe gradually adopted such a system in place of the far more cumbersome Roman numeral system which was in widespread use till then. It is also little known that the subject of Grammar as it is taught today is the result of the work of the greatest Grammarian of all time Panini, who is reputed to have completed this work several hundred years before the birth of Christ.

Sixth, there is considerable opposition, resulting in discord and disharmony within India to the notion that the dominant thread in the Indic Civilization today is the one generally recognized as the Dhaarmik Tradition. In fact the ruling dispensation as of this date subscribes vociferously to the absence of such a dominant thread. We do not have the place in this monograph to deal with the diagnosis of this syndrome, except to make a few preliminary remarks. It is quite obvious that, such a discord was fanned assiduously by the Colonial Overlord as we describe in these pages and is a consequence of the Colonial paradigm.

Last but not least, it is a widespread misconception among India watchers to mistake India's diversity as a weakness and seek to exploit the resulting heterogeneity of India for purposes that are less than noble. Ethnic diversity and cultural diversity are two different aspects of any society. While the Indian subcontinent has always been home to an ethnically diverse population, due to geographical, climatic and other reasons, India possesses and always has exhibited a cultural uniqueness that is unmistakable. Many have been the philosophers, journalists, and essayists that have remarked on the unique nature of the Indic civilization. Even as far back as the Greek invasion of Alexander in the 4th century BCE, observers not native to the subcontinent, have remarked on the propensity of the Indian to concern himself with the larger ontological issues relating to the nature of humankind and the place that the human species occupies in this universe. One must assume that such questions occupy one's mind only if other needs in the hierarchy[15] are met and that the Indian savant of antiquity was able to focus on such issues only because he was otherwise prosperous and had the time, inclination and the intellectual curiosity to pursue his inquiries.

A question that often occurs to the authors, and I am certain we are not unique in this respect, is to ask why the Indic civilization which had reached such lofty levels several millennia ago, has sunk to such depressed levels today. I am sure the answers to this question are manifold, but we have attempted to peel the layers of the onion to understand why we are where we are today. If we come across as placing the responsibility for such a transformation on others such as the British and the Islamic invaders, who marauded the land for over 7 centuries, that certainly is not the intent. The responsibility for being at the current state of affairs clearly lies with the people of the subcontinent, but we feel it is an obligation even a duty to seek the causes of this transformation and let the chips fall where they may. Civilization is a precious good, in the words of Will Durant, and its fragile structure and delicate fabric can easily be disturbed leading to extinction of cultures as we have seen repeatedly throughout History. The Indic civilization may have survived one onslaught but may not prove to be resistant to future such onslaughts should they occur. It behooves us therefore to seek to understand the nature of the threat(s) that the civilization faces as she enters a new millennium.

From diagnosis comes the hint of a cure, so that the Indic civilization can once again join the comity of nation states with her head held high and play a significant role in the future advance of the planet and the species which inhabit it. We believe the stakes are too high. A failure of the Indic civilization to resurrect herself will have disastrous consequences for humanity in general and the one and quarter billion who inhabit the subcontinent in particular. Success in

15. Abraham Maslow, http://www.ship.edu/~cgboeree/maslow.html.

Incidentally the similarities between Maslow's hierarchy of self actualization and the path to self realization presecribed in Vedantic *darshanas* (Weltanschauung, worldwide) have been remarked by quite a few scholars and observers. There is reason to believe that Maslow had studied Raja Yoga in the process of developing his psychological theories. http://vmission.org/docs/VS/2004/mar/

achieving the desired goals cannot be presumed and needs to be earned every step of the way. Hence, it remains our desire to share these insights with others in the subcontinent as well as those who belong to the Diaspora. The jury is still out on the nature of the recovery and the extent to which the Indic civilization will resurrect herself.

A word on terminology. We have used the word Indic as the qualifier for our civilization. By Indic we mean all the people who derive their heritage from the Indian subcontinent. Does the term include the Indian Muslim? The answer is yes, but much will depend upon the Indian Muslim himself. He should have a sense of ownership and belonging to the civilization of the subcontinent. If he does so, (it is) well and good. If he does not it is his choice.

The following is a synopsis of what we believe are the causes of where we are today as presented under the aegis of the India Research Foundation on January 27, 2006 in Milpitas, California.

A typical viewpoint amongst the Pakistani elite

I am against the imperial streak in the Indian psyche. The 1947 riots had a deep impact on my mind...About 5% to 6% Brahmanas dominate India. "India will give its land when it will be divided into many pieces. India will have to be broken up. If India does not give us our land we will go to war and divide India...believe me, India is so fragile. India has such weak joints that if we want we could strike these weak joints then India will dismember. ...Jinnah was right when he invited Ambedkar to join Pakistan. Where are the lower classes? I am an Islamist. Islam is the final destiny of mankind. Islam is moderate, Islam is progressive. Islam is everything that man needs. It is not necessary to become a Muslim but it is necessary to adopt the principles of Islam. Naseem Azavi and Iqbal's writings have influenced my thinking."

Hamid Gul, Director General Pakistan ISI in the 90's.[16] In the following pages we seek answers to some questions that stand out

16. The point to note here is that by 1857, most of the area in the Indian subcontinent with the exception of Hyderabad state was not under Islamic rule. The Muslims in India numbered around 10 million, mostly concentrated in the provinces of Avadh and Bengal. The relationship with the Hindu had reached a modus Vivendi and was one characterized by mutual tolerance and even respect for each other's fighting abilities. There was considerable intermarriage with Hindu women which altered the basic outlook of the Nawabs. While they were convinced of the superiority of their Islamic traditions they developed a grudging respect for their Hindu cohorts. Bahadur

How did this viewpoint come about and who or what nurtured such a weltanschauung?

When did this begin and what was the genesis?

What were the motives?

If there was a concerted effort, could it be termed a conspiracy?

How was it executed?

Why is it important to study this topic?

Where does that leave us now?

Shah the last of the Mughals was a far cry from his Turkish forefather Jalaluddin Mohammad Babar. His primary language was Urdu while Babar spoke only Chagatai Turk and he had a feeling for Hindustan his native land that was nowhere exhibited by his ancestor. So, the question is how this hubris and arrogance developed among some of the Muslims of the subcontinent by 1947. To assume that this was a consequence of Hindu misgovernance overlooks the fact that the land was under the total suzerainty of the Brits. He had completely disarmed the populace, who were forbidden to own or cary firearms. The British control over the land was total. Nothing transpired without this knowledge or approval. So, how did this transformation take place?

3. The Nature of the Colonial Paradigm

The redefinition of India began almost immediately after the British gained control of vast tracts of land as a consequence of winning the Battle of Plassey (Polashir Juddho) in 757 and control of Bengal. The fundamental motive for the British coming to India in the initial years was profit through plunder. India was one of the richest countries in the17th century. But by the time they left. India was unquestionably one of the poorest.

In the initial decades after gaining of control of Bengal[17], the British never felt secure, surrounded as they were by a vast sea of natives. This was even more so, especially after 1857. We need to recall that they were after all less than 100,000 in number and in all likelihood in the neighborhood of 20,000 at any given time (before the1857 uprising) spread over a vast area of the subcontinent As they learnt more about the subcontinent, the rationale for not leaving became ever more complex. Very soon after 1857 the goal of prolonging British rule in India and extending control of the Indian subcontinent as long as feasible became an end in itself.

Most in England like Moon[18], believed that the British Raj was in large part an Anglo Indian enterprise, and that Britain conquered India

17. What we have stumbled on is a series of actions by the British that make a coherent and logical narrative only if we assume that they had developed a worldwide (weltanschauung) about the subcontinent that was consonant with these actions.

18. It must be remembered that the average Englishman wsa surrounded by a sea of natives. At that time it was still uncommon for British women to travel to India. So he was bereft of female companionship (of European women). After 1830 he segregated himself from the natives into separate townships called sacntonments. It is not surprising that he set about systematically to develop the means to make himself secure and thereby prolong British rule.

in 'a fit of absentmindedness' (quote attributed to Sir John Seeley). Seeley[19] went on to declare that nothing as great was ever done by Englishmen as the conquest of India, which was *"not in the ordinary sense a conquest at all", and which he put on par "with the Greek conquest of the East", pointing out that the British who had a "higher and more vigorous civilization than the native races" founded the Indian Empire "partly out of a philanthropic desire to put an end to enormous evils" of the Ṣrobber-states of India"*. That the original motive was plunder, as exemplified by Robert Clive and Warren Hastings, was quickly shoved under their newly looted Persian Carpets and the rationale for staying on in India was given a new and noble higher purpose.[20]

> "The freebooters of the 18th century were giving way to the bureaucrats of the 19th century. Ironically, it is highly debatable which of the two, freebooters or bureaucrats were the most dangerous to the people of India. Treasure can be replaced. Cultures, once tampered with, are nearly impossible to reclaim" remarks a present day commentator Kevin Hobson, in his essay on "Ethnographic mapping and the Construction of the British Census in India."

---

19. Seeley, Sir John Robert (1834-1895), *Expansion of England* (1883).
20. Another theme that recurs in the book (Conquest and Dominion of India by Sir Penderel Moon) is the change that occured in British goals in India: First it was the unabashed aim of getting rich, then it was transformed into the idea of ruling well, and then finally it was thought judicious to settle on the ennobling concept of civilizing the unwashed and uncouth hordes of the subcontinent. The Mutiny changed all this, and whatever excuses were thereafter offered, the truth was simply that Britain kept India because it made has a world power. The main theme in the latter part of the history is the Indian demand for self-government and 'the cautious, tardy British response' with grudging reforms that only alienated Indians. Moon rescues from obscurity such men as Thomas Adams, who really won Bengal for the British. He shows that expansion was not always profitable for the East India Company (under Wellesley, who conquered more territory than any other governor, the company's debts almost doubled). He explains that in 1917 conservative ministers in Britain agreed to promise India 'responsible government' because, ignorant of dominion history, they thought they would be able to interpret the phrase to mean whatever they wished.

Plate 2: W S Blunt *(facing pg. 34)*

The Plan to create an Alternate Center of Sunni Islamic Power

The plan to create an alternate center of Sunni Islamic Power was mooted by an Englishman by the name of Wilfred Skawen Blunt in the 1800's. He laid the foundation for what became the British policy towards the Islamic world award special privileges to the Islamic Ummah within the subcontinent, encourage the extinction of the Indic civilization in its ancestral homeland thereby cutting off the Indic from the source of his tradition, Britain set about methodically and systematically to execute the plan during the ensuing several decades.

A key ingredient in British Policy towards India was the emasculation of the Indic civilization. The motivation for this sprang from the methods that the Europeans practiced and honed to a level of sophistication especially in the newly discovered Americas. Pizarro and the Incas, Cortes and the Aztecs, reconquista in Spain, elimination of native American traditions in North America, were some of the instances they were able to accomplish these goals. An additional factor especially after 1857 was the pressure from Missionaries to eliminate Pagan religions in all British dominions. This would ensure that the Indic was cut off from his own traditions. Let us recall the words of Friedrich Maximilian Müller.

Hinduism was dying or dead because it belonged to a stratum of thought which was long buried beneath the foot of modern man. He continued: "The worship of Shiva, Vishnu, and other popular deities was of the same and in many cases of a more degraded and savage character than the worship of Jupiter, Apollo or Minerva. 'A religion', he said 'may linger on for a long time, it may be accepted my large masses of the people, because it is there, and there is nothing better. But when a religion has ceased to produce defenders of the faith, prophets, champions, martyrs, it has ceased to live, in the true sense of the word; and in that sense the old orthodox Brahmanism has ceased to live for more than a thousand years." (Speech at the Christians Missions in Westminster Abbey in 1873).

We will have more to say about Max Müller (as he referred to himself and as Indians referred to him) later in this essay. Just as the justifications for ruling India were altering as their stay lengthened, so did the goals they set for themselves and for India and the plan to create an Islamic Ummah was the consequence of at least a few iterations, as they peeled the layers of the onion namely the riddle that lay behind the history of the subcontinent.

The chronology of events is significant and critical to the analysis

If any one event could be given precedence in the hardening of British resolve to craft a long term plan to enhance and perpetuate their power in the subcontinent it was 1857 and the events thereafter. The 1857 Great Uprising was the turning point. The British were astonished at the extent of the unity inherent in the uprising and realized they could not hold India against a united populace. Until then the Muslim sultans and their cohorts were held in great contempt. Henceforth the plan to create a rival Sunni power in the subcontinent and to emphasize and exploit the diversity of India and to create tectonic faults in the landscape took on an added urgency. The underlying assumption - control of the Indian subcontinent was essential for the well being and prosperity of Britain. What is noteworthy, is not the fact that they would craft such a plan, but the nature and grand scope of the plan to change the very nature of the civilization of the subcontinent.

Why was control of India important to the British?

The British Indian Empire bolstered Britain's self image as the legitimate successor to the Roman Empire. This was the age of enlightenment, yet there were precious few to ask themselves the crucial question why Britain needed an Empire in the first place. In one fell swoop, the King (or Queen) of England became an Emperor with sway and absolute sovereignty over vast lands and a huge proportion of the population of the globe. Britain became a world power despite the loss of the Americas and could claim global interests by virtue of its possession of India. For example, Britain could dictate to China to purchase opium grown in India in order to pay for imports from China. India was a heaven sent opportunity for Britain, the Crown jewel of the British Empire and in turn, formed the rationale for domination of other parts of the globe.

The Premise behind the Plan unveiled

In retrospect, it cannot be said that there was much that was surprising about the plan, once they had decided on their fundamental premise. Sir John Strachey (Finance minister 1874): "The existence side by side of these (Hindu and Muslim) hostile creeds is one of the strong points in our political position in India. The better classes of Mohammedans are a source of strength and not weakness." They constitute a comparatively small but an energetic minority of the population whose political interests are identical with ours." Sir James

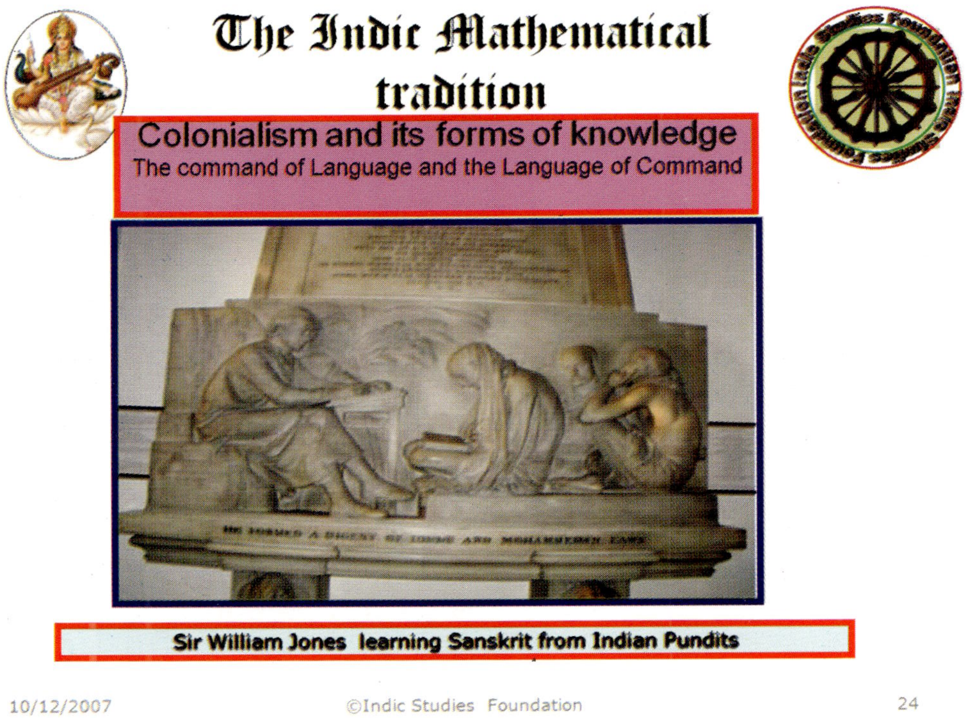

Plate 4: Colonialism and its form of Knowledge *(facing pg. 38)*

Sir William Jones (1746 - 94)

The real pioneer of Indology was Sir William Jones (1746-94), reputedly a scholar, gifted linguist and founder of the Royal Asiatic Society. Jones was appointed Judge of the Supreme Court and was a confidante of Warren Hastings (1732-1818.). Jones ostensibly became an ardent admirer of India. He wrote, ṢI am in love with Gopia, charmed with Crishen (Krishna), an enthusiastic admirer of Raama and a devout adorer of Brihma (Brahma), Bishen (Vishnu), Mahisher (Maheshwara); not to mention that Judishteir, Arjen, Corno (Yudhishtira, Arjuna, Karna) and the other warriors of the Mahabharat appear greater in my eyes than Agamemnon, Ajax and Achilles appeared when I first read the Iliad¿ (Mukharji, S.N., Sir William Jones: A Study in Eighteenth Century British Attitudes to India, Orient Longman, 1987).

This is the story we are told. What is the truth of the matter? He remained true to the Biblical dogma of Genesis which he took to be a literal account. His chronology for ancient India, including the dating of Chandragupta Maurya to the period of Alexander's invasion of India was dictated at least in part by the Biblical dogma. Jones may not have had an ulterior motive in doing this. All the same, his disinclination to go against his scriptures renders his conclusions suspect. In 1786, while delivering his third lecture, Sir William made the following statement which aroused the curiosity of many scholars and finally led to the emergence of comparative linguistics. Noticing the similarities between Sanskrit and the Classical Languages of Europe such as Greek and Latin he declared:

"The Sanskrit language, whatever be its antiquity, is of wonderful structure; more perfect than the Greek, more copious than the Latin, and more exquisitely refined than either, yet bearing to both of them a stronger affinity, both in the roots of verbs and in the forms of grammar, than could not possibly have been produced by accident; so strong indeed, that no philologer could examine them all three, without believing them to have sprung from some common source which, perhaps, no longer exists; there is a similar reason, though not quite so forcible, for supposing that both the Gothic and the Celtic, though blended with a very different idiom, had the same origin with the Sanskrit; and the old Persian might be added to the same family..." (Jones, Collected Works, Volume III: 34-5).

One must understand the milieu of the times, to fathom the motivations of the individuals and nuances of what happened. Who were these people who came to India so eagerly? What motivated them to do so? Prodosh Aich has documented the real story behind the study of Indology, the subject that Sir William was credited with initiating. There are many questions that he answers in the book Lunge mit Langen Beinen (Lies with Long Legs)[24]. For example the preponderance of individuals who served in the upper echelons of the British East India company were awarded the title Sir (or a Knighthood) before being sent to India, we presume to impress the Indians. A gentleman with the title Sir in front of his name was a Knight of the British Empire, reminiscent of the Knights of King Arthur. A Knight did not belong to the hereditary nobility, except on rare occasions. In order to become a Lord and sit in the House of Lords, one had to own a substantial estate and land was scarce in England and hence, while it was possible to impress the Indian by awarding a Sir, it rarely resulted in being elevated to the Peerage. We mention this to emphasize that the vast majority of official who came to India came from modest circumstances and only became wealthy after their stay in India. In other words, the instances where the individual was famous or a scholar before he came to India was rare indeed. So it was in the case of Sir William, whose primary motivation in coming to India was to achieve wealth, at a greatly accelerated pace, than he could hope to achieve in England.

As far as his mastery of languages is concerned, there appears to be considerable exaggeration when he is credited with knowing 32 languages. He apparently knew Greek and Latin and had learned Arabic. In fact so great was his ignorance of Indic languages that he was unable to distinguish any of the languages spoken in Bengal when he arrived in Calcutta in 1782. When we was advised by Charles Wilkins to learn Sanskrit, he is quoted as saying 'Life is too short and my necessary business too long for me to think at my age - he was then 38- of acquiring a new language, when those which I have already learned have such a mine of curious and agreeable information.

Thus began the study of Indo European languages as one family. Such a study falls under the rubric of a field known as Philology. Wikipedia defines Philology as *"Philology* is the study of ancient texts and languages. The term originally meant a love (*Greek philo-*) of learning and literature (Greek *-logia*). In the academic traditions of several nations, a wide sense of the term "philology" describes the study of a language together with its literature and the historical and cultural contexts which are indispensable for an understanding of the

24. Prodosh Aich '*Lies with Long Legs*', Sanskriti, New Delhi, 2004.

Plate 3: Map of India 1700-1792 *(facing pg. 36)*

Caird of Thanjavur, 1879: "there was no class except Brahmanas, which was so hostile to the English." Sir John Strachey again "this is the first and most essential thing to learn 'that there is not and never was an India or even any country of India, possessing according to European ideas any sort of unity, physical, political, about India.[21]

The Subtext

Exploit the ethnic diversity of India and encourage the notion that India was not one cultural entity with common traditions.

Assert that everything good in India came from somewhere else, that India was just a compilation of continuous invasions.

With the exception of a few martial races, that the Indic was incapable of defending himself.

Reinvent the caste system as a watertight system of stratified castes whose only interaction with one another was exploitive in nature.

Denigrate and ridicule the higher castes as the source of social stagnation and exploitation - this was truly a masterstroke - killed two birds with one stone deflected attention from themselves (the true exploiter) and placed it on the Brahmana. A tried and true tactic through the ages—destroys those in leadership positions among the competition and/or denigrates them endlessly.

Caste and the census of India

No indigenous equivalent to the word Caste in India. The English word Caste was derived from Portuguese word Casta which meant race, breed or lineage. Quite distinct from Varna

The British institutionalized the word Caste, using the decennial Census of India as a tool for ethnographic mapping and conjured up 100's of new castes.

The Census acted as a catalyst for an increased consciousness of caste as caste status became an increasingly significant factor in attaining material status.

See for instance Nicholas Dirks '*Castes of Mind*'

21. Note – the British public were sold on the notion that any kind of nationhood that India could aspire to was purely a consequence of the British conquest and dominion of India and the implication was strong that what Caesar giveth Caesar can take away. The plan was breathtakingly simple – work ceaselessly but circumspectly to see that there was no unity and then on the day of reckoning one could say 'see there is no unity, I have to divide the country accordingly'.

Caste and the Colonialist Enterprise

Caste (as we experience it today in India) is neither an unchanged survival of ancient India nor a single system that reflects a core cultural value. Rather than a basic expression of Indian tradition, caste is a modern phenomenon ș the product of a concrete historical encounter between India and British colonial rule Nicholas Dirks Castes of Mind, Colonialism and the Making of Modern India H. H. Risley[22], Commissioner of the 1901 census, also bared his underlying British prejudices in an 1886 publication which stated that race sentiment, far from being:

a figment of the intolerant pride of the Brahman, rests upon a foundation of fact which scientific methods confirm, that it has shaped the intricate grouping of the caste system, and has preserved the Aryan type in comparative purity throughout Northern India.[23]

Englishmen who Shaped Indic Thought

There were of course more than a few influential Englishman in this endeavor, but we have selected 3 who were especially successful in leaving a mark and initiated the processes which shaped Indic thought. These three gentlemen were in my view largely responsible for the worldview of the elite Indian of Modern India and in turn were also responsible for shaping world opinion of the Indians themselves. The language that we speak converse in, discuss, learn our technology from in India is in large part due to the initiative of Macaulay in his now famous minute on Education.

---

22. "In any case, the British administrators were, understandably overwhelmed by these figures and felt obliged to find a way to compartmentalize chunks of population into manageable groups. The most obvious way to do so was through the use of India's unique caste system **"Ethnographic Mapping and the Construction of the British Census in India *Kevin Hobson.***

    -This is a relatively charitable explanation. The more plausible one is that they needed an idea of the diversity of India in order to exploit it for the prolongation of their rule by use of an important dictum that went back to Roman times and to Julius Caesar.

23. When you examine this statement, it reveals:

1. Dislike of the Brahmana – that he is intolerantly proud (meaning the British who had completely segregated themselves into ghettos called cantonments, were the only ones entitled to be proud and be conscious of their caste)
2. That he believes in the racial purity of the Aryan
3. That the caste system was based on race

literary works and other culturally significant texts. Philology thus comprises the study of the grammar, rhetoric, history, interpretation of authors, and critical traditions associated to a given language. Such a wide-ranging definition is becoming rare nowadays, and "philology" tends to refer to a study of texts from the perspective of historical linguistics.

Thus inadvertently Sir William set in motion a chain of events beginning with the search for a proto Indo European Languages or PIE for short. The puzzling observation here is that it never occurred to him that possibly Sanskrit itself could be the grand ancestor to all the languages of the Indo European languages. Till then Europeans had assumed that the oldest language related to the European languages was Hebrew. Given the anti Semitic feelings that were always simmering underneath the surface in Europe, there was general relief that the roots of their heritage lay elsewhere than in Hebrew, but Sir William may have realized that the notion of the unwashed millions possessed the linguistic technology (in Panini's Ashtadhyayi) to explain the grammars of their own language would perhaps be equally unacceptable. Whatever the case may be, there are two major disservices that he did to the Indic Civilization. One was the possible misdating of Chandragupta Maurya by several centuries and the other was postulating the assumption of a PIE, which implied an Urheimat (an ancestral home) from where the Indo Europeans fanned out to the 4 corners of the Eurasian landmass. By so doing, he made the chronology of India captive to the evolution of the mythical Aryan in Europe and he laid the seeds for a fractured historical narrative for the Indics, which was not supported by any Indian legend or folklore. In short he saddled the Indics with perpetually having to refute dual falsehoods—a false chronology and an imposed 'Aryan Invasion or what has been light heartedly called the Aryan Tourist theory. Some might infer that the most significant corollary to this paradigm shift was the profound impact it had on the mind of the Indic people and the wide fissures it created in Indian society.

The introduction of English as a medium of instruction in India is in large part due to the initiative of Macaulay in his now famous minute on Education.

Thomas Babington Macaulay (1800 - 1859)

Thomas Babington Macaulay (1800-59) was one of the most brilliant men recruited by the East India Company and also credited with a prodigious memory and is best known for introducing English education in India. He is also remembered for drafting the Indian Penal Code, which remains pretty much intact to this day. Though not a missionary himself, he believed that Christianity held the key to the problem of curing India's ignorance. Although he confessed to have no knowledge of Sanskrit and Arabic, he did not hesitate to belittle the religious works of the East.[25]

Some quotes attributed to Macaulay

"A single shelf of a good European library was worth the whole native literature of India and Arabia".

"all the historical information which has been collected from all the books written in the Sanscrit language is less valuable than what may be found in the most paltry abridgments used at preparatory schools in England".

"It may safely be said, that the literature now extant in that language (English) is of far greater value than all the literature which three hundred years ago was extant in all the languages of the world together."

"The languages of Western Europe civilized Russia. I cannot doubt that they will do for the Hindoo what they have done for the Tartar".

It is surprising that even he admitted that India was as good as England (and that's the skies, right?) in philosophy, "In every branch of physical or moral philosophy, the relative position of the two nations is nearly the same".

Regarding teaching Hindu religion, he said, "We are to teach it because it is fruitful of monstrous superstitions. We are to teach false History, false Astronomy, false Medicine, because we find them in company with a false religion". Yet, one must admit that he was against the missionaries, "We abstain, and I trust shall always abstain, from giving any public encouragement to those who are engaged in the work of converting natives to Christianity".

---

25. To further this end Macaulay wanted a competent scholar who could interpret the Vedic scriptures in such a manner that the newly educated Indian youth would see how barbaric their native superstitions actually were. Macaulay finally found such a scholar in Friedrich Max Müller.

    The History of western (missionary) scholarship in Oriental Studies in India can be traced to William Carey, the pioneer of modern missionary enterprise in India. Carey was an English oriental scholar and founder of the Baptist Missionary Society. From 1801 onward, as Professor of Oriental Languages, he composed numerous philosophical works, consisting of 'grammars and dictionaries in the Mahratti, Sanskrit, Punjabi, Telugu, Bengali.'

He ridiculed those who wanted to teach Sanskrit and Arabic literature with, "when we can teach European science, we shall teach systems which, by universal confession, whenever they differ from those of Europe, differ for the worse; and whether, when we can patronize sound Philosophy and true History, we shall countenance, at the public expense, medical doctrines, which would disgrace an English farrier,-Astronomy, which would move laughter in girls at an English boarding school,-History, abounding with kings thirty feet high, and reigns thirty thousand years long,†and Geography, made up of seas of treacle and seas of butter".

He showed his generosity and magnanimity with, "at once stop the printing of Arabic and Sanskrit books, I would abolish the Madrassa and the Sanskrit college at Calcutta - If we retain the Sanskrit college at Benares and the Mahometan college at Delhi, we do enough, and much more than enough in my opinion, for the Eastern languages".

If an individual comes right out and says I wish to alter the wellsprings of the civilization of its subject people without giving them the option, just so that he can make it easier to dominate the subcontinent, there is not much left to say. We can only presume Macaulay was a bundle of contradictions. Furthermore, these were the cream of the crop of western civilization; we can only surmise how much more badly worse, the rest of the officials were in the service of the East India Company. So destructive was Macaulay's introduction of English as the medium of instruction to the vast population of India, that by the time the beginning of the 20th century rolled around, the literacy rate had plummeted to 6%.

In October 1844, Lord Hardinge, Governor General of India promulgated a resolution that all Government appointments in India should give preference to English speaking candidates. This along with Macaulay's minute on education was responsible for the adoption of the English language in India and for all practical purposes it became the language of commerce, government and university education and remains so even to this day almost 150 years after the death of Thomas Babington Macaulay.

Friedrich Maximilian Müller (1823-1900)

Friedrich Maximilian Müller (1823-1900) was born in Dessau and educated in Leipzig, where he learned Sanskrit and translated the Hitopadesa of Pandit Visnu Sarma before coming to England in 1846. Since he was penniless, he was under the tutelage of Baron von Bunsen, the Prussian Ambassador to England[26] who basked in the childishly pleasant and ubiquitous thought of converting the whole world to Christianity. It was in London that Max Müller met Macaulay who was still on the lookout for his 'right man'. Müller was first commissioned by the East India Company to translate the Rg Veda into English. The company agreed to pay the young Müller 4 Shillings for each page that was ready to print. He later moved to Oxford where he translated a number of books on Eastern religion. His magnum opus was his series *The Sacred Books of the East*, a fifty volume work which he began editing in 1875. It goes without saying that by the end of his career, Müller had amassed a comfortable sum of money. It is ironic that the man who has Bhavans named after him all over India and is treated with so much veneration there, probably did the most damage to uproot Vedic culture. At the time of his death he was venerated by none other than Lokamanya Tilak as 'Veda-maharishi Moksha-mula Bhatta of Go-tirtha' (Oxford).

Although Max Müller is on record as extolling India's ancient wisdom, his letters (printed in two volumes) tell an entirely different story. Excerpts from his letters are quoted in the appendix. Here is a sample.

"Large number of Vedic hymns are childish in the extreme; tedious, low,commonplace." "Nay, they (the Vedas) contain, by the side of simple, natural, childish thoughts, many ideas which to us sound modern, or secondary and tertiary. The Vedas are like the twaddle of idiots and the ravings of madmen. Their downright absurdity can hardly be matched

Letter to his wife , Oxford,December 9,1867

"...this edition of mine and the translation of the Vedas, will hereafter tell to a great extent on the fate of India and on the growth of millions of souls in that country. It (the Rg Veda) is the root of their religion and to show them what the root is, I am sure, the only way of uprooting all that has sprung from it during the last three thousand years."

See Appendix B for his real views along with the politically correct version as exemplified by the Indian Postal Department.

---

26. We recall that Germany had not been unified as yet and that Prussia was the most powerful of the Germanic principalities. It should also be recalled that the last Kaiser of Germany who abdicated after WW I was a grandson of Quenn Victoria, the Empress of India.

Plate 5: T B Macaulay (above), Stamp of Max Müller (bottom) *(facing pg. 44)*

Occidentals who studied Sanskrit, Indian History, and Indology

Sir William Jones (1746-1794) the founder of Indology, largely responsible for postulating a Proto Indo European language for which no speakers have been found and for misdating the chronology of ancient India.
Hermann George Jacobi (1850-1837) was the first to suggest that the Vedic Hymns were collected around 4500 BCE based on Astronomical observations made by the Vedics.
Thomas Babington Macaulay (1800-1859) decreed English to be the medium of instruction, drafted the Indian Penal Code.
Friedrich Maximilian Mýller (1823-1900) translated the books of the east. His private views of these books were vastly at variance with his public pronouncements.
Roberto Di Nobili (1577-1656), Jesuit Priest, posed as a Brahmana, posited a counterfeit Veda, called the Romaka Veda Rudolf Roth(1821-1893) studied rare manuscripts in Sanskrit.
Abbê Dubois, Jean Antoine (1765-18) went to India to convert the heathen returned discouraged that it was very difficult to accomplish William Carey[27] (1761-1834), Missionary.
Sir Charles Wilkins (1749-1836) Translated the Bhagavad Gita in 1785.
Colonel Colin Mackenzie (1753-1821) Collector of Indian Manuscripts.
Henry Thomas Colebrook (1765-1837) Studied Sanskrit from the Pundits and wrote on the Vedas.
Horace Hayman Wilson (1786-1860) First Boden Professor of Sanskrit at Oxford University wrote on the Puranas.
August Wilhelm Schlegel (1767-1845), Lecturer in Sanskrit, Bonn University.
Franz Bopp (1791-1867) Did detailed research leading to postulation of Proto Indo European (PIE).
James Mill (1773-1836). Completed The History of British India in 1817.
Colonel Boden who endowed the Boden Chair of Sanskrit Studies in 1811 with the purpose of debunking the Vedas.

Sir Monier Monier-Williams (1819-1899), Boden Professor of Sanskrit, Oxford.
Robert Caldwell (1815-1891) Collected Sanskrit manuscripts, a British missionary.
Sir Alexander Cunningham (1814-1893), member of Asiatic Society of Bengal.
Vincent Smith (1848-1920), author of Oxford History of India.
Frederick Eden Pargiter (1852-1897) published 'Purana texts of the Dynasties of the Kali age'.
Arthur Anthony McDonell (1854-1930), brought 7000 Sanskrit manuscripts from Kashi to Oxford University.
Sir Mark Aurel Stein (1862-1943), Archaeological Survey of India.
Maurice Bloomfield (1855-1928), interpreted the Vedas.
Arthur Barriedale Keith (1879-1944) published 'The religion of and philosophy of the Vedas' in 2 volumes in 1925, Cannot be regarded as a authentic or reliable translation.
Sir Robert Erie Mortimer Wheeler (1890-1976).
Alexander Basham.
Morris Winternitz (1863-1937), wrote History of Indian Literature.
Alain Danielou (1907-1994).
Sir John Hubert Marshall, (1876-1958) director general Archaeological Survey of India.
Joseph Campbell (1904-1987) follows in the tradition of Heinrich Zimmer, albeit he uses the word myth much too liberally.
Edwin Bryant (Ph.D. Columbia, 1997).
Heinrich Zimmer (1890-1943) author of Philosophies of India "Indian philosophy was at the heart of Zimmer's interest in oriental studies, and this volume therefore represents his major contribution to our understanding of Asia. It is both the most complete and most intelligent account of this extraordinarily rich and complex philosophical tradition yet written.¿

The Boden Chair of Sanskrit Studies at Oxford University

An interesting personality who championed the cause of Oriental Studies, with profound implications for the future of India was a Lt. Col. Boden of the Bombay Native Infantry who bequeathed his estates of about 25,000 Pounds to the University of Oxford to enable them to found a Chair of Sanskrit which the University named after him. In his will dated August 15, 1811, Boden stated most explicitly that the special object of his munificent bequest was to promote the translation of the scriptures into Sanskrit, so as ***"to enable his countrymen to proceed in the conversion of the natives of India to the Christian Religion"*** (Preface to Sanskrit-English Dictionary by Sir Monier-Williams, Boden Professor of Sanskrit, 1899, p.ix). It would not be out of place to state that Sir Monier-Williams mentions in this Preface, "He (Monier-Williams) has made it the chief aim of his professional life to provide facilities for the translation of our sacred Scriptures into Sanskrit". It may be mentioned that Prof. H.H. Wilson, the eminent Sanskritist and first occupant of the Boden Chair, wrote a book, "*The Religion and Philosophical Systems of the Hindus.*" Explaining the reasons for undertaking this work, he said," These lectures were written to help candidates for a prize...for a best refutation of the Hindu Religious System." To think that the man who wrote these words held one of the most prestigious professorships at Oxford! Monier Monier-Williams, the second holder of the Boden chair of Sanskrit at Oxford University and whose Sanskrit-English dictionary is still used, wrote in its preface that "the Boden chair of Sanskrit was set up by Colonel Boden to promote the translation of Christian Scriptures into Sanskrit, so as to enable his countrymen to proceed in the conversion of the natives of India to the Christian religion." He told the Missionary Congress held at Oxford on 2 May 1877,

> "The chief obstacle to the spread of Christianity in India is that these people are proud of their tradition and religion." His dictionary, he hoped, would enable the translation of the Bible into Sanskrit and "when the walls, of the mighty fortress of Brahmanism are encircled, undermined, and finally stormed by the soldiers of the Cross, the victory of Christianity must be signal and complete."

One can begin to see why under this constant barrage of anti-Brahmanism by the colonial overlord for almost 2 centuries, that many Indics have internalized this fear and loathing of Brahmanas to such a degree, leading to such grotesque legislative remedies as the Draconian anti Brahmana quota based affirmative action programs which are now in place in the country. It becomes increasingly clear why even conservative groups in countries such as America support such programs even though they would oppose them vociferously in their own country. So much for ideological consistency.

Discovery of Saraswathi Sindhu Civilization (SSC)

The Discovery of Harappa by Daya Ram Sahni (1921) and of Mohenjo Daro, by Rakhal Das Banerjee (1922) under the direction of John Marshall was the final confirmation of the existence and history of Indian civilization.[28] Prior to the discovery of these archaeological sites, there was generally no acceptance that India had any Civilizational heritage to speak of much less an ancient one. The prevailing mood is well described by Max Müller in this passage in 1883.

> "They would not have it, they would not believe that there could be any community of origin between the people of Athens and Rome, and the niggers of India. The classical scholars scooted the idea and I still remember the time when I was a student at Leipzig and begun to study Sanskrit, with what contempt my remarks on Sanskrit or comparative grammar were treated by my teachers 'No one ever was for a time so completely laughed down as Professor Bopp, when he first published his comparative grammar of Sanskrit, Zend, Greek, Latin, and Gothic. All hands were against him."

The notion that the British had something in common with the rickshaw puller of Calcutta much less a common linguistic heritage was not accepted with alacrity by almost all the academic community. The very notion that the humanity that they came across in the streets of India could teach them something was met with incredulity. Memories are short and the fact that Sir William Jones learnt Sanskrit from the

---

28. The discovery of the SSC in 1922 by Rakhal Das Banerjee was a momentous affair. Overnight the antiquity of India shot back in time by about 3 millennia. This was long before Stonehenge or anything comparable in Europe. The question was how to handle this new knowledge so that the resulting theory would further their political aims and prolong their presence in the subcontinent instead of shortening it. Thus was born the variant of the AIT that is current today.

    It was preceded by the discovery of seals of great antiquity in 1856, six miles from the river Ravi, in the foothills of the Himalayas, railway construction workers came upon a small crumbling hill of fire-baked bricks. These they quickly appropriated for the railway line's ballast. Along with the bricks, certain steatite (soapstone) seals were found. Archaeologists, notably Sir Alexander Cunningham, quickly confirmed their antiquity.

pundits of India was already a dim memory. However, the findings at Harappa and Mohenjo Daro forced Europeans to revise their views. But such acceptance was not unqualified. There was still the matter of degree of antiquity relative to the antiquity of the European civilizations.

One observation that was immediately obvious was that the Vedics (I prefer the use of this term rather than the ubiquitous Aryans, for the simple reason that there is no such ethnic group called Aryans) who had been dated as around1200 BCE had no extant archaeology till then, and that the newly discovered Harappan who were older than 2500 BCE had no written records. The obvious explanation, using Ockham's razor was that the 2 were one and the same. But that would never do, for by so doing, India would instantly be credited with having an unbroken civilization going back 6000 years. So, the invention of a new theory began, the so called Aryan Invasion Theory (AIT). While space constraints prevent us from going into detail, we will touch upon the basic postulates of the theory and what it sought to accomplish. The entire controversy is well documented by Edwin Bryant and Laurie Patton in the Indo Aryan Controversy[29]. We have encapsulated the main points of this hypothesis in appendix.

Colonial Paradigm of Indian History lingers today in the invasion theory of Indian history

The invasion theory of Indian History was first postulated by Hegel (1899) that India lacked historical agency [30] and that India was a *cultural cul de sac* from which nothing worthwhile ever emanated. The Aryan Invasion Theory (which has now morphed into Aryan Immigration or Influx Theory), based largely on linguistic conjectures and postulates is a narrative that was force fitted to Hegel's postulate. In one brilliant master stroke, the Brits killed several birds with one stone.

What were the Basic Postulates of AIT - that a race of nomadic Aryans came thundering across the passes of the Hindu Kush mountain range on horse drawn chariots and overcame the sedentary urban civilization of the Indus river valleys who happened to belong to the Dravidian race and then shortly thereafter in short order decided to compose the entire gamut of Vedic Literature from the Vedas, Puranas, the smritis, the Brahmanas the Upanishads and the Itihaas of India. If this is was what really happened, the transformation from Central Asian

29. Edwin Beryant and Laurie Patton 'The Indo Aryan Controversy'. The book contains as up to date bibliography.

30. See Appendix J.

Nomads to the intellectual speculations inherent in the Vedic literature must surely rank as one of the most rapid transformations in human history.

See for instance *http://www.boloji.com/architecture/00002.htm*

What did the postulation of AIT accomplish?

Postulated a discontinuity between the Vedics and the Saraswathi Sindhu Civilization, and assigned a much more recent date to the Vedics and hopelessly confused the issue of the precedence of the Vedics.

Ergo, the Vedics became aliens to the subcontinent and became associated with the mythical Aryans, with all its 20th century fascist connotations.

To top it off, the caste system was now associated with these marauding Aryans.

The conclusion was inescapable -the Brits were simply a latter version of the Aryans to have conquered India and had as much legitimacy to remain and rule India as did the original Vedics.

Meanwhile back at the ranch, the defeated and displaced Dravidians allegedly retreated to the south and formed the bulk of the downtrodden castes of modern India - gave rise to the plethora of Dravidian parties in the state of Tamilnadu. So much so that today no party can get elected in TN without the appellation of Dravidian tacked on to its name.[31]

Plans for future division of India

This may have firmed the resolve of the British to push through the plans for division of India. What greater irony than to divorce the

31. The simplicity and sweep of the theory is simply stunning and the effectiveness of such a narrative is that it continüs to be the History that is peddled in Indian History books even today. That it was received so unquestioningly is simply astonishing given the lack of any archaeological evidence to back up the theory. Never mind that there is no mention of these migrations anywhere in the sacred books of the Vedics.

Further, the AIT when it was first proposed by Friedrich Maximillian Müller, was merely regarded as a postulate or a hypothesis. Subsequently it took on a life of its own and was bestowed with the aura of incontrovertible truth and that to question it was to invite the wrath of the High priests of secularism, that such questioning was motivated by right wing Hindu nationalist ideology.

Indus valley, which would be later be known as the cradle of civilization and separate it from the heartland of India. Plans to divide the country were hatched when the Middle East was secure after the First World War and Saudi Arabia was already a state. The assessment of the colonial powers was that the game was up once the natives connected the Saraswathi Sindhu civilization with the Vedic tradition and that they would realize the true antiquity of their heritage. It would be difficult to keep the country colonized subsequently. In 1935 the GOVERNMENT OF INDIA ACT was passed by the British parliament and Burma and Aden were separated from India in anticipation that India would accelerate her demand for independence.

Phase II Post Independence

It is more difficult to fathom the motives for British antagonism towards India .After all the game was over. What could further be gained by trashing and containing the Indics? Or at least so it appeared to the Indics unschooled as they were to the finer points of the realist imperative driving Western civilization. It was more than a matter of simple spite against a former colony. The anti Indian moves were primarily orchestrated by Britain immediately after the war during the 50's and 60's with USA playing an increasingly dominant role thereafter, especially after 1971. Post independence plans were set in motion by Noel Baker (Commonwealth secretary) and Ernest Bevin (Foreign secretary) during the watch of Clement Atlee. Initially the US (esp. George Marshall, Post war US secy. of state), was well disposed towards India. Marshall made the assertion that the accession of Kashmir to India was final and legal. Marshall even offered India a UNSC seat, but soon thereafter was convinced otherwise by Britain.

When finally Britain was forced to relinquish control of India, they followed a variation of the dictum of the Romans, namely 'Divide and Quit'. In this case India was divided into 2 countries India and Pakistan. The British from long experience immediately recognized that India would be a major world power in the not too distant future. Why make it easier for the Indians and certainly why let a plum like Kashmir fall into their hands. There was also the suspicion, eventually to come true in later years that India would be the more difficult country to deal with because of its larger size. In addition, Britain did not expect that India would be so spectacularly successful in persuading all the Princely states in to joining the Indian Union. Certainly their expectation was that Kashmir would join Pakistan. To their chagrin, India finessed the whole issue thanks to Sardar Patel by accepting the instrument of accession from the Maharajah.

In the meantime the mantle for protecting the Western world from Russia (by then it was called the Soviet Union) and the Communist nations would fall on the newly emergent superpower the United States. The US, properly coached by Britain, also inherited the problem of containing the power of a potentially resurgent India. Thus began a 50-year sequence of events between India and the US, which while not making them bitter adversaries made them highly suspicious of each other. The US made it a point from day one to oppose India on the Kashmir issue. Despite periods of relative calm in the relationship, this adversarial relationship continued pretty much undisturbed till the present day.

The US and Americans are disingenuous when they suggest that the reason for the deterioration of relations had to do with a number of third party issues, such as the Non Aligned Movement etc. But this is really a chicken and egg issue. The US drew first blood by questioning the sovereignty of India over Kashmir and this was a fundamental issue of national integrity for India. The world's most powerful democracy was questioning the territorial integrity of the world's largest democracy. The issue of Nehru's intransigence does not arise, since at that time Nehru felt he had excellent relations with both the British and the US and it was not until after 1962 and the liberation of Goa that he changed his opinion on the matter.

It took many years for Indians to understand that the US was actually hostile to the Indian conception of India and in fact many Indians continued to blame Nehru, suggesting his woolly headed idealism was the cause of this rift between the 2 countries. It did not help matters much that India had a very free press and all the bickering that the Indians would indulge in were there for all the world to see.

In the early years, especially during the 50's and 60's it was common to read articles in the western newspapers that India was going to break up. They would contemptuously quote Indian newspapers talking about 'fissiparous tendencies' and predict that India would break up within 25 years. The 65 war was the first time that such preconceived notions would receive a rude shock. Both the US and Britain realized that India was not a banana republic and this was after all the true inheritor of the British Indian army which undertook major campaigns on behalf of Britain in both world wars. While at the beginning the US acted as a cheer leader for Pakistan during the first few days, when it realized that the Pakistanis were losing badly, they immediately went to the UN to stop India from doing further damage. This pattern of behavior was repeated during the 1971 war.

The Post Independence Plan

Continuously undercut India in all international fora such as the UNSC while professing keen interest in the future development and well being of India The US and UK shocked Nehru when they voted for Pakistan on the Kashmir issue in the UN.

Recommend that India's defenses were kept at ridiculously low levels and not commensurate with the large size of the country, the large number of bordering countries and its long coast line.

Encourage the notion that Pakistan and India were essentially at parity in terms of defense and military capabilities and keep India occupied perennially fending of threats from Pakistan. A Pakistan now armed with modern weaponry from the US.

Emphasize at every opportunity that whatever unity India exhibited was the result of British colonial rule and that India would breakup rapidly once the British left.

Refer to India as Hindu dominated India or predominantly Hindu India.

The Plan to create a New Khilafat

Process of creating new Khilafat out of the debris left after disintegration was expected to take not more than 2 to 3 decades after independence. There were setbacks almost immediately.

One of the main setbacks came in the form of Sardar Vallabhai Patel ş the geography of present day India was created by Sardar Patel. The annexation of the state of Jammu and Kashmir when Maharaja Hari Singh ceded his territory to India. Rapid, timely and complete integration of princely states including Hyderabad thanks to Sardar Patel. The decisive defeat of Pakistan in 1971, resulting in the surrender of 90.000 troops in one of the shortest wars in modern history demolished the myth of martial races within the subcontinent.[32]

The fourth setback (and I am certain not the last) was the declaration by India that she was a Nuclear Power in 1998. The prevention of India from becoming a nuclear power was a canonical commandment of the US State Department Mandarins. The resulting discomfiture is one from which they have yet to recover.

---

32. See for instance Chapter 9, of Nicholas Dirks, *Castes of Mind*.

The West and the Islamic World

Study the chronology of events in the Islamic world. Islam and Christianity share a common Semitic heritage fundamentally Abrahamic in nature. The British developed a relationship with the Ashraf and the Saudis and the Iranians for different reasons but in the latter two cases because of Oil, The Indic civilization was not appreciated till the 20th century and even then grudgingly with a lot of caveats (recall the slide on Colonialism and forms of knowledge).

The West has always had difficulty dealing with the Indics. He could not reconcile the intellectual pretensions of the upper class Indian with the widespread poverty of the Indic populace (see for example remark by Risley on the Brahmana).

When asked to rank the sacred books Max Mýller listed the new Testament and the Koran (the rationale being they were not much different) at the top and the Vedas and the Avesta last.

1971 India Pakistan War - a watershed event in the subcontinent

Notion of a two nation Theory ṣorigins in Islamic theology

Notion that India and Pakistan were roughly equal in military power

Psychological Boost for India- laid to rest the Martial races theory of the Brits

Kissinger/Nixon doctrine revealed overtly what had been the worst kept secret of the cold war ṣ the tilt towards Pakistan

There were unintended consequences magnified by Pokhran I ṣ the West was alarmed that India would elect to become another miltarized state

The term South Asia came into currency in a big way. The cold war against the Republic was resumed in earnest.

Why the tilt to the Islamic Ummah

To summarize

Oil

The Sub continental Muslim (especially the Ashraf) was considered more pliable, presumably because he was in a minority

Islam has a more well defined view of its Global presence. The educated Indian Muslim is no exception and looks outside India for his ideological moorings

Islam has traditionally been more assertive about its place in the world scene ş the squeaky wheel gets the grease

As Max Müller asserted the Koran was not that much different than the New Testament, not very surprising an observation, since both faiths claim to have evolved from the Prophet Abraham

Hinduism is not even recognized as an established religious faith in some countries, e.g. France

Depiction of the Indic traditions (in particular the Hindu tradition) both in text books and in media is demeaning, derogatory, misleading and plain false

Depiction of status of women is equally demeaning and false, see for instance[33]

By allowing Islam to spread eastward, it would remove or at least mitigate the historical threat that Islam had posed to Europe. We need to recall that Charles Martell had to defend against the Moor in the 8th century and that the Turks had to be turned back from the gates of Vienna as late as the 15th century. Turkey has not been admitted to the European Union even till today, despite repeated pleas to do so. This appears to be a characteristic propensity of the British to be generous with territory that does not belong to them in the first place

Meanwhile, the learning of Sanskrit in order to ridicule and denigrate the faith of the Hindus goes on with as much vigor as ever. Harvard Prof of Sanskrit Studies Michael Witzel's aversion to Hindus is well exemplified by the following quote. The broad stereotyping and the condescension that Witzel indulges in is astounding if not demeaning, especially in this day and age.

"Rajesh, I agree: The Hindus in North America (HINA's) are not just hiina, "lost, abandoned", but they (understandably) cling to their homeland in all manners they can come up with. "Reforming" our schoolbooks according to an imagined Golden Age (Ram Raj), hoary India is just one of the expressions we can observe. They also tell their daughters to study Classical Indian Dance. (Not exactly a highly regarded occupation back home), they build many temples and have Sunday schools (as many other ethnicities do). But, they hardly invest

---

33. David Freedholm, Women and Hinduism in US Text Books, *http://davidfreedholm.sulekha.com/blog/post/2003/02/women-and-hinduism-in-u-stextbooks.htm.*

in Higher Education as other successful Asians have done. Nor allow their children to study items outside Law or Medicine, such as Indian Studies, —the only way that members of their group could speak with real authority (for example, in school books)."

4. What's in a Name; India, South Asia and the Indic Identity

The term "South Asia" began to be used by the US State Department after the1971 war. The US established numerous grants to Universities to develop South Asian studies with emphasis on subaltern studies and to study the role of Muslim minorities in India.

The invention of the new nomenclatures served a twin purpose. It minimized the predominantly Indic nature of the civilization in the Indian subcontinent. Thereby there arose an opportunity to give prominence to the notion of a hyphenated subcontinent where Pakistan has an equal role. Thus it furthered the plan to establish a Sunni Ummah in "South Asia"

Nationhood and identity of India

India," Winston Churchill once barked, "is merely a geographical expression. It is no more a single country than the Equator." Churchill was rarely right about India, but it is true that no other country in the world embraces the extraordinary mixture of ethnic groups, the profusion of mutually incomprehensible languages, the varieties of topography and climate, the diversity of religions and cultural practices, and the range of levels of economic development that India does.[34]

Over the 2 centuries of their colonial rule over India, the British made a conscious effort to devalue the Indian identity, in particular its broad and unique Civilizational aspects, and to deny that there ever was a cohesive entity called India throughout its history. The word India itself is merely the latest avatar of the original Sindhu Sarasvati river valley civilizations. While the original connotation of Sindhu

34. Shashi Tharoor in India, From Midnight to the Millennium.

was local to what is now the Indus Valley, over the millennia it acquired a geographical connotation comprising the entire subcontinent. It may not have been the term the ancient Indics may have used to refer to themselves but by usage and custom it has acquired a broader connotation.

In denying such an identity for the people of the subcontinent, the British wished to take credit for the formation of the modern political nation state called India and perhaps more to the point, to deny an independent Civilizational status to the Indics. It would become very inconvenient to explain to the British public that given the antiquity of the cultural and Civilizational status of the Indics, there was any need for the British to exert the role of Colonial overlord in the continent much less a role where they assumed absolute suzerainty over the people of the subcontinent. It was far easier to keep up the faèade that Britain had a civilizing role in the subcontinent, if the presumption was made that there was no civilization to speak of prior to their arrival. Hence the constant attempt to deny any kind of Civilizational status and to say whatever there was in existence on their arrival was in large part due to the advent of the Moghals and prior conquests and invasions. It is also ironic that Pakistan tries its best to deny the existence of the Indian identity, given the fact that M A Jinnah wanted to appropriate the name for the territories he inherited from the British. "We know of course that the late Z A Bhutto, the former Prime Minister of Pakistan, known for his vitriolic hatred of India, was fond of quoting that consistency was the hobgoblin of little minds. The crowing irony amongst the ironies of History is that Bhutto was beheaded by the dictator who succeded him, a man who he himself had appointed, in a similar display of inconsistency, not to mention barbarism."

Furthermore, such an attempt flies in the face of history. In fact other Asian civilizations such as the Chinese have Civilizational memories of India, her culture and her people. Even the Arabs before Islam and after Islamic civilization have a Civilizational memory about the people of India through trade and commerce. However, such memories have been superseded by the viewpoints of the Anglo Saxon world. The rest of the world even today has views about India/Hindus set by Europeans [Anglo Saxons] and missionaries in the 1800 and 1900s. Hence the country and Indians/Hindus are already stereotyped with a particular set of images and perceptions for the most part from the British and colonial perspective. The British due to their interaction with India from the early 17th century and later their long experience with colonial rule became the global power by the end of 19th century and were able to influence and build a worldwide image of Hindus, the non-Muslims, along with India and the Indic civilization, an image that was in accord with their views of the world. This is very critical to understand in the 21st century. This British image of Indians and India was perpetuated throughout the 20th century with the advent of the communication revolution. India has never been able to change the perception appreciably after independence. Europeans by the time of World War II looked at India and Indians, Muslims and non-Muslims in a certain way from their historical experience.

"An English authority, Sir John Strachey, had this to say about India:[35] ...... *this is the first and most essential thing to learn about India -that there is not and never was an India or even any country of India, possessing according to European ideas, any sort of unity, physical, political.*[36] *His was not an isolated opinion. Reginald Craddock, Home Minister of the Government of India under Hardinge and Chelmsford, in The dilemma in India (1929) denied the existence of an Indian nation: An Indian Nation, if such be possible, has to be created before it can exist. It never existed in the past, and it does not exist now. Do we flatter ourselves that we created it? If so, it is sheer flattery. There is no word for 'Indian' in any vernacular tongue; there is not even any word for 'India'. Nor is there any reason why there should be an Indian Nation. The bond or union among the races to be found there is that they have for the last century and a half been governed in common by a Foreign Power.*[37] P. C. Bobb sums up Craddock's views nicely*: By this account 'Indian' was the same kind of misnomer, applied by the English, as the term 'European' when applied to the English (as it was in India). According to Craddock, India was merely, like Europe, a subcontinent within the vast single continent of Europe and Asia, whose peoples had "roamed over the whole" in prehistoric times. Down the centuries nationalities had become localized, until Europe and India, for example, each contained well over twenty separate countries, divided by race and language. India looked like one country only if seen from the outside, from ignorance or distance. India's cultural diversity, and lack of political unity has often invited its comparison with Europe.* "

---

35. Dileep Karanth, The Unity of India, *http://www.swaveda.com/articles.php?action=show&id=47.*

36. Radhakumud Mookerji, The Fundamental Unity of India (From Hindu Sources), Longmans, Green and Co. 1914.

37. P.C. Dobb, Muslim Identity and Separatism in India: The Significance of M.A. Ansari, *Bulletin of the School of Oriental and Aafrcian Studies*, Volume LIV, Part I, 1991, pp. 116-117.

These are indeed astonishing statements when viewed from an Indic perspective and certainly many Indian personalities such as Sankaracharya, who roamed the length and breadth o f India and what is more made himself perfectly understood wherever he went, through the ages would have expressed consternation to learn that India was not a unique cultural and civilizational entity. As we have already remarked, cultural diversity and ethnic diversity are two different aspects of society and one can have one without the other. It is our contention that India is culturally unique while being ethnically diverse.

"The renowned Islamic scholar, Mawlana Syed Sulaiman Nadwi develops a variant of a widespread idea about the origin of the name 'Hind': Before the advent of the Muslims, according to him, there was no single name for the country as a whole. Every province had its own name, or rather a state was known by the name of its capital. When the Turco Afghans, the upper classes among whom spoke Persian, conquered a province of this country, they gave the name 'Hindu' to the river, which is now known as Indus, and which was called Mehran, by the Arabs. In the Old Persian and also in Sanskrit, the letters 's' and 'h' often interchange. There are many instances of this. Hence Sindhu became in Persian Hindu, and the word 'Hind' derived from Hindu, came to be applied to the whole country. The Arabs, however, who were acquainted with other parts of the country, restricted the word 'Sind' to a particular province, while applying the word 'Hind' to other parts of the country as well. Soon this country came to be known by this name in distant parts of the world. The Western nations dropped the 'h' and called the country Ind or India. All over the world, now, this country is called by this name or by any one of its many variants. (Nadwi, Mawlana Syed Sulaiman Nadwi, Indo-Arab Relations (An English Rendering of *Arab O' Hind Ke Ta'alluqat*) (Translated by Prof. M. Salahuddin), The Institute of Indo-Middle East Cultural Studies, Hyderabad, India P. 8). An influential historian, Andrê Wink, writes about the fashioning of "India" from whatever geographical and cultural and human materials were present in the region now known as India: *We will see that the Muslims first defined India as a civilization, set it apart conceptually, and drew its boundaries. The early Muslim view of India includes, to be sure, a close parallel to the Western Mirabilis Indiae in the accounts of the "aja'ib al-Hind". It also includes a number of stereotypes which were already familiar to the ancient Greeks: of India as a land of self-absorbed philosophers, high learning, "wisdom", the belief in metempsychosis, of sacred cows, elephants, and, again, great wealth.*

The Arab geographers are perhaps uniquely obsessed with Indian idolatry and polytheism, "in which they differ totally from the Muslims". But the Arabs, in contrast to the medieval Christians, developed their conception of India in direct and prolonged contact with it. In a political-geographical sense, "India" or al-Hind, throughout the medieval period, was an Arab or Muslim conception. The Arabs, like the Greeks, adopted a pre-existing Persian term, but they were the first to extend its application to the entire Indianized region from Sind and Makran to the Indonesian Archipelago and mainland Southeast Asia. It therefore appears to us as if the Indians or Hindus acquired a collective identity in interaction with Islam. (Wink)[38]. *According to this view, the idea of "India" or "Hindus" itself emerged in interaction with Islam.* The Arabs must have called a vast land 'al-Hind' as a shorthand term, just as a modern textbook of geography might club diverse nations under the umbrella term 'Middle East'. Another example is the term Sudan. It was the Arabs who named a vast tract of land (without delimiting it exactly) as Bilad al-sudan -"land of the blacks". The various peoples of that region did not refer to themselves as 'Sudanese' until modern times" Yet the alert reader who reads the above excerpt would surely notice that the concept of an Indianized region stretching from Makran (Baluchistan) to Indonesia has somehow wriggled its way into a discourse which would deny (a priori) the existence of an 'India'. A question arises immediately: What was it about the region from Sind to Indonesia that merits the term 'Indianized', which caused the Arabs to call this region collectively as 'al-Hnd'? A partial answer to this question can be formulated by quoting what Vincent Smith, an authority on early India had said: *"India, encircled as she is by seas and mountains, is indisputably a geographical unit, and as such is rightly designated by one name."*

Wink's statement says: "*We will see that the Muslims first defined India as a civilization, set it apart conceptually, and drew its boundaries*". The fact that the word "India" is ostensibly of foreign origin is used to insinuate that the very idea of an Indian nation is a contribution by outsiders. No matter how the name India originated, it eventually came to mean something quite well-defined, and the use of a single term, India, is justified, and not only as a shorthand for a hazy notion. Vincent Smith[39] explains: "*The most essentially fundamental Indian unity rests upon the fact that the diverse peoples of India have*

38. Andre Wink, Al-Hind, The Making of the Indo-Islamic World, Oxford University Press, 1990, pp. 4-5.

39. Vincent Smith, Oxford History of India, 3rd Edition, 1958, p. 7.

developed a peculiar type of culture or civilization utterly different from any other type in the world. That civilization may be summed up in the term Hinduism. India primarily is a Hindu country, the land of the Brahmanas, who have succeeded by means of peaceful penetration, not by the sword, in carrying their ideas into every corner of India. Caste, the characteristic Hindu institution, is utterly unknown in Burma, Tibet, and other borderlands, dominates the whole of Hindu India, as well as in distant outposts of Indian civilization such as Bali, and exercises no small influence over the powerful Muslim minority. Nearly all Hindus revere Brahmanas, and all may be said to venerate the cow. Few deny the authority of the Vedas and other ancient scriptures. Sanskrit everywhere is the sacred language. The great gods, Vishnu and Shiva, are recognized and more or less worshipped in all parts of India. The pious pilgrim, when going the round of the holy places, is equally at home among the snows of Badrinath or on the burning sands of Rama's Bridge. The seven sacred cities include places in the far south as well as in Hindustan. Similarly, the cult of rivers is common to all Hindus, and all alike share in the affection felt for the tales of the Mahabharata and Ramayana. India beyond all doubt possesses a deep underlying fundamental unity, far more profound than that produced either by geographical isolation or by political suzerainty. That unity transcends the innumerable diversities of blood, color, language, dress, manners and sect."

The reader may not agree with all that Vincent Smith says but the idea of a culturally united India, call it a nation, or a civilization, clearly did not depend upon the Arabs/ Muslims. Nor was the idea born out of the labors of the Western Orientalist or the British colonial administrator; "India" --- the name which launched a thousand ships, and which has fired the imagination of explorers for ages, predates the emergence of Islam and Western Indology, by centuries, if not millennia."

5. Recent Initiatives to Arrive at an Entente

This was essentially a development initiated by A B Vajpayee's 'natural allies' speech at UN. His predecessors Rajiv Gandhi, P V Narasimha Rao and even Indira Gandhi in her second term, tried but were unsuccessful in overcoming the hostility of entrenched foreign policy mandarins, a legacy of the Nixon/Kissinger doctrine which institutionalized the anti -India tilt practiced with circumspection since the days of John Foster Dulles.

Towards a Strategic Partnership

India is no longer dismissed as a perennially underdeveloped country but is regarded as an Emerging Power

Despite almost five decades of hostility from the west the Indian republic has made significant strides in its geopolitical ranking

India has become self sufficient in feeding her vast population. There have been no famines since 1947. India is now the worlds largest producer of milk and other food products developed a respectable manufacturing infrastructure vaulted to the top rank countries in IT, and has become self sufficient in Prescription/OTC Drugs and has developed a strong infrastructure in Biotech

Whether the change in perception is merely cosmetic remains to be seen.

We need to see more such views from Americans before we are convinced there is a change in perception among the foreign policy mandarins.

Why what's Good for India Is Good for Us

by Charles Wheelan, Ph.D

I spent two weeks last month in India, one of the most fascinating places on the planet. Where else can you stroll through the gleaming high-tech Bangalore campus of Infosys only hours after getting stuck in a traffic jam on a major highway caused by a collision between a tractor and an ox cart?

Global Geopolitical Ranking (using multiple of GDP-using purchasing power parity and per capita GDP relative to USA)

1. United States (100%)
2. Japan (27%)
3. China (25%)
4. Germany (17%)
5. France (12%)
6. United Kingdom (12%)
7. Italy (11%)
8. **India (8.5%)**
9. Canada (7.8%)
10. Russia (6.5%)
11. Spain (6.4%)
12. Brazil (5.8%)
13. Korea (5.5%)
14. Australia (4.7%)

Ref: GLOBAL POWER FROM THE 18TH TO THE 21ST CENTURY: POWER POTENTIAL (VIP2), STRATEGIC ASSETS AND ACTUAL POWER (VIP).

By Dr Arvind Virmani, until recently, Director & Chief Executive of ICRIER (Indian Council for Research in International Economic Relations), New Delhi, was released in November 2005.

There are 4 possible scenarios

India and by association the Indic civilization) will be recognized for her Global sweep and reach.

India will be grudgingly recognized for her economic and (to a lesser extent) military clout.

India will always be consigned to the status of a'wannabe' great power and at best an emerging power (present status) and her civilization will also be under 'virtual' attack (present status).

Demographic conditions will reach a point where her civilization will have even less political backing within India than the currently abysmal state of affairs and where the preservation of her ancient traditions will become a moot issue. The Indic civilization will go the way of the Egyptian and Aztec civilization and may be remembered only in Museums (if it is remembered at all). The last and most ancient of the great civilizations will cease to be that, except as a memory.

Where does that leave us?

First and foremost we must individually arm ourselves with accurate and reliable information not only on our own History but the history of other nations and cultures. A Unity based on enlightened self interest is essential. It is not Islam but the Dharma that is on the front lines of battle (from an ideological perspective) with the Occident for most of recorded History. It is the Dharma that they will take careful aim at in the coming decades and not Islam to further their goal of establishing a Sunni Ummah in South Asia.

Conclusions

We have sought to establish that there is a common thread running through British policy towards the Indian subcontinent, ever since Sir William Jones came to India and with his prodigious curiosity and command of language(s) established the Royal Asiatic Society, and that such a thread has had its sequel in the policy of the Anglo/US/NATO alliance the virtual successor to the paramount British power in the19th century. It has not been our contention that there ever was a conspiracy whatever that term may imply in this context. But the record of consistency of such a policy has been staggering and is too coincidental to overlook. Till 1947 the objective of such a policy was to prolong British rule in India as long as was feasible with as few concessions as they could get away with. It is not as if the British were a particularly mendacious or greedy or mercantilist as Napoleon often described them. After all they had granted Dominion status to their possession in Canada and Australia with a large measure of self government, But India was different. She was different in skin color, manners, traditions, language and according to the British in Civilization. After 6 horrendous centuries of particularly brutal rule, the Indic was in comatose condition despite the last hurrah by the Marathas. Long centuries of material deprivation coupled with loss of self esteem had taken its toll. This much is hardly surprising at least to the Indic who bore the brunt of the resulting grinding poverty.

What is astonishing is the systematic manner in which the British went about the business of undermining what was left of his/her self esteem by some of the methods described above. That such a consistency was observed for several generations by intelligent men coming from varied backgrounds is a remarkable testament to the national character of the British and their unwavering faith in the righteousness of their endeavor.[40] This is despite the fact that a large majority of the people had come to accept British rule as a respite from far more arduous time. In this I would have to agree with Sir Penderel Moon, that Britain could not have ruled India for such a length of time without substantial collaboration from the Indic. Which is what it makes so difficult to comprehend; the enormous indifference and callousness to the desperate conditions of the population, accompanied by no fewer than 70 famines during their reign. Truly I would have to conclude that the British had left behind their humanity during their stay in India.

It has been a long term goal of the Western (read US/Anglo) alliance to emasculate the Indic civilization and to establish a South Asia Islamic Ummah and to prevent the development of a harmonious and militarily powerful Indic power in the Indian ocean region.

It should be the endeavor of every Indian Government to take counter measures one of which is to establish a significant trading and political partnership with the West so that the continuing motivation for the above will eventually dissipate.

The US must be made to realize that its policy of backing corrupt dictators in the land of the pure is anachronistic, impresses neither friend nor foe, and bound to fail but old habits die hard.

US must be made to realize that the Indic civilization has staying power and will outlast any obstacles put before it.

40. Sarila, Narendra Singh, *The Shadow of the Great Game*, Caroll and Graff Publishers, NY, 2005.

This is how I interpret Vajpayeeji's historic statement that "India and US are natural allies"

To summarize we have attempted to answer the questions we posed at the outset

How did this viewpoint come about and who or what nurtured such a weltanschauung?

When did this begin and what was the genesis?

What were the motives?

If there was such a concerted effort, could it be termed a conspiracy?

How was it executed?

Why is it important to study this topic?

Where does that leave us now?

Further Reading

Future of Islam by Wilfred Scawen Blunt (available from Amazon)

Imagining India by Ronald B Inden

The Dominion and Conquest of India by Sir Penderel Moon

Castes of Mind, Colonialism and the making of Modern India by Nicholas Dirks

The History of India as told by its own Historians by Elliot and Dowson

Pakistan flawed not Failed State by Dennis Kux - the politically correct view peddled by the west

Colonialism and its forms of Knowledge by Bernard Cohn

Further reading (Continued)

Refer to e-book The Indic Civilization for elaboration of many topics touched on here vepa.us/dir20

If asked for userid and password, use Userid Arjuna password sarathy. Book contains an extensive bibliography

Contact me at *Kaushal44@gmail.com*

Plate 6: Robert Clive *(facing pg. 68 (i))*

Plate 7: Mir Jaffar and Clive *(facing pg. 68 (ii))*

Appendix A Chronology Of The Colonial Period

1498 - Vasco Da Gama lands in India vîa the sea route. During this time there existed an elaborate Indian Ocean economy.

1599 - English East India Company formed.

1602 - Dutch East India Company formed.

1658 - French East India Company formed.

1707 - Death of Aurangzeb and virtual end of Mughal rule.

1744 - Robert Clive travels to India.

1757 - Battle of Plassey,(Polashir Juddho in Bengali) 23 June 1757 at Palashi, West Bengal, India.

1770 - The great Bengal Famine , where 1/3rd of Bengal died of slow starvation, the first of many famines in the Colonial era.

1835 - Macaulay plans to civilize the natives so that a class of people is created who think and do exactly like their masters. "I have no knowledge of either Sanskrit or Arabic. But I have done what I could to form a correct estimate of their value. I have read translations of the most celebrated Arabic and Sanskrit works. I have conversed both here and at home with men distinguished by their proficiency in the Eastern tongues. I am quite ready to take the Oriental learning at the valuation of the Orientalist themselves. I have never found one among them who could deny that a single shelf of a good European library was worth the whole native literature of India and Arabia. The intrinsic superiority of the Western literature is, indeed, fully admitted by those members of the Committee who support the Oriental plan of education."

The main philosophy was to incrementally indoctrinate the children with principles that are sympathetic to colonizer's philosophy. Make future generations uncertain of their own heritage Avoid teaching children the basic facts about their own history. Teach them that natural aggression is wrong and docile submission is right. Teach them that any basis of a moral foundation, like the principles of religion, is a weakness to be avoided in the name of freedom and also redefine the concept of patriotism to support colonizer's views.

1853 - Sir Alexander Cunningham was the first to archeologically examine Harappa in 1853 and 1856. Finding some Kushana coins in the site, he attributed the city to the Kushana period (Imam 1966) It is shocking to note that about one hundred miles of the Lahore-Multan railway was ballasted by bricks retrieved from the ruins at Harappa by rapacious railroad contractors; "No invader of India had ever so ruthlessly and wantonly destroyed her ancient remains as did the railway contractors in the civilized 19th century" (Edwin Bryant— *Quest for the origins of the Vedic culture,* pp. 331-332). This made the Anglo Saxon realize that the Indians have the remains of civilization just like the Mesopotamia. The big plan for India was created to change the course of history of India. The British by this time were already doing research on all the other ancient civilization such as Egypt, Mesopotamia etc. It was his concerted attempt to show that India did not have an antiquity greater than that of Egypt and Mesopotamia.

1857 - The Great Uprising of 1857- (portrayed by the East India Company as the sepoy mutiny to make it appear as an act of disloyalty) made the British aware that a united India would be disastrous for their rule in the subcontinent. This was when they laid the groundwork for a divide and rule policy for the Indian sub-continent. After the war, Whitehall assumed direct responsibility for the administration of India, ending 250 years of rule by the British East India Company. This war changed the resolve of the British towards Indians and made them racist towards the native population. Till then the practice of marriage with the local women was considered normal (especially Punjabis and Muslims) and mixed blood was not frowned upon. After the change in attitude the British made sure that they segregated the native population from themselves and their family and created a class system for privileges and favor. This was also the beginning of the creation of cantonments where the British segregated themselves.

1863 - Max Muller proposes the Aryan Invasion Theory - Probably due to the absence of finding any archaeological remains of a civilization this concocted theory was proposed and it took a life of its own. Since the native version of the history was discarded ,the Harappan phase of Indian civilization was brushed aside as being related to Mesopotamia.

1867 - Creation of Deoband Muslim school so that Ashrafs can come closer to the rest of the local Muslim converts and create a united Muslim front against the British, Till then the Ashrafs looked upon themselves as the higher and the ruling class. Syed Ahmed Khan starts the Aligarh Muslim education center to bring Muslims to the forefront of the European education. Deobandis who were Muslim reformers who setup the first madrassahs for the purpose of training future clerics were not in agreement with the Aligarh School of reformers.

1875 - First seals of Indian civilization found by Sir Alexander Cunningham in 1875(Source: Ancient Civilizations by Hugh Bowden) - This made the Anglo Saxons realize that the Indians have the remains of civilization just like the Mesopotamia. The big plan for India was created to change the course of history of India by influencing the elite class of the Indian society and to shape future generations, control the schools. The British by this time were already doing research on all the other ancient civilization such as Egypt, Mesopotamia etc. They had for the last few centuries already studied the Islamic civilization (the first Arabic chair in the west was set up in 1630s). Indus civilization was not pursued rigorously in case a large section of Indians get nationalistic feelings. The British had committed a great mistake in 1857 by accidentally uniting Moslems and Hindus against them in some areas by their policies. They were more careful in their game after that. However, they saw that the true danger to their dominance were the educated Hindus who were in possession of both Western and traditional Indic knowledge. This was the class that could easily challenge them, as it was still wedded to the Hindu ways and capable of using the power of the newly acquired Western knowledge against the British. Sir John Strachey (Finance minister 1874): "The existence side by side of these (Hindu and Muslim) hostile creeds is one of the strong points in our political position in India. The better classes of Mohammedans are a source of strength and not weakness. They constitute a comparatively small but an energetic minority of the population whose political interests are identical with ours." Sir James Card of Thanjavur, 1879: "there was no class except Brahmins, which was so hostile to the English."

1881 - The first census in British India done. This is a massive project to really classify the largest human group into various classes by their origins and social strata supposedly for benign motive. This has helped the British and later the west to target individual groups for various religious and military purposes. This census also helped the British to map the kinship pattern among various social groups, which they continued to monitor till the 20th century.

1877 - 1906 Repeated Famines in India 26 million die of slow starvation.

1885 - Indian National Congress formed as a tool of the British government to influence the course of the Independence movement and for the emancipation of the suffering Indians. The main reason for forming this organization is to create a platform to dissipate the nationalistic sentiments and to control the nature of the debate and pace of the changes in the political class of the Indians. The political consciousness of the Hindus could be molded and controlled with such platform. The terms of debate between the Hindus and Muslims were also influenced with the help of key people in the party as it evolved in the next 50 years. The main philosophy was to shape the political philosophy, infiltrate the government: Whenever and wherever possible place those sympathetic to your philosophy into office at all levels-the higher, the better-so they can sway the direction of the country within every function of government, promising solutions and benefits for all. In such a way you can tilt legislation toward incrementally increasing the control of and dependency on government-a government that you are shaping.

1906 - split of Bengal during The Great Game at the height of rivalry between the Russians and the British in the Eurasian landmass. The British needed an ally who would be able to resist the thrust of the Tsars. Russian expansion started in 1582 and continued to central Asia and the pacific till late 1700s. The next target of the Russians was Tibet and British were worried about Tibet coming under the influence of Russia. The long-term plan was to keep India under the British dominion for the next 500 years and was expressed in commonwealth speeches in early 1900-1910.

1911 - Capital shifts from Calcutta to New Delhi. This was done to reduce the increasing demands for independence in the enlightened Bengal, which had the most interaction with the west. This was a diversion so that the seat of power should be perceived similar to the Mughal Empire. This also broke the deep intellectual nationalist discourse in Bengal and weakened it. The ultimate aim is to make sure that the Muslims would also start seeing a Muslim homeland in Indian sub-continent.

1917 - First World War. Fall of Ottoman Empire and creation of Middle Eastern states under the direct influence of the British. British looked at the Muslims of the Middle East and the Muslims of the India as one and built relationship with the Arabs and the ashrafs of the sub-continent. The British oust the Ottomans from Jerusalem and Baghdad; in the Balfour Declaration, Britain declares its support for the establishment of a 'national home for the Jewish people' in Palestine. In return, the unwritten agreement with the Arabs is the creation of a Muslim homeland in the Indian sub-continent.

1920s -Discovery of Mohenjo-Daro, Harappa by Rakhal Das Banerjee and Daya Ram Sahni- final confirmation of the existence and history of Indian civilization. This may have made the British to push through the plans for division of India.

1930 - Plans to divide the country hatched when the Middle East was secure after the First World War and Saudi Arabia was already a state. The assessment of the colonial powers was that the history of the natives has been discovered with archeology and they would eventually realize the richness of their own civilization. It would be difficult to keep the country colonized for a long time.

1935 - The GOVERNMENT OF INDIA ACT passed by the British parliament. Burma and Aden were separated from India. British India was divided into 11 provinces, each under an appointed governor and an appointed executive council. Each province was to have an elected legislature (bicameral in six provinces and unicameral in five), with a ministry responsible to it. Representation was to be based on the communal award. The provincial governments were to enjoy wide autonomy, though the governors retained certain emergency powers. The ultimate objective was the establishment of an All-India Federation, to include the Indian states as well as. The provinces of British India.

1939 - Second World War - British still to recover from the First World War and willing to lessen their burden in the empire.

1940 - Lahore resolution for a separate Muslim homeland. Secretly British were siding with the Muslim League/Ashrafs to create a homeland for them for future collaboration. There is increasing evidence that Lahore resolution was made in that location and time so that the future homeland of the Pakistan will have Punjab as the cultural/political and military center.

1947 - Indian Independence/partition. Creation of Pakistan.

1950 - the Birth of the Modern Republic.

1971 - Split of Pakistan the largest Muslim nation into Pakistan and Bangladesh.

Appendix B Proposed Skeleton Or Scaffolding Of Indian Chronology

Key Dates

Event	Individual or detailed description	Date
Era	The Vedic Era	7000 to 4000 BCE
Era Sarasvati Sindhu Civilization	Mehrgarh Culture, early phase	7000 BCE
Dynasty	The Ikshvakus and the Ramayana	7000 BCE
Era	Brahmana Era, Beginning of	5000 BCE
Era	Puranic Era	5000 BCE - 3000 BCE
Birth	Veda Vyaasa	3200 ~ 3300 BCE
Observation Vernal Equinox in Rohini	Observation of Nakshatra in which the Vernal Equinox occurs	-3100 BCE
War	The Great Bharata War	Nov 22, 3067 BCE
Era	Era of the Sulva Sutras. Sutras of the cord, development of geometry, trigonometry	4000 ~ 2000 BCE
Birth	Apastambha	-3000 BCE
Birth	Baudhayana	-3000 BCE

Era	Kali Yuga	3102 BCE
Writings	Pingala	2900 BCE
Writings	Panini's Ashtadhyayi, codification of Vyakarana and other Vedangas	2900 BCE
Paradigm shift	Use of Decimal Place Value system (Panini , Pingala). Catalyzed Indic contribu. to algebra, number theory, infinite series, spherical trigonometry	2900 BCE
Era Sarasvati Sindhu civil.	Mature Phase	3000 BCE - 1700 BCE
Dynasty (Magadha)	Brhihadratha Dynasty (22 kings, 1007 years)	3139 BCE- 2132 BCE
Birth	Aryabhata	2765 BCE, 337 Yugabda
Writings	Yajnavalkya, Brihat-AranyakaUpanishad, Satpatha Brahmana	-3000BCE Astronomical evidence
Writings	Aryabhata wrote the Aryabhatiyum when he was 23 years old	2742 BCE
Dynasty	Pradhyota Dynasty (5 kings, 138 years)	2132 to 1994 BCE
Dynasty	Sisunaga Dynasty (10 kings, 360 years)	1994- 1634 BCE
Lifespan	Gautama Buddha	1887-1807 BCE, puranic and astronomical evidence
Dynasty	Nanda Dynasty (Mahapdmananda and his sons)	1634 - 1534 BCE
Coronation	Chandragupta Maurya	1534 BCE -1500 BCE
Coronation	Asoka Maurya	1472 BCE
Dynasty	Maurya (12 kings, 316 years Kushan Empire	1534-1218 BCE 1298 BCE -

Dynasty	Sunga Dynasty (10 kings, 300 years)	1218 - 918 BCE
Writings	Patanjali's Mahabhashya	1218 BCE
Writings	Nagarjuna	1294 BCE
Reign	Kanishka	1298-1237 BCE
Dynasty	Kanva Dynasty (4 kings, 85 years)	918-833 BCE
Era	Andhra Satavahana (32 kings, 506 years)	833 BCE -327 BCE
Birth	Kumarila Bhatta	557 BCE
Era	Sakanripa Kala (era of Cyrus the great of Persia	550 BCE
Birth	Adi Sankaracharya	509 BCE-477 BCE
Coronation	Alexander of Macedonia	336 BCE
Coronation	Chandragupta of Gupta dynasty	327 BCE
War	Alexander initiates an inconclusive battle with Purushottam, regional kshatrap in the Punjab and is forced to retreat short of his goal of vanquishing the great empire of India	326 BCE
Dynasty	Imperial Gupta Dynasty (7 kings, 245 years)	327 BCE- 82 BCE
Writings	VarahaMihira Pancha Siddhanta	123 BCE
Reign	Vikramaditya	102 BCE to 78 BCE
Era	Vikrama Saka	57 BCE
Birth	Brahmagupta	30 BCE
Era	Salivahana Calendar (Punwar dynasty)	78 CE
Writings	Bhaskara II Siddhanta Siromani	486 CE
Dynasty	Punwar Dynasty (23 Kings, 1111 years)	82 BCE- 1193 CE

Era	Christian Era	0 (Yugabda 3102)
Era	Salivahana (Saka Calendar)	78 CE
Dynasty	Pala Empire	750-1174 CE
Dynasty	Chola Empire	848 CE - 1279 CE
Beginning of Islamic Era	Prithviraj Chamahana the last major indic dynasty in North India	1192 CE
Era	Delhi Sultanate	1192 CE - 1526 CE
Era	The Hoysalas	1040 CE-1346 CE
Reconquista begins and the Fall of Toledo	Toledo, the great Muslim center of learning falls into Christian hands	1085 CE
Era	The Kakatiyas	1083 CE-1323 CE
Era	Bahmani Confederation	1390 CE-1596 CE
Era	Vijayanagar Empire	1339 CE-1625 CE
Era	The Moghal Empire	1526 CE - 1757 CE
Dynasty	The Maratha Confederacy	1674 CE - 1818 CE
Dynasty	The Sikh Confederacy	1716 CE - 1849 CE
Dynasty	The British Empire	1757 CE - 1947 CE
Era	The Modern Republic	1950 CE

Appendix C Select Dynasties Who Ruled India In The 'Modern' Era After The Start Of Kali Yuga February 17, 3102 BCE

There is no attempt at completeness here and this list or lists are not exhaustive by any means. But the dynastic lists available to us are far more complete, than our English Language text books would have you believe. So when Indian History Books written by Englishmen, studiously avoid mentioning dynastic lists, methinks they have a reason and that being the need to indulge in and foster the illusion that the Indic had no sense of history. Our response is what is the gold standard for the respective eras we are talking about? How many accurate Dynastic lists do we have in the world going back to to 3000 BCE and earlier?

Descendants of the Kuru Pandavas (from Yudhistira 3067 BCE - 1634 BCE)

Yudhistira	Parikshit
Janamejaya	Sataneeka
Ashwamedadata	Adhseema Krishna
Nichaknu	Ushna
Chitra ratha	Suchirata
Krushnimanta	Sushena
Suneetha	Nrupegakshu
Sukhibala	Pariplava
Sumaya	Medhavi

Ripunjaya	Urva
Tigma	Bruhadradha
Kasudana	Saranika II
Udayana	Kihinara
Dandapani	Nivamitra
Kshemaka	

Table From Dating in Indian Archaeology, Problems and Perspectives, Bharatiya Itihaas Sankalan Samiti, T P Verma Ed.

Chart I : INDUS - SARASWATI CIVILIZATION : STAGES OF DEVELOPEMENT (4000 B.C. - 1500 B.C.)

PERIOD	APPROXIMATE TIME BRACKET	REGION AND CULTURES					
		PUNJAB	SINDH	RAJASTHAN	HARYANA	GUJARAT	BALUCHISTAN
LATE PERIOD	1500 B.C. To 1900 B.C.	Cemetery - H	Jhukar	Kudwala Lurewala Gamanwala Siddhuwala Shahiwala	Mitathal - II B Bhagwanpura - I B - Sanghol - I	Dholavira - VI Kuntasi - II Surkotada - I C Rojdi Lothal B	Mehargarh - VIII Sibri
MATURE PERIOD	1900 B.C. To 2600 B.C.	Harappa - III C B A	Mohenjodaro (Upper Levels) Balakot - II	Kalibangan - II Ganeshwar - II	Banawali - II Kunal I C	Dholavira - IV Kuntasi - I Surkotada I A - I B Padri II Rojdi Lothal A	Nausharo - II
TRANSITION PERIOD	2600 B.C. To 2800 B.C.	Harappa - II	Mohenjodaro (Intermediate Levels) Balakot - II (Lower Levels)	Kalibangan (I - II Overlap)	Banawali - I C Kunal I B (Upper Level)	Dholavira - III Surkotada - I A (Lower Levels)	Nausharo - II - I C
EARLY PERIOD	2800 B.C. To 3500 B.C.	Kot Diji - I Harappa-I	Kot Diji - I Mohenjodaro (Lower Levels) (Pre-Defence)	Kot Diji - I Kalibangan - I Ganeshwar - I Sothi Culture	Kunal I B Kot Diji Banawali I A - I B	Dholavira - I - II Padri - I	Mehargarh - V - VII Nausharo I A & B
FORMATIVE PERIOD	3500 B.C. To 4000 + B.C.	Pre-Harappa - I " Ravi Culture " (Pre - Kot Diji) Level Jalilpur - I	Amri Culture Miri Kalat - II Bala Kot - I	Hakra Culture Lathwala - I Bhostanwala Ambrawali Chikrala	Kunal Culture Kunal - I A	Padri I Loteshwar	Mehargarh - IV - V

Dynastic Lists of the Magadha Empires

Dynasty	Number of kings	Period	Total number of years ruled	Cumulative Total
Brhadratha	22	3136 to 2132 BCE	1006	
Pradhyota	5	2132 to 1994 BCE	138	1144
Sisunaga	10	1994 to 1634 BCE	360	1504
Nanda	9	1634 to 1534 BCE	100	1604
Maurya	12	1534 to 1218 BCE	316	1920
Sunga	10	1218 to 918 BCE	300	2220
Kunwa	4	918 to 833 BCE	85	2305
Andhra Satavahana	33	833 to 327 BCE	506	2811
Imperial Gupta	77	327 to 82 BCE	245	3055
Punwar or Pramara	24	82 BCE to 1193 CE	1275	4330
Totals	206	3136 BCE to 1193 CE	4330	

The Brihadratha Dynasty

Serial No.	Name of King	Regnal Period	Begins Kali Era KE or Yugabda	Begins BCE
1	Marjari	58	36 before KE	3138
2	Srutasrava	64	22	3080
3	Apratipa or Ayutayu	36	86	3016
4	Niramitra	40	122	2980
5	Sukrutha or Sukshatra	58	162	2940
6	Brihatkarma	23	220	2882
7	Syenajit	50	243	2859

8	Srutanjaya	40	293	2809
9	Mahabala or Vibhau	35	333	2769
10	Suchi	58	368	2734
11	Kshemya	28	426	2676
12	Anuvrata or Suvrata	64	454	2648
13	Dharmanetra or Sunetra	35	518	2584
14	Nirvriti	58	553	2549
15	Suvrata	38	611	2491
16	Dhrudasena or Mahasena	58	649	2453
17	Sumati or Mahanetra	33	707	2395
18	Suchala or Subala	22	740	2362
19	Sunetra	40	762	2340
20	Satyajit	83	802	2300
21	Veerajit or Viiswajit	35	885	2217
22	Ripunjaya	50	920	2182

The Pradyota Dynasty

Serial No.	Name of King	Regnal Period	Begins Kali Era KE or Yugabda	Begins BCE
1	Pradyota or Balaka	23	970	2132
2	Palaaka or Paalaka	24	993	2109
3	Visakhayupa	50	1017	2085
4	Jamaka or Suryaka	21	1067	2035
5	Nanivardhana	20	1088	2014

The Sisunaga Dynasty

Serial No.	Name of King	Regnal Period	Begins Kali Era KE or Yugabda	Begins BCE
1	Sisunaga	40	1108	1994
2	Kakavarma	36	1148	1954
3	Kshemadharma or Kshemavarma	26	1184	1918
4	Kshemajit	40	1210	1892
5	Vidhisarta or Bimbisara	38	1250	1852
6	Ajatasatru	27	1288	1814
7	Darsaka or Vamsaka	35	1315	1787
8	Udayana or Udasina	33	1350	1752
9	Nandivardhana or kakavardhana	42	1383	1719
10	Mahanandi	43	1425	1677

The Nanda Dynasty

Serial No.	Name of King	Regnal Period	Begins Kali Era KE or Yugabda	Begins BCE
1	Mahapadmananda	88	1468	1634
2	Sumalya etc, 9 brothers	12	1556	1546

The Maurya Dynasty

Serial No.	Name of King	Regnal Period	Begins Kali Era KE or Yugabda	Begins BCE
1	Chandragupta Maurya	34	1568	1534
2	Bindusara	28	1602	1500
3	Asoka	36	1630	1472
4	Suparsva or Suyasa	8	1666	1436
5	Dasaradha or Bandupalita	8	1674	1428
6	Indrapalita	70	1682	1420
7	Harshavardhana	8	1752	1350
8	Sangata	9	1760	1342
9	Salisuka	13	1769	1333
10	Somasarma or Devasarma	7	1782	1320
11	Satadhanva	8	1789	1313
12	Brihadradha or Brihadaswa	87	1797	1305

The Sunga Dynasty

Serial No.	Name of King	Regnal Period	Begins Kali Era KE or Yugabda	Begins BCE
1	Pushyamitra	60	1884	1218
2	Agnimitra	50	1944	1158
3	Vasumitra	36	1994	1108
4	Sujyeshta	17	2030	1072
5	Bhadraja or Andhraka	30	2047	1055
6	Pulindaka	33	2077	1025
7	Ghoshavasu	3	2110	992
8	Vajramitra	29	2113	989
9	Bhagavata	32	2142	960
10	Devabhuti Kshemabhumi	10	2174	928

The Kanva Dynasty

Serial No.	Name of King	Regnal Period	Begins Kali Era KE or Yugabda	Begins BCE
1	Vasudeva Kanva	30	2184	918
2	Bhumimitra	24	2223	879
3	Narayana Kanva	12	2247	855
4	Susarma	10	2259	843

The Satavahana Andhra Dynasty

Serial No.	Name of King	Regnal Period (Years)	Period of Reign in Kali Era (Solar Tropical Year)	Period of Reign BCE (Before the Common Era)
1	Simukha Saatakarni	23	2269-2292	833 - 810
2	Sri Krishna Saatakarni	18	2292- 2310	810-792
3	Sri Malia Saatakarni	10	2310 - 2320	792 - 782
4	Puurnothsanga	18	2320 - 2338	782-764
5	Sri Satakarni	56	2338 - 2394	764 - 708
6	Skandha stambhi	18	2394 - 2412	708 - 690
7	Lambodara Saatavaahana	18	2412 - 2430	690 - 672
8	Apiitaka Saatavaahana	12	2430 - 2442	672 - 690
9	Meghaswaati Saatavaahana	18	2442 - 2460	660 - 642
10	Saata Swaati Saatavaahana	18	2460 - 2478	642 - 624
11	Skanea Saatakarni	7	2748-2485	624-617
12	Mrigendra Saatakarni	3	2485 - 2488	617 - 614
13	Kuntala Saatakarni	8	2488 - 2496	614 - 606

14	Soumya Satakarni	12	2496-2508	606-594
15	Saata Saatakarni	1	2508 - 2509	594 - 593
16	Puloma or Puloma I	36	2509 - 2545	593 - 557
17	Megha Satakarni	38	2545 - 2583	557 - 519
18	Arishta Satakarni (in the tenth year of his reign in B.Ç. 509, Sri Sankara was born.)	25	2583 - 2608	519 - 494
19	Haala Saatavahana	5	2608 - 2613	494 - 489
20	Mandalaka Saatavahana	5	2613 - 2618	489 - 484
21	Purindrasena Saatavahana	21	2618 - 2639	484 - 463
22	Sundara Saatakarni	1	2639 - 2640	463 - 462
23	Chakora Saatakarni Mahendra Saatakarni	1/2 1/2	2640 2640 2641 - 2641	462-461 462-461
24	Siva Saatakarni	28	2641 - 2669	461-433
25	Gautamiputra Saatkarni	25	2669-2694	433-408
26	II Puloma Saatakarni	32	2694-2726	408-376
27	Siva sri Saatakarni	7	2726-2733	376-369
28	Sivaskanda Saatakarni	7	2733-2740	369-362
29	Yajna Sri Saatakarni	19	2741-2759	362-343
30	Vijayasri Saatakarni	6	2759- 2765	343-337
31	Chandra Sri Saatakarni	3	2765-2768	337-334
32	III Puloma Sri Saatakarni	7	2768-2775	334 - 327

The Imperial Gupta Dynasty

Serial No.	Name of King	Regnal Period	Begins Kali Era KE or Yugabda	Begins BCE
1	Chandragupta I or Vijayaditya	7	2775	327
2	Samudragupta or Asokaditya	51	2782	320
3	Chandragupta II or Vikramaditya	36	2833	269
4	Kumaragupta I or Mahendraaditya	42	2869	233
5	Skandagupta or Pratapaditya	25	2911	191
6	Narasimha gupta Baladitya	5 35	2936 2941	166 161
7	Kumaragupta II Kramaditya	44	2976	126

Source: Chronology of Ancient Hindu History Part 1. author and publisher, Bharata Charitra Bhaskara, Vimarsakagresara, Pandit Kota Vankatachela paakayaaji Kali 5058, AD 1957- Arya Vignana Grantha Mala, Publication No 23.

The List of Chola Kings[41]

Early Cholas, Interregnum (circa 200-848 CE)

Ilamcetcenni . Karikala Chola, Nedunkilli . Nalankilli

Killivalavan . Kopperuncholan, Kocengannan . Perunarkilli

Medieval Cholas

Name	Regnal Period,CE
Vijayalaya Chola	848-871(?)
Aditya I	871-907
Parantaka Chola I	907-950
Gandaraditya	950-957
Arinjaya Chola	956-957
Sundara Chola	957-970
Uttama Chola	970-985
Rajaraja Chola I	985-1014
Rajendra Chola I	1012-1044
Rajadhiraja Chola	1018-1054
Rajendra Chola II	1051-1063
Virarajendra Chola	1063-1070
Athirajendra Chola	1067-1070

Chalukya Cholas

Kulothunga Chola I	1070-1120
Vikrama Chola	1118-1135
Kulothunga Chola II	1133-1150
Rajaraja Chola II	1146-1163
Rajadhiraja Chola II	1163-1178
Kulothunga Chola III	1178-1218
Rajaraja Chola III	1216-1256
Rajendra Chola III	1246-1279

41. Dating and dynastic lists need to be examined.

The Dynastic list of the Vijayanagar Empire (1336 - 1672 CE)

1Vira Harihara I Sangamas 1336 (CE unless otherwise noted)	1354 2 Bukka Raya I Sangamas 1354	1377 3 Vira Harihara Raya II Sangamas 1376	1404 4 Virupaksha Raya I Sangamas 1404
1405 5 Bukka Raya II Sangamas 1405	1406 6 Deva Raya I Sangamas 1406	1422 7 Bukka Raya III Sangamas 1422	1423 8 Deva Raya II Sangamas 1423
1446 9 Vira Deva Raya Sangamas 1446	1447 10 Mallik arajuna Raya Sangamas 1465	1465 11 Viru paksha Raya II Sangamas 1465	1486 12 Suluva Narasinga Raya I Suluva 1486
1493 13 Suluva Narasinga Raya II Suluva 1493	1501 14 Vira Sarasimha Raya I Tuluva 1501	1502 15 Vira Narasimha Raya II Tuluva 1502	1509 16 Krishna Deva Raya Tuluva 1509
1530 17 Achy-uta Deva Raya Tuluva 1530	1542 18 Venk-ata Deva Raya I Tuluva 1542	1543 19 Vira Sadashiva Raya Tuluva 1543	1568 20 Tirumala Deva Raya II Aravidu 1568
1572 21 Sri Ranga Deva Raya I Aravi-du 1572	1586 22 Venk-atapati Deva Raya II Aravidu 1586	1614 23 Sri Ranga Deva Raya II Aravidu 1614	1615 24 Rama Deva Raya Aravidu 1615
1633 25 Ve-nkata Deva Raya III Aravidu 1633	1646 Sri Ranga Deva Raya III Aravidu 1646	1672	

The Vijayanagar Empire was the last of the major Hindu Kingdoms.

The Satavahana Andhras

Ed.Note

The history of the Andhra Kingdoms has been much neglected in the Eurocentric descriptions of our past. Furthermore , there has been an assumption that Andhra has been synonymous with the Telugu language. While the Telugu language has an extensive literature of its own , our current knowledge of the matter suggests that the Andhra Kingdoms predate the language by at least a millennium. Here is one account of the history of the Andhras. To verify this chronology we need to cross check references to Adi Sankara during this period.

The Andhra Dynasty of Emperors of Magadha

(Kota Venkatachalam)

506 (TOTAL YEARS OF THE SATAVAHANA DYNASTY)

As per the list above the 32 Andhra Satavahana emperors of Magadha ruled for 506 years on the whole from Kali2269 - 2775 or B. C. 833 to 327 B. C. After them the founder of the Gupta or Andhra Bhritya Dynasty, Chandragupta occupied the throne in B. C. 327 after putting to the sword the last two princes of the Aandhra dynasty, Chandra Sri and Puloma III. The king who then got himself crowned at Pataliputra, having annexed a considerable part of the Magadha state was this Chandragupta 1 of the Gupta dynasty and not Chandragupta Maurya, founder of the Maurya dynasty, as is commonly and erroneously supposed now-a-days. By this erroneous identification by the western (European) historians of India, and as a consequence of it to be in accord with that. By pushing forward and locating in B. C. 1500 the Mahabharata war which took place actually in B. C 3138 and the coronation of Chandra Gupta Maurya of B. C. 1534 to B. C. 324, the antiquity of the entire history of ancient India has been reduced by more than 12 centuries.

Details of this distortion (partly due to mistake and partly to deliberate mischief) are given in our other publication in English with the title 'The plot in Indian Chronology'. In B, C. 327 the Aandhras lost their power in the Magadha state, the Paramount power in Bharat at the time. Their empire came to an end; but not the Saatavahana dynasty of Aandhra princes. The princes of the dynasty indulged in mutual quarrels, cut up the empire into bits, each declared himself independent and all reduced themselves to the position and status of rules of petty principalities. The royal dynasty split up into 12 branches according to the Puranas.

Aandhraram samsthitaha panch tesham vasashcah ye punaha saptaivatu bhavisyanti iti (Brahmanda Purana Chap 77, Verse 171 or Vayu Purana Ghapt. 99-3517- Verse.)

Thereafter the princes of the Agni dynasty (a branch of the Saatavahana dynasty) might have branched off into various further subdivisions. Pallava, Cheta, Sena. Kadamba, Rashtrakuta, Vishnulu Kundina. Brihatphalayana, Baana. Gaanga, Hosala, Rajaputra, Saalamkayana, Vakataka. Vallabhi. Vaidumba, Nolamba dynasties were all connected with the Andhra Saatavahana dynasty' Even from earlier times as the eldest sons at. The Saatavahana kings only succeeded to the throne by the principle of Primogeniture, the younger sons and sons in law of the kings of the different generations were perhaps provided for by being made the chiefs of small principalities in Rajputana (current day Rajasthan).

The present Rajput royal dynasties might have thus come into being. Such as Pramara or Paramara Chapahani or Chahuman. Sukla or Chalukya, Parihara or pratihara) the four Agni dynastieg. These royal dynasties are otherwise known as Brahma-Kshatriyas, as the founders of the above named four dynasties were all Brahmanas well versed in the Vedas.

The Bhavishya Purana-Pratisarga parva declares Pramara was a student of Saama. Chapahaani of Yajus. Sukla was versed in the three Vedas (Rig, Yajus and Sarna) and Parihara was a student of Adharvana. In Kali 2710. ie. B. C. 392, these four scholar s and sages were made to perform sacrifices on Mount Arbuda or Abu in Raajaputana, with the object of developing in them the martial spirit (Kshatra Tejas) and they were made the kings of the four parts of the country. Details of this account of the origin of the royal families of the Agni dynasty are available in the last chapter of this book "Kings of Agni Vamṣa".

Kalhana in his Raja tharangini says Princes descended from the Andhra Saatavahana dynasty were ruling in the eighth century after Christ, in Kashmir. Lahore, Abhisaara, Draga, Simhapura, Divyakataka, Uttara Jyotisha, —the first two now forming part of Kashmir and the last three in modern Afghanistan, all the five, Yavana kshatriya kingdoms. The Lohaar and Hindu Saahi princes are descendents of the Andhra Saatavahana and the Thomara dynasty derived from it. The famous emperors Vikramaditya, Saalivahana and Bhoja belonged to the Pramara or Paramara or more well known as Panwar dynasty deriving from the Andhra Saatavahanas. The Chapahanis were also known as Chahumans, those of the Thomara branches followed the Kshatriya, traditions and customs and were reckoned as Kshatriyas proper in the Puranas too. The famous historical personages Prithviraj, Jayachand and Rani Samyukta all belong to the Thomara dynasty.

The Sukla or Chalukya princes are well-known among the rulers of Southern India. Of them one branch known as the Eastern Chalukya ruled over the regions of the eastern coast land and another known as the Western Chalukya ruled in the west. The famous king Raja Rajanarendra, who patronized and sponsored the literary effort of the translation of the Mahabharata into Telugu, belonged to the Eastern Chalukya dynasty. During the centuries after Christ, the Chalukya princes deemed it more honorable to style themselves as Kshatriyas and managed to link up the founders of their dynasties with ancient Kshatriya princes and got such lists of their descent recorded in the inscriptions of their times. The Pariharas ruled in Bengal the Brahmanas of the Sakti worship cult in Bengal belong to this branch of Agni Kshatriyas or Brahma-Kshatras.

The Kings of The Kadamba Dynasty

Mayuura Sarma, founder of the Kadamba dynasty of princes who ruled in Kerala or Malayala country, also belonged to the Aandhra Saatavahana dynasty and became the ruler of that part of the country in the 6th century B. C. Kaakutsa Varma a prince of this dynasty was ruling there in B. C. 550 (Vide Ancient Dekkan P. 27)

As there were no Brahmanas in Kerala at that time king 'Mayuura sarma' sponsored the migration of a group of Brahmana families from his birth place Ahi kshetra [Sarpavaram as it is now called) a village in Godavari District and settled them in his kingdom. In the '*Castes and Tribes of Southern India*' a publication of the Madras Government in seven volumes, it is stated with reference to the Brahmanas of Kerala : —In some of the ancient texts of Brahmanas in manuscript, it is recorded that, in the reign of king Mayuravarma of the Kadamba dynasty, some Aandhra Brahmanas were encouraged to migrate to south Kanara. Subsequent to the legendary curse of Parasurama till this migration of Brahmanas from Ahi kshetra in Aandhra under the patronage of king' Mayura sarma of Kadamba dynasty, there were no Brahmanas in Kerala.

Inscriptions reveal that, the founder of the Kadamba dynasty of princes who ruled at Banavasi in North Kanara as the Capital, was Mayuravarma (the name is variously recorded, as Mayura varma and Maurya Sarma). He was the Founder of the Brahmana dynasty of princes known as "Kadamba,"

The traditions and written record's of the Nambudri Brahmanas of Kerala extend back to 'Mayuravarma.' The Brahmanas imported by Mayura Varma were at the time of their migration the disciples and followers of the famous Kumarila Bhatta or Bhattacharya. but after the migration they accepted the principles and became the adherents of the philosophy of Sri Sankara (birth 509 BCE) which prevailed in Kerala.

In the fifth volume of the same publication Sri Subramanya Ayyer writes:-"':The Danta 'Kadha list in 'Kerala Mahatmya declares that the Nambudri Brahmanas of Kerala" were the descendents of immigrants from" Ahikshetra.

The sentences are a quotation from the ancient Sanskrit books 'Kerala Mahatmya' and 'Keralotpatti'. Andhra praehalana or 'Andhra movements', a small publication of the Andhra Mahasabha, immediately after the first conference of the Andhra Sabha, also claims that 'the famous historical personages of Mayura varma, Bhattacharya and Sri Sankara were all Andhras. Several of the Dantna stories also support the claim.

Even V. A. Smith[42] admits in p. 43 of his history of India that the kings of the Kadamba dynasty who ruled over the region comprising the Kanara and the northern districts of Mysore from the 3rd to the 6th centuries after Christ were Brahmanas. Thus the Kadamba princes who ruled over Kerala from the 6th century before Christ to the 6th century after Christ and the Brahmanas who migrated to the Country along with them and under their patronage were all Aandhras.

Among the Brahmanas who thus migrated from Ahikshetra or Sarpavaram, a village in the Godavari District) to Kerala under the patronage of Mayura-Sarma the Brahmana ruler of Kerala. there was a Brahmana scholar of the name Siva guru who settled down in the village Kaladi in Kerala. To him, after he had settled in Kerala was born 'Sri Sankara the first.' So Sri Sankara the Great Advaitic Philosopher and the Nambudri Brahmanas were all of Andhra descent, 'Sri Ramanuja' the Great protagonist of 'Visishtadwaita' bore the surname (family name) "Aasuuri". Surnames or house names constitute a distinguishing feature of the Aandhras, among the different peoples of south India.

Tamilians have no surnames or house names. So Sri Ramanuja should be deemed to belong to a family of Andhra Brahmanas, who had

---

42. Smith, Vincent, *A Oxford History of India*.

migrated to the Tamil country and settled down there some generations previous to him. Even so, 'Madhva-Acharya,' the great exponent of the 'Dvaita system' of philosophy bore the surname of Nadiminti. (Madya geh) He should be similarly deemed to belong to an Andhra Brahmana family that had migrated to the Kannada country and settled down there. Sri Tallapaka Annamacharya, and his son Sri Tiruvengalayya who lived in the 15th century, and Kshetrayya of the 7th century who composed the songs known after him and the famous Thyagaraja of the 18th century, author of the immortal songs inculcating and expressing at the same time the principles of devotion (Bhakti) enlightenment (Jnana) and renunciation (Vairagya) all these celebrated musical composers were of Andhra descent though belonging to families that had migrated to and settled down in several parts of the other regions in South India. The great scholar Kumarila Bhatta of 557 BCE" who stemmed the advancing tide of the Jaina and Bouddha religions and safeguarded the ancient Vaidic religion of the country, was an Andhra. The great savant 'Vidyaranya who wrote authoritative commentaries on the four Vedas and preserved for us knowledge of the contents of the Vedas to this day was an Andhra.

Hence the sage 'Appayya Dikshitha:' declares "It should be deemed a great good fortune to be born an Andhra, to claim the Andhra language as ones mother tongue; to' 'live in Andhra Desha, further to the Vaidic cultural tradition and then to be a student of the Yajurveda'. It is a good fortune possible only for one with rare accumulated merit." It need not be mentioned that he himself was an Andhra (though he is said. by some. to belong to the Dravida branch: even if it is conceded; it only means he belongs to a group of Dravida or Tamilian families that migrated to Andhra in the remote past. settled down there in such remote past that they had long ago forgotten and given up the use of the Tamilian language even in their homes, and made the Andhra language their mother tongue. Even then we have every right to claim him to be an Aandhrai. There are several other great personages among Andhras in every period Ancient and modern.

Source: Chronology of Ancient Hindu History Part 1. author and publisher, Bharata Charitra Bhaskara, Vimarsakagresara, Pandit Kota Vankatachela paakayaaji Kali 5058, AD 1957- Arya Vignana Grantha Mala, Publication No 23.

MAX MUELLER (SANSKRIT SCHOLAR)

Max Mueller was born at Dessau in Germany in 1823, the only son of Wilhelm Mueller, a distinguished poet, some of whose poems were set to music by Franz Schubert. Max Mueller attended the gramer school in his native town till 1836. He than entered the University of Leipzig in 1841 with the intention of studying Latin and Grek. However studying these languages proved somewhat tiring to him, and when he heard of the foundation of a Chair in Sanskrit, he took to the study of the language with deep devotion and started learning that language. Taking has decorate in philosophy in 1943, Max Mueller proceded to the University of Berlin in 1844 to continue his work on Sanskrit and philosophy under Franz Bopp, the founder of the Science of Comparative Philosophy, and under Friendrich von Schelling, te eminent philosopher. In 1846, he went to England, with an introduction to the Prussian Minister in London, Baroon Bunsen, who later became his well-wisher, to copy and collate manuscripts in Sanskrit. The greatest difficulty he faced was money for the publication of the Rig-Veda which he in a meanwhile, had begun to translate. This difficulty was, however, overcome with the help of Baron Bunsen adn H.H. Wilson, the first Boden Professor of Sanskrit at Oxford who ecommended him to East India Company for financial support. As his Rig-Veda was being printed at the iversity Pres, he migrated to Oxford in 1848 and spent the rest of his life there. The first volume of Max Mueller's edition was apeared in 1849, the sixth and the last in 1874. This printed Rig-Veda caused great ethusiasm in India. With the translation of the Rig-Veda, and innumerable publications on Indian religion and literature, Max Mueller ushered in renaissance of India's culture and was its greatest interpreter to the Western world. Later it was specially the Vedanta which attracted him so much that Swami Vivekananda said for him: "Max Mueller is a Vedantist of Vedantists. He has, indeed, cought the real soul of the melody of the Vedanta." Gradually, Mueller's reputation spread in India. His book 'India: What it can teach us' has a special place among his publications. It contains a series of lectures given by Mueller at the University of Cambridge. When reading these books, the reader will find it difficult to believe that Max Mueller was never in India. Max Mueller did not only delve into India's past but also took the liveliest interest in her political reawakening. He regualrly corresponded with prominent Indians who prepared the path for India's freedom. When he died in 1900, India had indeed lost a great friend, on whom she rightly bestowed the title "Moksha Mula." The Posts and Telegraphs Department is privileged to bring out a stamp in honour of Max Mueller.

Plate 8: Max Müller Letter *(facing pg. 96)*

Appendix D Friedrich Maximilian Müller

Friedrich Max Müller

Friedrich Maximilian Müller (1823-1900) was born in Dessau and educated in Leipzig, where he learned Sanskrit and translated the Hitopadesa of Pandit Visnu Sarma before coming to England in 1846. Since he was penniless, he came under the tutelage of Baron von Bunsen, the Prussian[43] ambassador to England who basked in the childishly pleasant thought of converting the whole world to Christianity. It was in London that Max Müller met Macaulay who was still on the look out for his 'right man'. Müller was first commissioned by the East India Company to translate the Rg Veda into English. The company agreed to pay the young Müller 4 Shillings for each page that was ready to print. He later moved to Oxford where he translated a number of books on Eastern religion. His magnum opus was his series *The Sacred Books of the East*, a fifty volume work which he began editing in 1875. It goes without saying that by the end of his career, Müller had amassed a comfortable sum of money. It is ironic that the man who has Bhavans named after him all over India and is treated with so much veneration there, probably did the most damage to uproot Vedic culture. At the time of his death he was venerated by none other than Lokamanya Tilak as 'Veda-maharishi Moksha-mula Bhatt of Go-tirtha' (Oxford).

Although Müller is on record as extolling India's ancient wisdom, his letters (printed in two volumes) tell an entirely different story. Generally personal letters give a true picture of the writer's inner mind. We present herein some of Müller's many statements in which his true view on Indian culture is glaringly obvious.

"History seems to teach that the whole human race required a gradual education before, in the fullness of time, it could be admitted to the

43. We recall that the German nation was not unified as yet.

truths of Christianity. All the fallacies of human reason had to be exhausted, before the light of a high truth could meet with ready acceptance. The ancient religions of the world were but the milk of nature, which was in due time to be succeeded by the bread of life.

'The religion of Buddha has spread far beyond the limits of the Aryan world, and to our limited vision, it may seem to have retarded the advent of Christianity among a large portion of the human race. But in the sight of Him with whom a thousand years are but as one day, that religion, like the ancient religions of the world, may have but served to prepare the way of Christ, by helping through its very errors to strengthen and to deepen the ineradicable yearnings of the human heart after the truth of God.

"Large number of Vedic hymns are childish in the extreme; tedious, low, commonplace." "Nay, they (the Vedas) contain, by the side of simple, natural, childish thoughts, many ideas which to us sound modern, or secondary and tertiary.

"...this edition of mine and the translation of the Vedas, will hereafter tell to a great extent on the fate of India and on the growth of millions of souls in that country. It (the Rg Veda) is the root of their religion and to show them what the root is, I am sure, the only way of uprooting all that has sprung from it during the last three thousand years".

"Hinduism was dying or dead because it belonged to a stratum of thought which was long buried beneath the foot of modern man. He continued: " The worship of Shiva, Vishnu, and other popular deities was of the same and in many cases of a more degraded and savage character than the worship of Jupiter, Apollo or Minerva. 'A religion', he said 'may linger on for a long time, it may be accepted by large masses of the people, because it is there, and there is nothing better. But when a religion has ceased to produce defenders of the faith, prophets, champions, martyrs, it has ceased to live, in the true sense of the word; and in that sense the old orthodox Brahmanism has ceased to live for more than a thousand years." (Speech at the Christians Missions in Westminster Abbey in 1873). In 1876, while writing to a friend, Müller said that he would not like to go to India as a missionary since that would make him dependent upon the government. His preference was this -"I would like to live for ten years quite quietly and learn the language, try to make friends, and then see if I was fit to take part in this work, by means of which the old mischief of Indian priest craft could be overthrown and the way opened for the entrance of simple Christian teaching-India is much riper for Christianity than Rome or Greece were at the time of Saint Paul."

"The rotten tree for some time had artificial supports ...but if the English man comes to see that the tree must fall...he will mind no sacrifice either of blood or of land...I would like to lay down my life, or at least lend my hand to bring about this struggle".

"I do not claim for the ancient Indian literature any more that I should willingly concede to the fables and traditions and songs of savage nations. I simply say that in the Veda we have a nearer approach to a beginning, and an intelligent beginning, than in the wild invocations of the Hottentots and Bushmen,"

"This edition of mine and the translation of the Veda will hereafter tell to a great extent... the fate of India, and on the growth of millions of souls in that country. It is the root of their religion, and to show them what the root is, I feel sure, the only way of uprooting all that has sprung from it during the last 3000 years." When Duke of Argyll was appointed Secretary of State for India in December 1868, Max Müller wrote to him "India has been conquered once, but India must be conquered again and that second conquest should be a conquest by educationṀthe ancient religion of India is doomed, and if Christianity does not step in, whose fault will it be?"

In another letter, Müller wrote to his son 'Would you say that any one sacred book is superior to all others in the world? ....I say the New Testament, after that, I should place the Koran, which in its moral teachings, is hardly more than a later edition of the New Testament. After these two, would follow according to my opinion the Old Testament, the Southern Buddhist Tripitaka, the Tao-te-king of Lao-tze, the Kings of Confucius, the Veda and the Avesta.'

In an audacious letter to N.K. Majumdar, Müller wrote -'Tell me some of your chief difficulties that prevent you and your countrymen from openly following Christ, and when I write to you I shall do my best to explain how I and many who agree with me have met them and solved them...From my point of view, India, at least the best part of it, is already converted to Christianity. You want no persuasion to become a follower of Christ. Then make up your mind to work for yourself. Unite your flock - to hold them together and prevent them from straying. The bridge has been built for you by those who came before you. STEP BOLDLY FORWARD, it will break under you, and you will find many friends to welcome you on the other shore and among them none more delighted that you old friend and fellow labourer F. Max-Müller.'

Müller harshly criticized the view of the German scholar, Dr. Spiegel, who claimed that the Biblical theory of the creation of the world is borrowed from the ancient religion of the Persians or Iranians. Stung by this statement Max Müller writes : 'A writer like Dr. Spiegel should know that he can expect no money; nay, he should himself wish for no mercy, but invite the heaviest artillery against the floating battery which he has launched in the troubled waters of Biblical criticism.

Dr. Spiegel was not the only target of Müller's bigotry. In 1926 the French scholar Louis Jacolliot, Chief Judge in Chandranagar, wrote a book called 'La Bible dans l'Inde'. Within that book, Jacolliot theorized that all the main philosophies of the western world originated from India, which he glorified thus 'Land of ancient India! Cradle of Humanity. hail! Hail revered motherland whom centuries of brutal invasions have not yet buried under the dust of oblivion. Hail, Fatherland of faith, of love, of poetry and of science, may we hail a revival of thy past in our Western future.'

Müller said while reviewing Jacolliot's book that, 'The author seems to have been taken in by the Brahmins of India.

Müller may also be credited with the popularization of the Aryan racial theory, Writing for the Anthropological Review in 1870, Müller classified the human race into seven categories on an ascending scale —with the Aborigines on the lowest rung and the "Aryan" type supreme. However, he recanted later on when his professional reputation as a Sanskrit scholar was in peril.

"I have declared again and again that if I say Arya, I mean neither blood nor bones, nor hair, nor skull; I mean simply those who speak an Aryan language...to me an ethnologist who speaks of Aryan race, Aryan blood, Aryan eyes and hair, is as great a sinner as a linguist who speaks of a dolichocephalism dictionary or a Brach cephalic grammar." Max Müller cannot be placed in the same category as inexperienced Ideologists such as Christian Lassen and Albrecht Weber whose Aryan race conceptions were chiefly fueled by their ardent German nationalism, Müller's motivations were just as diabolical. Müller had been paid to misinterpret the Vedic literatures in order to make the Indians look, at best silly, and at worst, bestial.

However, not everyone was taken in by the academic prowess of the man who was known as 'Moksamula Bhatta'. Swami Dayananda Saraswati, the founder of the Arya Samaja, was so disgusted with the level of Müller's knowledge of Sanskrit that he likened him to a "toddler learning to walk.

He wrote: "Prof. Max Müller has been able to scribble out something by the help of the so called 'tikas' or paraphrases of the Vedas current in India." Another revealing incident of Müller's glaring ignorance was when a Brahmana came from India to meet the famous Sanskrit scholar. When he came face to face with Müller and spoke to him in chaste Sanskrit, Müller admitted that he couldn't understand what the gentleman was saying! No wonder Schopenhauer acerbically said, "I cannot resist a certain suspicion that our Sanskrit scholars do not understand their texts any better than the higher class of school boys their Greek and Latin,"

Appendix E Thomas Babington Macaulay (1800-1859) : On Empire And Education

THE FIRST SELECTION A SPEECH ON THE INDIA BILL OF 1833 AND EXPRESSES HIS VIEW OF THE ACHIEVEMENTS AND GOALS OF THE BRITISH EMPIRE IN THE EAST. BETWEEN 1834 AND 1838 HE LIVED IN CALCUTTA AND SERVED ON THE BRITISH "SUPREME COUNCIL FOR INDIA". HIS "MINUTE ON EDUCATION, " FROM WHICH THE SECOND SELECTION BELOW COMES, TOUCHES ON THE RELATION OF WESTERN AND INDIAN CIVILIZATIONS.

Education and the English Empire in India

I feel that, for the good of India itself, the admission of natives to high office must be effected by slow degrees. But that, when the fullness of time is come, when the interest of India requires the change, we ought to refuse to make that change lest we should endanger our own power; this is a doctrine of which I cannot think without indignation. Governments, like men, may buy existence too dear. "Propter vitam vivendi perdere causas," ["To lose the reason for living, for the sake of staying alive"] is a despicable policy both in individuals and in states. In the present case, such a policy would be not only despicable, but absurd. The mere extent of empire is not necessarily an advantage. To many governments it has been cumbersome; to some it has been fatal. It will be allowed by every statesman of our time that the prosperity of a community is made up of the prosperity of those who compose the community, and that it is the most childish ambition to covet dominion which adds to no man's comfort or security. To the great trading nation, to the great manufacturing nation, no progress which any portion of the human race can make in knowledge, in taste for the conveniences of life, or in the wealth by which those conveniences are produced, can be matter of indifference. It is scarcely possible to calculate the benefits which we might derive from the diffusion of European civilization among the vast population of the East. It would be, on the most selfish view of the case, far better for us that the people of India were well governed and independent of us, than ill governed and subject to us; that they were ruled by their own kings, but wearing our broadcloth, and working with our cutlery, than that they were performing their salams to English collectors and English magistrates, but were too ignorant to value, or too poor to buy, English manufactures. To trade with civilized men is infinitely more profitable than to govern savages. That would, indeed, be a doting wisdom, which, in order that India might remain a dependency, would make it an useless and costly dependency, which would keep a hundred millions of men from being our customers in order that they might continue to be our slaves.

This much has to be said about Macaulay. Misguided and naðve he may have been in his goal of creating brown Englishman (or would he be ecstatic at the results of his policy) but mendacious and mean spirited he was not in comparison to many of his countrymen.

"Are we to keep the people of India ignorant in order that we may keep them submissive? Or do we think that we can give them knowledge without awakening ambition? Or do we mean to awaken ambition and to provide it with no legitimate vent? Who will answer any of these questions in the affirmative? Yet one of them must be answered in the affirmative, by every person who maintains that we ought permanently to exclude the natives from high office. I have no fears. The path of duty is plain before us: and it is also the path of wisdom, of national prosperity, of national honor.

Source: From Thomas Babington Macaulay, "Speech in Parliament on the Government of India Bill, 10 July 1833," Macaulay, *Prose and Poetry*, selected by G.M. Young (Cambridge, MA: Harvard University Press, 1957), pp. 716-18.

On Indian Education

We now come to the gist of the matter. We have a fund to be employed as Government shall direct for the intellectual improvement of the people of this country. The simple question is, what is the most useful way of employing it?

All parties seem to be agreed on one point, that the dialects commonly spoken among the natives of this part of India contain neither literary nor scientific information, and are, moreover, so poor and rude that, until they are enriched from some other quarter, it will not be easy to translate any valuable work into them. It seems to be admitted on all sides, that the intellectual improvement of those classes of the people who have the means of pursuing higher studies can at present be effected only by means of some language not vernacular amongst them.

What then shall that language be? One-half of the Committee maintain that it should be the English. The other half strongly recommend the Arabic and Sanskrit. The whole question seems to me to be, which language is the best worth knowing?

I have no knowledge of either Sanskrit or Arabic. But I have done what I could to form a correct estimate of their value. I have read translations of the most celebrated Arabic and Sanskrit works. I have conversed both here and at home with men distinguished by their proficiency in the Eastern tongues. I am quite ready to take the Oriental learning at the valuation of the Orientalist themselves. I have never found one among them who could deny that a single shelf of a good European library was worth the whole native literature of India and Arabia. The intrinsic superiority of the Western literature is, indeed, fully admitted by those members of the Committee who support the Oriental plan of education.

It will hardly be disputed, I suppose, that the department of literature in which the Eastern writers stand highest is poetry. And I certainly never met with any Orientalist who ventured to maintain that the Arabic and Sanskrit poetry could be compared to that of the great European nations. But when we pass from works of imagination to works in which facts are recorded, and general principles investigated, the superiority of the Europeans becomes absolutely immeasurable. It is, I believe, no exaggeration to say, that all the historical information which has been collected from all the books written in the Sanskrit language is less valuable than what may be found in the most paltry abridgements used at preparatory schools in England. In every branch of physical or moral philosophy, the relative position of the two nations is nearly the same.

How, then, stands the case? We have to educate a people who cannot at present be educated by means of their mother-tongue. We must teach them some foreign language. The claims of our own language it is hardly necessary to recapitulate. It stands preeminent even among the languages of the west. It abounds with works of imagination not inferior to the noblest which Greece has bequeathed to us; with models of every species of eloquence; with historical compositions, which, considered merely as narratives, have seldom been surpassed, and which, considered as vehicles of ethical and political instruction, have never been equaled; with just and lively representations of human life and human nature; with the most profound speculations on metaphysics, morals, government, jurisprudence, and trade; with full and correct information respecting every experimental science which tends to preserve the health, to increase the comfort, or to expand the intellect of man. Whoever knows that language has ready access to all the vast intellectual wealth, which all the wisest nations of the earth have created and hoarded in the course of ninety generations. It may safely be said, that the literature now extant in that language is of far greater value than all the literature which three hundred years ago was extant in all the languages of the world together. Nor is this all. In India, English is the language spoken by the ruling class. It is spoken by the higher class of natives at the seats of Government. It is likely to become the language of commerce throughout the seas of the East. It is the language of two great European communities which are rising, the one in the south of Africa, the other in Australasia; communities which are every year becoming more important, and more closely connected with our Indian empire. Whether we look at the intrinsic value of our literature, or at the particular situation of this country, we shall see the strongest reason to think that, of all foreign tongues, the English tongue is that which would be the most useful to our native subjects.

The question now before us is simply whether, when it is in our power to teach this language, we shall teach languages in which, by universal confession, there are no books on any subject which deserve to be compared to our own; whether, when we can teach European science, we shall teach systems which, by universal confession, whenever they differ from those of Europe, differ for the worse; and whether, when we can patronize sound Philosophy and true History, we shall countenance, at the public expense, medical doctrines, which would disgrace an English farrier [note: a maker of horse shoes] -Astronomy, which would move laughter in girls at an English boarding school, History, abounding with kings thirty feet high, and reigns thirty thousand years long, and Geography, made up of seas of treacle and seas of butter.

We are not without experience to guide us. History furnishes several analogous cases, and they all teach the same lesson. There are in modem times, to go no further, two memorable instances of a great impulse given to the mind of a whole society,-of prejudices overthrown,-of knowledge diffused,—of taste purified,—of arts and sciences planted in countries which had recently been ignorant and barbarous.

The first instance, to which I refer, is the great revival of letters among the Western nations at the close of the fifteenth and the beginning of the sixteenth century. At that time almost everything that was worth reading was contained in the writings of the ancient Greeks and Romans. Had our ancestors acted as the Committee of Public Instruction has hitherto acted; had they neglected the language of Cicero and Tacitus; had they confined their attention to the old dialects of our own island; had they printed nothing and taught nothing at the universities but Chronicles in Anglo-Saxon, and Romances in Norman-French, would England have been what she now is? What the Greek and Latin were to the contemporaries of More and Ascham [note: English humanists of the 16th century] our tongue is to the people of India. The literature of England is now more valuable than that of classical antiquity. I doubt whether the Sanskrit literature be as valuable as that of our Saxon and Norman progenitors. In some departments,-in History, for example, I am certain that it is much less so.

In one point I fully agree with the gentlemen to whose general views I am opposed. I feel with them, that it is impossible for us, with our limited means, to attempt to educate the body of the people. We must at present do our best to form a class who may be interpreters between us and the millions whom we govern; a class of persons, Indian in blood and color, but English in taste, in opinions, in morals, and in intellect. To that class we may leave it to refine the vernacular dialects of the country, to enrich those dialects with terms of science borrowed from the Western nomenclature, and to render them by degrees fit vehicles for conveying knowledge to the great mass of the population.

Source: From Thomas Babington Macaulay, "Minute of 2 February 1835 on Indian Education," Macaulay, *Prose and Poetry*, selected by G. M. Young (Cambridge MA: Harvard University Press, 1957), pp-721-24,729.

This text is part of the Internet Modern History Sourcebook. The Sourcebook is a collection of public domain and copy-permitted texts for introductory level classes in modern European and World history.

Appendix F A Perspective on Indo US Relations

In Greek Mythology Prometheus is the God of Fire, chained to a craggy rock in the Island of Scythia. His crime—Prometheus had shared the secret of fire with mankind, thereby giving them the means for sustenance, warmth and to provide material goods with the metals that could be forged with fire. This so angered Zeus that he had him chained to the rock. So also did the US try to punish India for trying to harness the fire of the nucleus in the service of the poorest of mankind and in the defense of its people.

Part I -US/India Bilateral Relations

The relationship between the 2 largest democracies has not been a happy one during the last half of the 20th century and is not going to alter dramatically at the stroke of midnight at the beginning of the millennium or any time shortly thereafter. But improve these relations; the 2 nations must, for there is no alternative. We are all aware by now of the reasons for this long ranging hostility and I do not wish to go into them here. Suffice it to say that a lot of these reasons have long since ceased to be valid, among them not least the cold war.

It is also true that many of these reasons for the overt hostility between the 2 nations still remain. There is the mutual propensity to deliver moral judgments, although with the passing of the Nehru era, India no longer indulges in this superfluous pastime. There is also a perception that what happens in India is not of great vital interest to America, arguably a very superficial judgment.

One where the 2 countries have differed almost from day one is Kashmir. Ever since India's disastrous experience at the UN, and it needs to be recalled that India was the one to take the Kashmir problem to the UN, India has been extremely chary since then of 'Internationalizing' the Kashmir issue and extremely suspicious of any US offers to mediate in this dispute. India feels that countries that mediate bring in their own set of agendas, and are less interested in solving the problems according to the merits of the case. However, suspicious Indians maybe of this kind of mediation, this does not mean that India should stop publicizing its viewpoint in the world arena. India in fact has a very strong case based on the legal accession of the state of Kashmir, much as was the case of accession in the case of Alaska, or Texas and certainly a stronger case than the accession of Hawaii or the accession of the vast areas of Asia to Russia in the 19th century.

But what has changed dramatically is the perception that the US relationship with India's neighbor Pakistan not only does not offer any tangible benefits, but is also turning out to be a liability. Pakistan, it is being realized is a major exporter of not only illegal opium and heroin, but a particularly virulent kind of Islamic fundamentalism that views as its goal the suppression of all cultures and religions other than its own. India has been particularly unfortunate in that a succession of events have convinced the US to use Pakistan in a variety of roles during the last 50 years.

So what should India's relationship with the US be in the new millennium ? Can 50 years of irritation and overtly hostile moves be forgotten and a new beginning be made. The answer is good relations between the 2 countries are essential not only for each other but for the whole planet, not only because the 2 represent a very large portion of humanity (India is the 2nd largest country and the US is the 3rd in population) but also because this hostility has far reaching effects not only in the well being of the subcontinent and the many nations within it, but also because of lost opportunities to act in concert where democratic values provide a platform for common action.

Part II - US, India, Pakistan & Kashmir

The Kashmir issue remains one of the thorniest issues not only between India and Pakistan but also between India and the US. We need to look at the genesis of the issue in some detail before we can understand the reasons for the US stance on Kashmir. The origins of the Kashmir issue are fairly clear. Kashmir acceded to the Union of India and this accession was signed by Maharaja Hari Singh of Kashmir, whose Dogra family had ruled Kashmir for approximately 100 years, initially as a general in the army of Ranjit Singh. India then sent troops to Kashmir to clear invaders from Pakistan who were pillaging and looting the countryside. India eventually took the issue to the UN hoping that the rest of Kashmir still occupied by Pakistan would be returned to India. To India this was a clear-cut case of invasion and theft of land. But to the consternation of India and Indians nothing of the sort happened.

To understand the reasons why, one has to go back to the Great Game that Britain had played with Russia for much of the previous 100 years. The great game involved preventing the spread of Czarist Russian ambitions. Czarist Russia had become the country with the largest landmass on this planet. To travel on the Trans Siberian Railway, you had to cross 13 time zones. Clearly this land and the country to which it belonged was a power to be reckoned with. Britain, as the predominant naval and colonial power naturally took a dim view of any potential rival. Kashmir and Afghanistan were important strategic outposts for the British in preventing the Russians from acquiring a warm water port, something that the Czars had been trying to acquire since the time of Peter the great.

When finally Britain was forced to relinquish control of India, they followed the dictum of the Romans—Divide and Quit. In this case India was divided into 2 countries India and Pakistan. The British from long experience immediately recognized that India would be a major world power in the not too distant future. Why make it easier for the Indians and certainly why let a plum like Kashmir fall into their hands. There was also the suspicion, eventually to come true in later years that India would be the more difficult country to deal with because of its larger size. In addition, Britain did not expect that India would be so spectacularly successful in persuading all the Princely states in to joining the Indian Union. Certainly their expectation was that Kashmir would join Pakistan. To their chagrin, India finessed the whole issue thanks to Sardar Patel by accepting the instrument of accession from the Maharajah.

In the meantime the mantle for protecting the Western world from Russia (now the Soviet Union) and the Communist nations would fall on the newly emergent superpower the United States. The US, properly coached by Britain, also inherited the problem of containing the power of a potentially resurgent India. Thus began a 50-year sequence of events between India and the US, which while not making them bitter adversaries made them highly suspicious of each other. The US made it a point from day one to oppose India on the Kashmir issue. Despite periods of relative calm in the relationship, this adversarial relationship continued pretty much undisturbed till the present day.

The US and Americans are disingenuous when they suggest that the reason for the deterioration of relations had to do with a number of third party issues, such as the Non Aligned Movement etc. But this is really a chicken and egg issue. The US drew first blood by questioning the sovereignty of India over Kashmir and this was a fundamental issue of national integrity for India. The world's most powerful democracy was questioning the territorial integrity of the world's largest democracy. It took many years for Indians to understand that the US was actually hostile to the Indian conception of India and in fact many Indians continued to blame Nehru, suggesting his woolly headed idealism was the cause of this rift between the 2 countries. It did not help matters much that India had a very free press and all the bickering that the Indians would indulge in was there for all the world to see.

In the early years, especially during the 50's and 60's it was common to read articles in the western newspapers that India was going to break up. They would contemptuously quote Indian newspapers talking about 'fissiparous tendencies' and predict that India would break up within 25 years. The 65 war was the first time that such preconceived notions would receive a rude shock. Both the US and Britain realized that India was not a banana republic and this was after all.the true inheritor of the British Indian army which undertook major campaigns on behalf of Britain in both world wars. While at the beginning the US acted as a cheer leader for Pakistan during the first few days, when it realized that the Pakistanis were losing badly, they immediately went to the UN to stop India from doing further damage.

Many have asked why the US continues to support Pakistan. After all this is the country that has had more Anti American demonstrations than even Beijing or even most Latin American countries. This was the country that burnt down their embassy. This was a country that killed and raped embassy personnel, an act that Theodore Roosevelt would surely have replied with some vigor. This was a country that trained people to bomb the World trade Center in New York. This was and is a country exporting huge amounts of drugs to the US. This continues to be a country that exports a virulent kind of fundamentalist Islam that has difficulty coexisting with other cultures and religions. What possible benefit could the US derive from patronizing such a country? Americans have given all the usual answers, that Pakistan was a bulwark against communist Russia (hmm...someone needs a reality check here), acted as a travel agent for Henry Kissinger when he went on his trip to Beijing (an expensive travel agent), acted as a conduit for weapons to the Afghan mujahedeen during their war against the Soviet Union (was the result worth it?) and so on. For most Indians these seem bizarre explanations for bizarre behavior. A democratic superpower aligning itself with a medieval theocratic state against the World's largest democracy for benefits of a dubious nature .

More than one exasperated Indian has asked why the US doesn't declare Pakistan to be what it blatantly is - a rogue state. The answer is that the US is not a church and this is not a morality play. The US does what it perceives to be in its best interests. Till now, the US has deemed it to be, rightly or wrongly that supporting Pakistan was in its best interest. It is my belief that this era is now coming to a close. The US is beginning to question its half a century of investment in this country and is now asking, where is the beef. The US is not a country prone to admitting mistakes, and it certainly will never come out and say we were wrong for 50 years. Of course very little of this change in policy had to do with anything that India did, although many will argue that India's entry into the nuclear club had something to do with it. In the next segment, we will examine what precipitated these changes, the nuclear issue and what the future holds for US Indian relations.

Part III The Future of Indo/US Relations

Where do the US and India go from here. But before we get to that, how eager are the 2 countries to improve relations. Despite misunderstandings, there remains a considerable amount of admiration in each of the 2 countries for the other. In India figures like Abraham Lincoln, Thomas Jefferson, Franklin Roosevelt and John F Kennedy evoke considerable admiration. Even lesser known Black Americans like George Washington Carver of the Tuskegee Institute in Alabama form part of the American folklore, known to Indians.

On the American side there is less awareness of India, other than as a distant country with elephants, snakes, palaces, tigers and a somewhat unusual individual by the name of Gandhi. But almost every university in the US now has faculty from India. Large proportions of motels and hotels in the US are now owned by Indians. A very large proportion of the US population has had contact with at least one physician from the Indian subcontinent. More recently, there are increasing numbers of Indian entrepreneurs in High Technology areas such as Silicon Valley, many of whom have become wealthy using the 'great American wealth builder' called the IPO, the Initial Public Offering. Every Research Lab in the US has a fair representation of scientists and engineers from the Indian subcontinent, and we need not mention the virtual explosion of software engineers without whom America could not have done the giant audit need for Y2K compliance. Indian companies are making their appearance increasingly on American stock exchanges and are proving to be good wealth makers for their American investors.

Despite this, the distrust between the 2 governments remains and is particularly acute in geopolitical issues relating to the Defense and Military. There is however considerable eagerness on both sides to improve relations and the realization that the potential for much warmer relations is there. The question is to how to get to that point from where we are today.

From the Indian side there is now evident a new pragmatism. In the early days there was considerable resentment that the US always took sides with Pakistan ever since 1947 when the US voted against India in the UN Security council resolutions on Kashmir. But now India realizes, that it is unrealistic to expect the US to abandon its long standing ally, even though it has not been a democracy for most of its life. India wants to build a relationship with the US quite independent of Kashmir. While this may sound difficult at first blush, recent pronouncements from the National Security Council (John Daley) that the relationship with the 2 largest countries in the subcontinent would take different trajectories sound promising. By this it is assumed by the Indians that the relationship with each of the 2 countries would be less dependent on the other. One particularly irritating habit of the Americans of referring to both countries in the same sentence on almost every occasion, may become a casualty of this new approach (we hesitate to call it a doctrine yet) much to the relief of the Indians. Despite the recent developments in Pakistan leading to military rule, I remain optimistic that the distance between the US and India on this question is not as far as it appears on first blush.

The proper approach as far as America is concerned is to stop looking at India through the narrow prism of Sub continental South Asian politics and as the 20th century inheritor of the British Raj. India has to be recognized for what she is, the 2nd largest country in the world, and the 5th largest economy with a diverse and arguably versatile industrial base. Militarily India is no slouch either, although I would caution Americans from being beguiled into thinking that India will somehow be a military superpower much like China and therefore that would be reason enough to improve relations. The fact of the matter is. that it will be many decades, if ever that India can be regarded as a military superpower and it would be misleading to use that as the excuse for improving relations. Far better to leverage on the immense purchasing power of the Indian populace, probably the largest in the world and build up strong commercial ties that will be more enduring.

A word needs to be said here on the larger question of the different perspectives each country has on global security in general and non-proliferation (NP) in particular. For the US NP means Nuclear Weapons should be restricted to the P5. In enunciating such a doctrine, the US basically does not answer the question uppermost in the mind of Indians. How should India find security when sandwiched between 2 hostile powers? Most in the American foreign policy establishment brush this aside with a bland statement that India's security concerns are not alleviated by resorting to nuclear weapons. They never offer a positive prescription which says this is what India should do to ensure her security. Furthermore, India's perception of NP, driven as it necessarily is by reasons of geography and geopolitics, is basically that it means a world shorn of all nuclear weapons. This is an unbridgeable gap between the 2 countries. The only way this can be finessed is for the US to realize that India cannot pose a threat to the US or any of its NATO allies for several decades if ever. It must also be accepted by the US that India has no ulterior designs on US allies such as Australia, and does not covet the real estate there as a safety valve for its own population.

To conclude, it is evident that the picture that emerges is hardly crystal clear in terms of where the relationship is going between the 2 countries. If that were the case, either India or the US would have been close allies or bitter enemies. Alas, reality intrudes as always and simplicity is the first victim. The surprise really is the extent of the hostility between the two given that neither country has ever attacked the other or spilt the blood of the other or has burnt down a consulate or an embassy or has colonized the other. I predict realism will dawn on the policy makers of both countries and with the right touch of pragmatism; there is every reason to hope for brighter days ahead for the checkered US/India courtship.

Appendix G Famines During Colonial Era

Table 1 Incidence of Famines in India

1770:	territory ruled by the British East India Company experienced the first Bengal famine of 1770. An estimated 10 million people died.
1780-1790s:	millions died of famine in Bengal, Benares, Jammu, Bombay and Madras.
1800-1825:	1 million Indians died of famine
1850-1875:	5 millions died of famine in Bengal, Orissa, Rajastan and Bihar
1875-1902:	26 million Indians died of famine (between 1876-1878 alone 10 million died of starvation)
1905-1906:	famine raged in areas with the population of 3,3 million.
1906-1907:	famine captured areas with the population of 13 million
1907-1908:	famine captured areas populated by 49,6 million Indians.
In 1943:	India experienced the second Bengal famine of 1943. Over 3 million people died.

Famines in British India

One of the forgotten stories of yesteryear is that of the ubiquitous occurrence of Famines during British rule in the Indian subcontinent. Our primary focus remains the accurate portrayal of the Indic civilization. However there are reasons why we do not wish to gloss over the holocausts that took place during British rule and during the 500 years of Islamic domination of the Indian subcontinent. As the quote by Will Durant aptly encapsulates, there is only so much abuse that a civilization will take before there is mortal damage to the ethos of the civilization and the psyche of the survivors. Our purpose here remains one of reaching an understanding of the durability and resilience of the Indic civilization, but at the same time one must have an accurate description of the massive damage inflicted on this civilization during the last 800 years. No Indian should forget the horrors of the destruction and genocide wrought by Tamer Lang in Delhi in 1398 CE, the consistent enslavement of the Indic population over several centuries, the naming of an entire mountain range in Afghanistan the Hindu Kush, for what it signified, the death of millions of slaves as they were carried away to the slave markets of Samarqand, Damascus, Isfahan and Bokhara, the Great Bengal famine of 1770, which initiated a whole cycle of famines in India over a 175 year period, culminating in the Great Bengal Famine of 1943, the rapacity of Warren Hastings and Robert Clive and the subsequent enrichment of the British landed gentry, resulting in the countryside of Great Britain being dotted with mansions dating from 1770 onwards. There has been no apology forthcoming. It is perhaps audacious of the children of a lesser God to expect such apologies, but surely it is important, the British public should not remain blissfully oblivious of the pernicious and penurious effects of their sustained impoverishment of India. The holocaust under British rule was of a lesser magnitude than the Holocaust under Islamic domination but the rate at which human beings were killed each century was significantly higher during the British Raj if we include all manmade causes such as famines.

We reiterate once again the reasons for reliving the past; it is mainly to learn the right lessons and to undertake actions and measures to avoid a repetition of the more horrific events of the past. It is often asserted that one should not dwell on the past, since it would unnecessarily hurt the sentiments of fellow Indian Muslims of today, who had little to do with the happenings of the past. To this we say, that a little bit of hurt sentiment never did any damage to anyone, and it would be more horrifying if we were to find out that there was no hurt sentiment at all. Certainly to speak of hurt sentiments in the same breath as one glorifies the period o f Islamic domination of the subcontinent signifies a cognitive dissonance which deserves an explanation and we feel there are the beginnings of thoughtful Indian Muslims who take the same view of our history as we do as exemplified by Dr. Abdul Kalam, the erstwhile President of India.

We begin by referring to two articles one, from an address by Dr. Babu Suseelan in a symposium on the Roots of Terrorism, and another by Dr. Gideon Polya on the Great Famines of India. The links are to be found in the new section on *Holocausts and Famines in India*.[44]

---

44. *http://indicethos.org/Indian%20Epics/HolocaustsandFamines/index.html*

Plate 9: The Famine of 1877 *(facing pg. 118)*

In a land laced with numerous rivers and noted for its agricultural bounty, famine was a rare occurrence in India till late into the medieval era, and was usually the consequence of major natural or manmade catastrophes. All that changed after the British conquered the territories of the subcontinent. The frequency of famine was especially high in areas directly administered by the British. There were many great famines where millions died, and famine occurred with dreadful regularity after the British Crown assumed the overlordship of the subcontinent. The present picture of India as a land bedeviled with extreme poverty is a direct legacy of the massive incompetence of the British in their stewardship of the subcontinent. The British destroyed the dignity of the vast portions of the population and reduced them to a undernourished and poverty stricken populace, where almost 90% of the population was under the grim levels of poverty. The pathetic story of the inhumanity of the colonial overlord is chronicled by Davis.[45] The estimate of total killed in all the famines in India during British rule is approximately 50 million. When coupled with the 70 million killed during the era of Islamic domination of the subcontinent, one wonders how the Hindu, who formed the bulk of the rural population survived at all. But unlike the American Indian, survive he did. Not satisfied with the grim statistics of the resulting holocaust, the Occidental Powers are now busily backing Pakistan, to further undermine India.

> "This year marks the 63rd anniversary of the end of World War 2 and the world will reflect on the human cost of this conflict. In particular we will remember the enormous loss of civilian life, particularly in Poland (6 million dead), the Soviet Union (20 million dead) and China (35 million dead). The Holocaust involving the deliberate extermination of 6 million Jews and half a million Gypsies has seared the human conscience, never to be forgotten. However a major man-made tragedy of similar proportions that occurred in Bengal in World War 2 has been effectively ignored by the world from the time it occurred. The man-made famine in Bengal in 1943-1944 killed an estimated 3.5 to 5 million people.
>
> The British brought an unsympathetic and ruthless economic agenda to India. Economic exploitation damaged the indigenous Indian economy and resulted in a decline in the standard of living. The British disinclination to respond with urgency and vigor to food deficits resulted in a succession of about 2 dozen

45. Davis, Mike, '*Late Victorian Holocausts*', Verso, 2002.

appalling famines during the British occupation of India. These famines swept away tens of millions of people [1-10]. One of the worst famines was that of 1770 that killed an estimated 10 million people in Bengal (one third of the population) and which was exacerbated by the rapacity of the East India Company. Bengal suffered further famines in 1783, 1866, 1873-74, 1892, 1897 and 1943-44".

The extraordinary continuing aspect of this 2 century Holocaust was the exacerbation and indeed the creation of famine by the sequestration and export of food for enhanced commercial gain. Thus in severe Indian famines in the mid-19th century (by which time the British authorities were thoroughly familiar with this sort of event) export of grain was permitted on the grounds of non-intervention in trade 6. This horrendous scourge continued into the 20th century. Thus Rajasthan suffered a succession of severe scarcities and famines from 1899-1941, a very severe famine occurring in 1939-1940 [8]. The culmination of this saga of immense human suffering was the Bengal famine of 1943-44".(*ibid*)

The famine in India - the sufferers at Bellary, Madras Presidency, October 20, 1877

10 million died in this famine in India. This is the same region of India where once the famed and opulent Vijayanagar Empire ruled a vast area of South India for over 200 years.

Some British citizens such as *William Digby* agitated for policy *reforms* and famine relief, but *Lord Lytton*, the governing British *viceroy* in India, opposed such changes in the belief that they would stimulate shirking by Indian workers. Reacting against calls for relief during the 1877-79 famine, Lytton replied,

> "Let the British public foot the bill for its 'cheap sentiment,' if it wished to save life at a cost that would bankrupt India," substantively ordering "there is to be no interference of any kind on the part of Government with the object of reducing the price of food," and instructing district officers to "discourage relief works in every possible way.... Mere distress is not a sufficient reason for opening a relief work." (quoted in Davis 2001:31, 52).

In 1877 and 1878, at the height of the famine, grain merchants exported a record 320,000 tonnes of wheat. As the peasants began to

Plate 10: The famine in India–the sufferers at Bellary, Madras Presidency, October 20, 1877 *(facing pg. 120 (i))*

Plate 11: The Famine of 1877 *(facing pg. 120 (ii))*

Plate 12: Lord Lytton *(facing pg. 120 (iii))*

starve, officials were ordered "to discourage relief works in every possible way." The Anti-Charitable Contributions Act of 1877 prohibited "at the pain of imprisonment private relief donations that potentially interfered with the market fixing of grain prices." The only relief permitted in most districts was hard labour, from which anyone in an advanced state of starvation was turned away. In the labour camps, the workers were given less food than inmates of Buchenwald. In 1877, monthly mortality in the camps equated to an annual death rate of 94 per cent.

As millions died, the imperial government launched "a militarized campaign to collect the tax arrears accumulated during the drought." The money, which ruined those who might otherwise have survived, was used by Lord Lytton to fund his war in Afghanistan. Even in places that had produced a crop surplus, the government's export policies, such as Stalin's in Ukraine, manufactured hunger. In the north-western provinces, Oud, and the Punjab, which had brought in record harvests in the preceding three years, at least 1.25 million died.

> It is rare to see any censure of Lord Lytton, the Viceroy by traditional British historians like Sir Penderel Moon, but clearly his callousness towards the extinction of human life by slow starvation especially if it was Indian, even on such a massive scale, bordered on the bestial.

The Famine Commission of 1880 observed that each province in *British India*, including *Burma*, had a surplus of foodgrains, and the annual surplus amounted to 5.16 million tons (Bhatia, 1970). At that time, annual export of rice and other grains from India was approximately one million tons. At about the same time the British devised the first ever *famine scales* and engaged themselves in a series of canal building and irrigation improvements. The results were that the mortality rate decreased rapidly. There was the threat of famine but after 1902 there was no major famine in India until 1943. In 1907 and in 1874 the response from the British was better: in both cases rice was imported from abroad and famine was averted.

The Famine of 1877

People dying of starvation. Altogether around 26 million people died between 1876 and 1906 during the 'benign' colonialism of the British.

Famine in Madras province, 1877

This section is specially dedicated to Will Durant,

He tried to improve understanding of viewpoints of human beings and to have others forgive foibles and human waywardness. He chided the comfortable insularity of what is now known as Eurocentrism, by pointing out in "Our Oriental Heritage" that Europe was only a "a jagged promontory of Asia." He complained of "the provincialism of our traditional histories which began with Greece and summed up Asia in a line" and said they showed "a possibly fatal error of perspective and intelligence." In the "Age of Faith", he wrote a highly accessible history of Islam for the general North American reader in an effort to create greater tolerance and understanding.

He was awarded the Presidential Medal of Freedom by President Ford in 1977.

He had a great love of the intellectual traditions of ancient Indian philosophy. His article on Vedanta and Adi Sankara can be found at the website www.indicstudies.us in the page on Philosophy.

1. It is true that even across the Himalayan barrier India has sent to us such questionable gifts as grammar and logic, philosophy and fables, hypnotism and chess, and above all our numerals and our decimal system. But these are not the essence of her spirit; they are trifles compared to what we may learn from her in the future.

2. Perhaps in return for conquest, arrogance and spoliation, India will teach us the tolerance and gentleness of the mature mind, the quiet content of the un-acquisitive soul, the calm of the understanding spirit, and a unifying, a pacifying love for all living things.

3. India was the motherland of our race, and Sanskrit the mother of Europe's languages: she was the mother of our philosophy; mother, through the Arabs, of much of our mathematics; mother, through the Buddha, of the ideals embodied in Christianity; mother, through the village community, of self-government and democracy. Mother India is in many ways the mother of us all. Nothing should more deeply shame the modern student than the recency and inadequacy of his acquaintance with India....This is the India that patient scholarship is now opening up like a new intellectual continent to that Western mind which only yesterday thought civilization an exclusive Western thing.

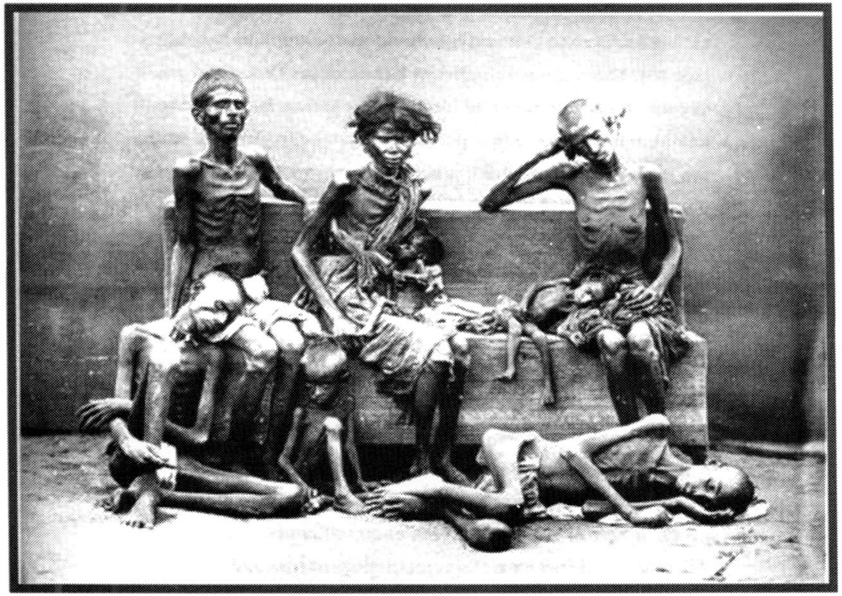

Madras Famine 1877-1878
Willoughby Hooper - Album print private collection
(source: Indian Art - By Vidya Dehejia p. 399-402).

***

Plate 13: Famine in Madras Province, 1877 *(facing pg. 122)*

4. "As flowing rivers disappear in the sea, losing their name and form, thus a wise man, freed from name and form, goes to the divine person who is beyond all." Such a theory of life and death will not please Western man, whose religion is as permeated with individualism as are his political and economic institutions. But it has satisfied the philosophical Hindu mind with astonishing continuity.

5. Even in Europe and America, this wistful theosophy has won millions upon millions of followers, from lonely women and tired men to Schopenhauer and Emerson.

Thought for the Day

It may be true that you can't fool all the people all the time, but you can fool enough of them to rule a large country. -Will Durant

Plate 14: The Great Uprising of 1857 *(facing pg. 124)*

Plate 16: Secundra Bagh after the Great Indian Uprising 1857 *(facing pg. 126 (ii))*

Plate 17: The Indians were strapped to canon and blown to bits as retribution for 1857 *(facing pg. 126 (iii))*

Appendix H The Great Uprising of 1857

This was an uncoordinated spontaneous uprising against the tyranny of the British rule in India. There is no question that the British would have been overwhelmed had there been a coordinated attack by the Indians. The total number of British were less than 30,000 at that period. But that was not to be. Significant sectors of the population remained apathetic to the uprising. The result was that there was a terrible reprisal of Indian lives by the British, when they went on a rampage killing thousands of Indians. The underlying premise behind the British actions and their reprisal was 'how dare they rebel against our rule'.

"The discovery unleashed an "all but national cry for unmitigated vengeance" (Ball 2:168); the "retributive impulses of our people," as the historian Sir John Kaye calls them (2:170), were given even freer rein than before. One primary instrument of these impulses was the sternly pious Colonel (subsequently rewarded for his vengefulness by being promoted to Brigadier General) James Neill, who already had made a name for himself for the ferocious retribution he had inflicted elsewhere upon mutineers and their suspected sympathizers. Left in command at Cawnpore as Havelock moved on to attempt the relief of Lucknow, Neill invented a form of extra punishment for condemned men thought to have been implicated in the massacre. Before being taken out to the gallows, each was forced to clean up with his own hands or to lick up a small square of dried blood from the courtyard pavement where the prisoners had been slaughtered-an appalling pollution for a high-caste Hindu, as most of the sepoys were. Neill proudly expressed his conviction that God was at work in the "strange law" that he had instituted (Ball 2:400). This was only one of the best publicized of many instances of merciless reprisals visited by British authorities, often on the flimsiest legal pretexts, upon Indian combatants and civilians in the course of the fierce campaign to restore British supremacy in India."

Some estimate that as many as a million Indians were hanged or otherwise massacred by the British.

http://www.amazon.ca/Our-Bones-Are-Scattered-Massacres/dp/product-description/0805024379

"A skillful retelling of a celebrated Victorian military engagement: the rebel siege of the north Indian city of Cawnpore during the Indian Mutiny of 1857. When Indian soldiers rose up and slaughtered their own officers, the British public was stunned at their treachery. Astonishment turned to horror as rebels killed European civilians and Indian Christians who had taken refuge in North Indian cities. The slaughter of European women and children led to a far more brutal and indiscriminate British retaliation. Readers in Victorian England had an insatiable appetite for harrowing tales of the mutiny, and European survivors of these events published dozens of histories and memoirs. Journalist Ward follows them closely in his story of the shocking events at Cawnpore, where European soldiers were massacred after being guaranteed safe passage by the local ruler, Nana Sahib, and his treacherous adviser, Azimullah. After harsh imprisonment, the surviving women and children were hacked to pieces and their bodies stuffed into a well. *Enraged at the discovery of what had been done, and inflamed by false accusations of rape, British soldiers forced defeated Indian rebels to lick up the blood of European victims, then executed thousands of them. Some were strapped to cannons and blown to bits.* For decades after the mutiny, any publication presenting the Indian point of view was banned by the British ruler of India. Ward (whose 1985 novel, Blood Seed, dealt with the aftermath of the mutiny) recognizes the British bias of his sources and tries to read between the lines in search of an Indian point of view. But it is perhaps inevitable that the passion of his book comes from its European sources. Ward's gripping account of heroism and cruelty falls short in its attempt to be fair to Indian as well as British victims. (40 illustrations, not seen).— *Copyright ©1996, Kirkus Associates, LP. All rights reserved.*"

We quote Heather Streets[46]

"British public opinion seemed to concur. Many people agreed that the East India Company had made its bed and was now lying in it. Company officers were blamed for excessive conversion efforts among their Hindu and Muslim sepoys as "one cause of the outbreak."[47]

---

46. Heather Streets, The Rebellion of 1857:Origins, Consequences, and Themes. *http://www.mssu.edu/projectsouthasia/tsa/VIN1/Streets.htm*

47. Aberdeen Herald and General Advertiser, Saturday, August 22, 1857, p. 3.

Plate 15: Interior of Fort Taku immediately after capture in 1860 *(facing pg. 126 (i))*

Blackwood's Magazine, a respected journal with clear connections to an imperially-minded audience, suggested in addition that "our leaders were unequal to their duty" in the crisis.[48]. So great was the general contempt for the *perceived blunders of the East India Company* that the Anglo-Indian *Delhi Gazette Extra* was forced to concede, "[t]he British public remain utterly impassive and indifferent, and become impatient when the subject is broached in conversation. They have made up their mind that it was entirely owing to the insolence and incompetency of the Regimental Officers, and seem rather glad that they have suffered for their supposed dereliction of duty."[49]

But when news of the Kanpur massacre began to filter into Britain by the late summer of 1857, the mood of the British public shifted abruptly away from its previous critical mode. In the wake of the murders, the Rebellion metamorphosed from a military conflict on the imperial periphery to a popular national struggle in which even ordinary Britons felt invested. The specter of British women and children being murdered by colonial men proved to be a catalyst by which ideologies of gender and race became both inseparable and central to the British 'cause' in India.[50]

Coverage of the event was widespread and sensational in national, provincial, and local papers all over Britain. *The London Times* alone carried one hundred eight stories on the massacre between August 15, 1857 and February 3, 1860. All of the largest national newspapers, regardless of political affiliation, featured intensive coverage of the murders-including *Reynolds's, Lloyd's*, and *News of the World*. In addition to selling newspapers, these 'horrors' also inspired unprecedented local action, by prompting packed meetings to pledge money for the victims of the Rebellion.[51]

The depth of public reaction to the murders was due in large part to the lurid nature of the published accounts. Though papers frequently argued that the 'vile tortures' practised upon British women and children should "be remembered, not told," all of them did in fact 'tell' of rape and torture in graphic detail.[52] Letters and telegraphs flooded the papers with accounts of women being raped in front of their children before being killed, of matted blood, gory remains of children's limbs, and of

---

48. "The Bengal Mutiny," Blackwood's Magazine 82 (September 1857), 382.

49. "London Correspondent," The Delhi Gazzette Extra, 10 July 1857.

50. Patrick Brantlinger, Rule of Darkness, 202.

51. Aberdeen Free Press and Buchan News, Friday, Sept. 11, 1857, 5.

52. Quoted from "Retribution," The Delhi Gazette 1857.

the suffocation of living children among their dead mothers when the victims were thrown into a well.[53]

Such graphic tales of rape and murder inflamed public sentiments calling for vengeance on a massive scale.[54] *The Illustrated London* News voiced its indignation in tandem with most other national, provincial, and local papers when it claimed that "every British heart, from the highest to the humblest of the land, glows with honest wrath, and demands justice, prompt and unsparing, on the bloodyminded instruments of the Rebellion."[55] Leading national and provincial papers went so far as to advocate the 'extermination' of Muslim and Hindu rebels.[56] In India, the *Delhi Gazette* also proclaimed that "the paramount duty of the British Government is now retribution-a duty to the dead and living."[57]

This vengeance was imagined against perpetrators who had come to represent a potent mixture of masculine, racial, and religious depravity. Sepoys were represented in the press not as men, but as "demons" and "fiends," led by their "passions" to "faithlessness, rebellion, and crimes at which the heart sickens."[58] Their apparent thirst for innocent blood-and their reported lust for forbidden women-had unmanned them, and placed them outside the boundaries of masculine honor. Moreover, their decision to operate outside these rules of conduct absolved the British from addressing their grievances or from showing them mercy. A poem in the Anglo-Indian *Delhi Gazette* put it plainly when it cried, "No mercy's shown to men whose hands/ With women's blood yet reek!"[59]

---

53. Alison Blunt, "Embodying War: British Women and Domestic Defilement in the Indian Mutiny, 1857-8," Journal of Historical Geography 26:3 (2000), 412-414.
54. Both Jenny Sharpe and Nancy Paxton call attention to the focus on rape of contemporary accounts and fictions of the Uprising. See Jenny Sharpe, "The Unspeakable Limits of Rape: Colonial Violence and Counter-Insurgency," Genders 10 (Spring 1991); Nancy L. Paxton, "Mobilizing Chivalry: Rape in British Novels About the Indian Uprising of 1857," Victorian Studies (Fall 1992).
55. "Progress of the Indian Rebellion," Illustrated London News, 5 September 1857.
56. These included the Times, the Morning Post, and the Newcastle Chronicle. Dawson, Soldier Heroes, 94.
57. "Retribution," *The Delhi Gazette*, December 1857.
58. General Orders India, October 7, 1857, in General Orders for the Military for 1857, OIOC,L/MIL/17/2/306.
59. R. Jacket, "The Indian Mutiny," *The Delhi Gazette* 1858.

That rebel sepoys would commit such unspeakable crimes against women was attributed both to racial characteristics and to religion. In India, the conflict had hardened racial hatreds among British officers long before Kanpur. Correspondence reveals widespread use of the word 'nigger' and other racially antagonistic language when referring to natives, and officers writing home frequently echoed the contention that "[t]he race of men in India are certainly the most abominable, degraded lot of brutes that you can imagine, they don't seem to have a single good quality."[60] In the British and Anglo-Indian media, such language received almost unqualified sanction in the wake of Kanpur. Despite the fact that a majority of high-caste Bengal army sepoys were traditionally recruited for their tall physiques and light skin, British sources depicted "gangs of black satyrs" raping and dismembering British women, and called rebel Indians "that venom race," "in heart as black as face."[61]

These 'black' villains were also believed to be depraved because of their religion, whether Hindu or Muslim, for in both cases religion was presumed to have encouraged the rape and murder of British women. Rumors circulated that some of the women at Kanpur were raped, kidnapped, and forced to convert to Islam.[62] High-caste Brahmins were said to be slaves to the requirements of caste, which supposedly included debased notions of masculine honor. Shortly after Kanpur, the *Delhi Gazette* bellowed:

We shall never again occupy a high ground in India until we have put a yoke upon the Brahmins. We have conceded too much to the insolence of caste. Not one high caste man should henceforward be entrusted with a sword.... He has been trusted with power, and how has he betrayed it? The graves of 100 English women and children-worse, the unburied bones of those poor victims-are the monuments of high bred sepoy chivalry.[63]

By their crimes at Kanpur, then, both Hindu and Muslim sepoys had given up all claims to manliness, to honor, to bravery, and to chivalry. Moreover, both their 'race' and their religion were increasingly called upon to explain the loss of those claims.

---

60. Brevet-Major R. Poore, MS letters by Brevet-Major R. Poore in Indian Mutiny. (1854-1858) 9504-22, National Army Museum, March 9, 1857.

61. Jacket, "The Indian Mutiny," *The Delhi Gazette*, January 1858; "Retribution," *The Delhi Gazette*, December 1857.

62. William Forbes-Mitchell, The Relief of Lucknow (London: The Folio Society, 1962). Mitchell was a soldier in the 92nd Gordon Highlanders, and was in Kanpur days after the murders. His diary was unpublished until 1962.

63. "Retribution," *The Delhi Gazette* 1857.

The effects of such narrative constructions were not merely textual- instead, they had real effects in the material world. Perhaps most importantly, they legitimated acts of appalling vengeance by British forces. At the same time, however, British control over these narratives either glossed or completely ignored the extent of British acts of brutality against Indian soldiers and civilians. As one of the conflict's most influential historians put it in 1864, the Rebellion had been fought by "English heroes" who, in the end, "marched triumphantly to victory."[64]

More recently, a growing number of historians have acknowledged that these "English heroes" were responsible for savage acts of retribution in India. Once it was clear that the Rebellion might induce any number of Bengal army regiments to mutiny, for example, many British officers lost no time making examples of the mutineers through execution.[65] Punishment was sometimes general, involving the slaughter of whole, or nearly whole, regiments. This was the fate of the 51st and 26th regiments, who both fell victim to the "unceasing vigilance" of John Lawrence in his proactive efforts to stem the Rebellion in the Punjab.[66] Of the 26th, Lawrence noted in August 1857 that, "we have killed and drowned 500 out of the 600 men of the...regiment."[67]

In addition to military executions, the British also exacted severe reprisals on civilian populations in north-central India. The notorious actions of Colonel James Neill, called to Bengal from the Madras army to help suppress the Rebellion, bear directly on the events surrounding the Kanpur massacre. After arriving in Allahabad on June 11, 1857, Neill was responsible for thousands of murders both of sepoys and suspected rebels as well as innocent men, women, and children. Describing the actions of Neill's troops around Allahabad, one officer wrote:

Every native that appeared in sight was shot down without question, and in the morning Colonel Neill sent out parties of regiment [?]...and burned all the villages near where the ruins of our bungalows stood, and hung every native that they could catch, on the trees that lined the

---

64. Sir John Kaye, Kaye s and Malleson s History of the Indian Mutiny of 1857-8, Volume I ed. Colonel Malleson (Westport: Greenwood Press, 1971), p. xii. (originally published 1897-98, Longmans, Green & Co.)

65. Edward Spiers, The Army and Society, 129.

66. The words "unceasing vigilance" were those ascribed to Lawrence by the Governor-General in General Orders for the Military for 1857, October 7, 1857. OIOC, L/MIL/17/2/306.

67. John Lawrence, August 1, 1857, Correspondence of Lord Lawrence, OIOC, MSS EUR C 203/1.

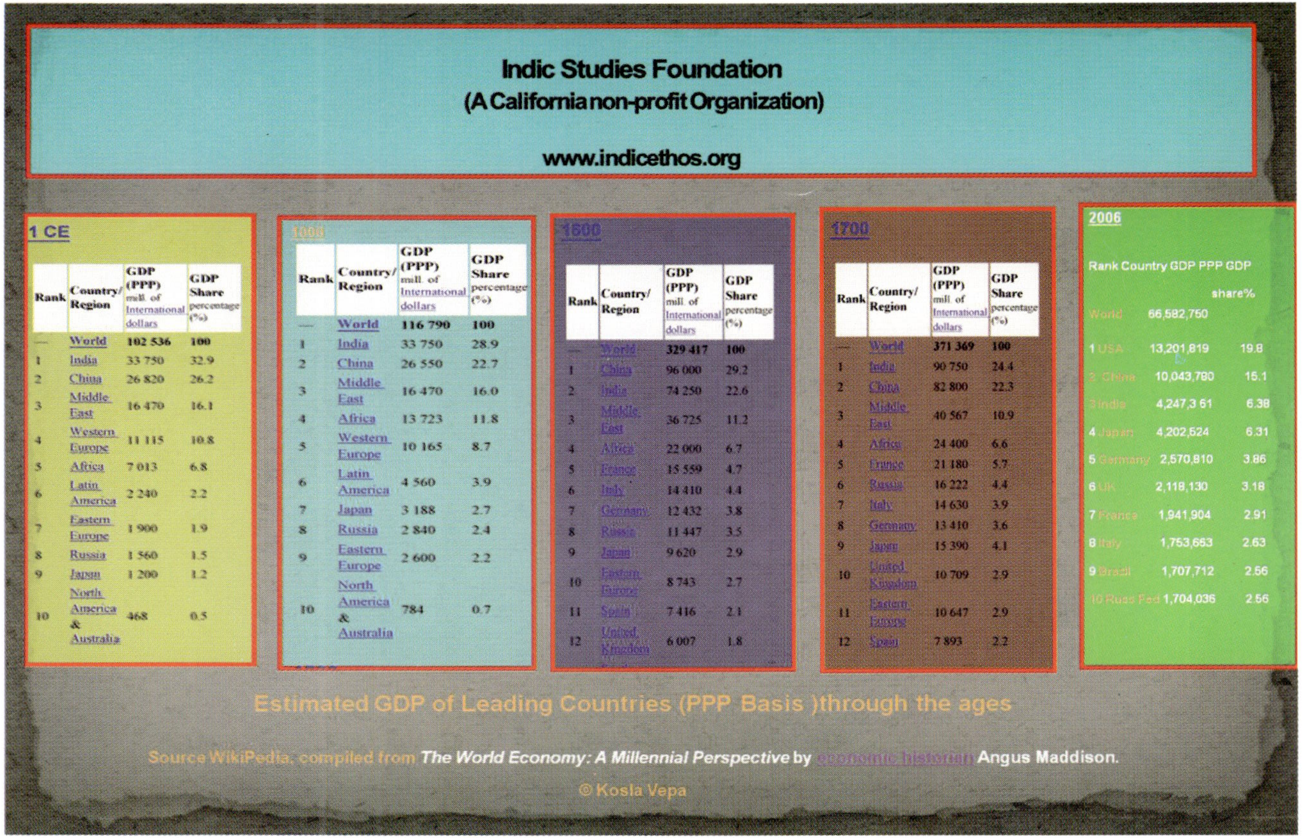

Plate 18: Estimated GDP PPP Basis through the ages *(facing pg. 130)*

road. Another party of soldiers penetrated into the native city and set fire to it, whilst volley after volley of grape and canister was poured into the fugitives as they fled from their burning houses.[68]

On June 29 1857, Neill ordered "the village of Mullagu and neighborhood to be attacked and destroyed-slaughter all the men-take no prisoners." He added, "all insurgents that fall into good hands hang at once-and shoot all you can."[69]

Significantly, Neill's 'bloody assizes' around Allahabad (as they came to be known) occurred before, not after, the massacre of British women and children at Kanpur on July 15. Some scholars have speculated that the murders were ordered in retaliation for the Indian civilians whose murders Neill personally supervised.[70] Whether or not such a contention can be proven, it is nevertheless clear that Neill's brutality could not have been justified by the Kanpur massacre as was so often contended, for his own excesses preceded the event.[71]

Yet while British atrocities preceded the massacre at Kanpur, once news of the killings spread they were used to justify retaliatory murders and punishments on an astonishing scale. Neill himself, who was with the first British force to enter the city two days after the massacre, invented macabre executions for both Hindu and Muslim sepoys that were designed to ensure both intense suffering before death and eternal damnation afterwards.[72]

British soldiers sent to India offered ample testimony to the scale of British retaliation against both military and civilian targets. Sergeant David McAusland of the 42nd Highland Regiment recalled that during his service in Bareilly during the Rebellion, "three scaffolds and six whipping posts stood outside of the town along side of the jail and there [took place] executions to the number of six every day." The

---

68. Quoted from Mukherjee, "The Kanpur Massacres in India," 182.

69. Instructions issued by Colonel Neill on 29 June, 1857 to Major Renaud, James George Smith Neill Papers, Rare Book, Manuscript and Special Collections, Duke University.

70. Sen, Eighteen Fifty-Seven, 150; Spiers, The Army and Society, 131; Patrick Brantlinger, "The Well at Cawnpore: Literary Representations of the Indian Mutiny of 1857," in Rule of Darkness: British Literature and Imperialism, 1830-1914 (Ithaca: Cornell University Press, 1988), 201.

71. Rudrangshu Mukherjee, Spectre of Violence, 32.

72. These included the notorious punishments of requiring sepoys to lick the blood of the slain women before being hanged. See Neill's orders for 25 July, 1857 at Kanpur, James George Smith Neill Papers, Duke University.

judge in charge of trials had lost his wife during the conflict, and had told McAusland, "if ever I get the chance of [judging] these Black rebels I will hang a man for every hair that was in my wife's head." McAusland responded by asking him how many men he had executed already, "he told me close on 700 well I said if you just continue you will have made good your work and turning to Sergt...Aden I said you mind what Sir Colin [Campbell] said to us at Cawnpore that every man that had a black face was our enemy and we could not do wrong in shooting him so you know how to act here."[73]

Private Alexander Robb, also of the 42nd, described the first summary hanging of an Indian civilian he witnessed during the Rebellion, adding, "that was the first man I saw dancing on nothing in India, but it was not the last, for I saw some awful sights in that line."[74] Lieutenant Robert Bruce McEwen of the 92nd Gordon Highlanders recorded, on numerous days, routinely shooting large numbers of prisoners and in taking part in actions where between 500 and 700 rebels were killed.[75] And when British forces finally attacked and re-took the city of Delhi in September, 1857, they were merciless in their treatment of soldiers and civilians alike.[76]

As these stories indicate, the history of the Rebellion-like all historical subjects-is continually in the process of being revised and re-interpreted. Scholars in the post-colonial period in particular have challenged British-centered accounts of the Rebellion, emphasizing instead the widespread nature of the conflict among Indian civilians as well as soldiers, and the scale of British retribution and violence. In recent years, historians of gender and racial theory have also contributed to the re-interpretation of the Rebellion by emphasizing the important consequences of the conflict for imperial ideologies. All of these approaches have helped to deepen our understanding of this bloody, brutal, but significant conflict. For the Rebellion was both a military mutiny and a peasant rebellion; it included murders and atrocities on both the British and the Indian sides; and it was significant not just in military terms but in ideological and historiographical terms as well.

---

73. David McAusland, Diary While in the 42nd, Accession #0214, Black Watch Museum, p. 84.

74. Alexander Robb, *Reminiscences of a Veteran: Being the Experiences of a Private Soldier in the Crimea, and During the Indian Mutiny.* (1888), p. 98. Catalog #: O/NO795, accession #6161, Black Watch Museum.

75. Robert Bruce McEwen diary, PB 157, Gordon Highlanders Museum. Entries include October 9, 11, 19, 25, 26, and 27, 1858.

76. Spiers, *The Army and Society*, 131-132.

Appendix I Bibliography (Post Independence)

A History of Pakistan and Its Origins (Anthem South Asian Studies).

Agrarian Conflict, Religion and Politics: The Moplah Rebellions in Malabar in the Nineteenth and Early Twentieth. Centuries." Past and Present 74 (1977): 112-41.

Armstrong,Karen, *Battle for Gods*, Karen Armstrong.

Arnold, David (4): *Police power and colonial rule, Madras, 1859-1947* (Delhi and New York : Oxford University Press, 1986).

Baer, Robert, *House of Saud*.

Baer, Robert, *See No Evil*.

Beaumont Gillian (Translator), Christoph Jaffrelot (Editor).

Behera, Navnita Chadha, *India Prospects for Conflict and Peace.*

Bhadra, Gautam (3). Dipesh Chakrabarty (3): *Rethinking working-class history : Bengal, 1890-1940* (Princeton, N.J.: Princeton University Press, 1989).

Bhure Lal, *The monstrous face of the ISI.*

Black and Benny Morris, *Israel's Secret Wars*.

Bloomfield, Maurice, *The Religion of the Veda*, New York,G P Putnam.

Bowden, Hugh, *Ancient Civilizations*.

Bracken, Paul, *Fire in the East: The Rise of Asian Military Power and the Second Nuclear Age* (HarperCollins, 1999).

Braudel, Fernand, *A History of Civilizations* (Penguin 1988/1963, pp.232-236).

Bryant, Edwin and Laurie L Patton, Ed. By (2005) *Indo-Aryan Controversy: Evidence and Inference in Indian History* (Hardcover), Routledge, London.

Bryant, Edwin, *The Quest for the Origins of Vedic Culture : The Indo-Aryan Migration Debate* (Hardcover), Oxford University Press.

Brzezinski, Zbigniew K, *The Grand Chessboard: American Primacy and it's geo-strategic imperatives.*

Buchanan, Pat, *Death of the West.*

Chomsky, Noam, *Pirates and Emperors, Old and New: International Terrorism in the Real World.*

Chomsky, Noam, *Understanding Power: The Indispensable Chomsky.*

Chomsky, Noam, *For Reasons of State.*

Chomsky, Noam, *Media Control: The Spectacular Achievements of Propaganda (Open Media Series)* Seven Stories Press; 2nd edition (December 2002).

Chomsky, Noam, *Chomsky Papers.*

Choudhary Sukhbir, *Moplah uprising, 1921-23*, Delhi : Agam Prakashan, 1977; Stephen F. Dale, "The Mappilla Outbreaks: Ideology and Social Conflict in Nineteenth Century Kerala," *Journal of Asian Studies*, 35, 1, 1975, 85-98; Conrad Wood, "*Peasant Revolt: An Interpretation of Moplah violence in the Nineteenth and Twentieth Centuries.*

Cohn, Bernard, *Colonialism and its forms of knowledge*, Oxford university Press, Delhi, 1997.

Contesting the Nation: Religion, Community, and the Politics of Democracy in India, Edited by David Ludden, Philadelphia: University of Pennsylvania Press; published in India as *Making India Hindu: Community, Conflict, and the Politics of Democracy*, Delhi: Oxford University Press, 1996.

Crile, George, *Charlie Wilson's War: The Extraordinary Story of the Largest Covert Operation in History.*

David, Deepak Lal, *Unfinished Business: India in the World Economy* (New Delhi: Oxford University Press, 2000).

Des Ball and Jeffrey T. Richelson, *The Ties That Bind.*

Desikachar, S V, *Hinduism and Islam in India From antiquity to modern times.*

Diamond, Jared, *Guns, germs and Steel.*

Dirks, Nicholas, *Castes of Mind, Colonialism and the Making of Modern India,* Princeton University Press.

Dixit, J.N., *India-Pakistan in War and Peace*, The India Today Group, New Delhi, 2002.

Douglass C. North, Robert Paul Thomas, *The Rise of the Western World: A New Economic History.*

Dubois,J.A., Abbe, (1906) *Hindu Manners, customs, and Ceremonies,* tr. H. K.Beeauchamp, Oxford Clarendon Press.

Dumont, Louis,(1980) *Homo Hierarchus*, Chicago, University of Chicago Press.

Durant, William, *History of Civilization* Volume I and II.

Eddy, William, *FDR Meets Ibn Saud.*

Elst, Koenrad, *Saffron Swastika: The notion of Hindu Fascism.*

Ferguson, Neill, *Empire: The Rise and Demise of the British World Order and the Lessons for Global Power.*

Friedman Thomas L., ''*The World Is Flat: A Brief History of the Twenty-First Century*,'' Farrar, Straus & Giroux.

Fukuyama, Francis, *End of History and the Last Man.*

Ghosh, S K, *Pakistan's ISI: Network of Terror in India.*

Globb, J.B., *War in Desert A soldier with the Arabs.*

Gold, Dore, *Hatred's Kingdom: How Saudi Arabia Supports the New Global Terrorism.*

Guha, Ranajit (4): *Elementary aspects of peasant insurgency in colonial India* (Delhi : Oxford, 1983); and *An Indian historiography of India: a nineteenth-century agenda and its implications* (Calcutta : Bagchi,K P., 1988).

Hardiman, David (4) *Peasant nationalists of Gujarat: Kheda District, 1917-1934* (Delhi and New York : Oxford University Press, 1981).

Hardy, Peter, *The Muslims of British India*, Cambridge: Cambridge University Press, 1972.

Harvey, Robert, *Global Disorder: America and the Threat of World Conflict*.

Hasan, Mushirul, *Communal and pan-Islamic trends in colonial India*, edited by, Delhi: Manohar, 1981.

Hasan, Mushirul, *Legacy of a divided nation : India's Muslims since independence*, Boulder: Westview Press, 1997.

Hickman, John, *Nationalism without a Nation in India: Contemporary South Asia*, Abingdon: Mar 2000, Vol. 9.

Hitchens,Christoffer, *The Trial of Henry Kissinger*.

Hopkirk, Peter, *The Great Game*, Kodansha International, New York, 1994.

Hourani, Albert, *A History of Arab Peoples*.

http://india.medinf.com/society/

http://koenraadelst.bharatvani.org

http://koenraadelst.bharatvani.org/Ayodhyaandmedia.html

http://shikshanic.nic.in/cd50years/g/T/GV/0TGV0101.htm

http://web.clas.ufl.edu/users/gthursby/ind/subalter.htm

http://web.pdx.edu/~kinsella/papers/isamw97.pdf Study of Symbols of power in India (1997)

http://www.acdis.uiuc.edu/homepage_docs/pubs_docs/S&P_docs/S&P_Fa-94.html

http://www.aryasamaj.org/eng_art/A_clouds_over_understanding.htm

http://www.bharatvani.org/books/dist/ch2.htm#8

http://www.education.nic.in/htmlweb/natpol.htm

http://www.globalresearch.ca/articles/SIM311A.html "Worldview Warfare" and The Science of Coercion

http://www.gwu.edu/~nsarchiv/NSAEBB/NSAEBB79/ - The Tilt: The U.S. and the South Asian Crisis of 1971, National Security Archive Electronic Briefing Book No. 79. Edited by Sajit Gandhi. December 16, 2002.

http://www.infinityfoundation.com/

http://www.infinityfoundation.com/mandala/society_essays_frameset.htm

http://www.isn.ethz.ch/researchpub/publihouse/fast/crp/2000/crp_india_2000.htm#_edn33, 2002 swisspeace and Swiss Agency for Development and Cooperation (SDC) ñ Federal Department of Foreign Affairs.

http://www.lib.virginia.edu/area-studies/subaltern/ssallau.htm - Entire library index

http://www.mssc.edu/projectsouthasia/international_affairs/other/CIAReport--GlobalTrends2015.htm

http://www.propaganda101.com/Propaganda/NewsMediaPropaganda/NewsMediaPropFrame.htm

http://www.sas.upenn.edu/casi/reports/perkovich042303.html

http://www.sulekha.com/expressions/column.asp?cid=218625

http://www.sulekha.com/expressions/column.asp?cid=239156

http://www.sulekha.com/expressions/column.asp?cid=305890

Huntington, Samuel, *The Soldier and the State*.

Huntington, Samuel, *Clash of Civilization*, Touchstone Books, New York, 1996.

Ignatius, *Agents of Innocence*.

Isaacs, Harold R., *Scratches on Our Minds: American Images of China and India*.

Jaffrelot, Christoffe, *India's Silent Revolution.*

Jaffrelot, Christoffe, *The Hindu Nationalist Movement and Indian Politics, 1925-1994: Social and Political Strategies*.

Jaffrelot, Christoffe, *The Hindu Nationalist Movement in India*.

Johnson, Paul, *Modern Times World from the Twenties to the Nineties*.

Johnson, Paul M., *Intellectuals*.

Kagan, Robert, *Of Paradise and Power: America and Europe in the New World Order*.

Kalavai, Venkat, *http://indiastar.com/venkat1.html* A Critical Review of Romila Thapar's Early India: From the Origins to AD 1300.

Kaplan, Robert, *The Arabists*.

Kaplan, Robert, *Coming Anarchy*.

Kaplan, Robert, *Warrior Politics*.

Kaplan, Robert, *http://www.theatlantic.com/issues/2001/12/kaplan.htm* - - Looking the World in the Eye.

Karnad, Bharat, *Nuclear weapons and Indian security*.

Keay, John, *India: A History*.

Kennedy, Paul, *Rise and Fall of Great Powers*, Random House, New York, 1987.

Kevin, Phillips, *Wealth and Democracy: A Political History of the American Rich*.

Khidhir, Hamza, *Saddam's Bomb maker*.

Kissinger, Henry, *Diplomacy*.

Kissinger, Henry, *Does America Need a Foreign Policy?: Toward a Diplomacy for the 21st Century*.

Kotkin ,Joel Tribes, *How Race, Religion, and Identity Determine Success in the New Global Economy.*

K.S. Lal, *Indian Muslims Who are they*.

Kupchan, Charles, *At the End of the American Era: U.S. Foreign Policy and the Geopolitics of the Twenty-first Century*.

Lakshmikantham,V.,and S.Leela, (2000) "*The Originof Mathematics*", University Press of America, Lanham, NewYork, Oxford.

Lal, K.S., *http://www.bharatvani.org/books/imwat/ Indian Muslims Who Are They*.

Lal, K.S., *http://www.bharatvani.org/books/tlmr/ The Legacy of Muslim Rule in India*.

Larry P. Goodson, *Afghanistan's Endless War: State Failure, Regional Politics, and the Rise of the Taliban*.

Lawrence, T E, *The Seven Pillars of Wisdom*.

Lewis, Bernard, *The Shaping of the Modern Middle East*.

Lewis, Bernard, *Crisis in Islam*.

Lewis, Bernard, *Islam and the West*.

Lewis, Bernard, *Islam in History*.

Lewis, Bernard, *The Middle East*.

Lewis, Bernard, *The Muslim Discovery of Europe*.

Lewis, Bernard, *What Went Wrong? : The Clash Between Islam and Modernity in the Middle East*.

Lewis, Bernard, *http://www.theatlantic.com/issues/2003/05/lewis.htm - Islam and Christianity*.

Maids, Hayat Siddiqi, *Agrarian Unrest in North India: The United Provinces, 1918-1922*, New Delhi: Oxford University Press, 1978.

Malhotra, Rajiv, *Columns - Lila series*.

Malhotra, Rajiv, *RASA Lila - 2 - Limp Scholarship and Demonology*.

Malhotra, Rajiv, *The Axis of Neocolonialism*.

Mark Adkin, Brig., *Mohammed Yousaf The Bear Trap*.

Marshall, Sir John, et al (1931)"*MohenjoDaro and the Indus Valley Civilization*" London, A Probsthain.

Mead, Walter, *Special Providence - American Foreign Policy*.

Mearsheimer, John J, *The Tragedy of Great Power Politics*.

Meyer, Karl Ernst, *The Dust of Empire: The Race for Mastery in the Asian Heartland*.

Michael, Griffin, *Reaping The Whirlwind: The Taliban Movement in Afghanistan*.

Michael, Klare, *Resource Wars*.

Middle East Illusions.

Mike, Davis, *Late Victorian Holocausts: El Nino Famines and the Making of the Third World*.

Modern India, 1885-1947 (Delhi : Macmillan, 1983; second edition with foreword by D.A. Low, New York : St. Martin's Press, 1989)

Mohammad Yousef, *Silent Soldier*.

Moorhouse, Geoffrey, *India Britannica: A Vivid Introduction to the History of British India*.

My White House Years by Henry Kissinger.

Nehru, Jawaharlal, *Discovery of India*.

Neugebauer, O., (1962), *The Exact Sciences of Antiquity*, New York.

Pandey, Gyanendra, *The ascendancy of the Congress in Uttar Pradesh*.

Partha Chatterjee (4): *Bengal, 1920-1947: The Land Question* (Calcutta: Published for Centre for Studies in Social Sciences by K.P. Bagchi, 1984); and *Nationalist thought and the colonial world : a derivative discourse?* (London: Zed Books, 1986), Past Director & Chief Executive of ICRIER (Indian Council for Research in International Economic Relations), New Delhi, was released in November 2005.

Perkovich, George, *India's nuclear Bomb*.

Peterson, Peter G, Grey, Dawn, *How the coming age wave will transform America and The World*.

Popular movements and middle class leadership in late colonial India : perspectives and problems of a history from below (Calcutta: Bagchi, K.P. 1983).

Posner, Steve, *Israel Undercover*.

Program in Arms Control, Disarmament, and International Security

Project for New American Century:*http://www.newamericancentury.org/*

Rajaram, N. S., *Distortions in Indian History*.

Rajayyan, K., *South Indian Rebellion: The First War of Independence, 1800-1801*, Mysore: Rao and Raghavan, 1971.

Rashid, Ahmed, *Taliban:Militant Islam, Oil, And Fundamentalism*.

Raviv, Dan and Yossi, Melman, *Every Spy a Prince*.

RISA Lila - 1: *Wendy's Child Syndrome*.

Rise and fall of the poligars of Tamilnadu, Madras: University of Madras, 1974.

Rushdie, Salman, *Shame*.

Saunders, Frances Stoner, *The Cultural Cold War: The CIA and the World of Arts and Letters*.

Schulze Reinhard A Modern History of the Islamic World.

Seeley, John Robert, *'The Expansion of England"*, University of Chicago Press,1883.

Sengupta, Kalyan Kumar, "*Agrarian Disturbances in Eastern and Central Bengal in the Late 19th Century*," Indian Economic and Social History Review 8, 2, 1971, pp. 192-212; and Pabna Disturbances and the Politics of Rent, 1873-85.

Seidenberg, A., (1978), *The origin of Mathematics*, Archive for History of Exact Sciences, vol.18, pp.301-342.

Sethna, K.D.,(1992) *The Problem of Aryan Origins*, Aditya Prakashan, New Delhi.

Shahid Amin (3): *Sugarcane and Sugar in Gorakhpur: an inquiry into peasant production for capitalist enterprise in colonial India* (Delhi, New York: Oxford University Press, 1984).

SOUTH ASIA - PRIMARY SOURCES, *Islam's impact - 950 to 1740s http://www.thescotties.pwp.blueyonder.co.uk/primary-3.htm* -

Strmecki, Marin J, *Holy War Inc.*

Subaltern Studies and bibliography.

Subaltern Studies: Writings on South Asian History and Society (volume VIII is subtitled Essays in Honour of Ranajit Guha), published by Oxford University Press, from 1982 until 1999.

Subramanian Swamy, *Economic Reforms and Performance: China and India in Comparative Perspective*.

Tellis, et al, *Measuring National Power in the Postindustrial Age: Analysts Handbook* (Santa Monica: Rand, 2000), p. 4.

Terrill, Ross, *The New Chinese Empire: And What It Means for the United States*.

The ascendancy of the Congress in Uttar Pradesh, 1926-34: a study in imperfect mobilization (Delhi and New York : Oxford University Press, 1978).

The Causes and Nature of Current Agrarian Tensions, in A.R.Desai, Editor, *Agrarian Struggles in India After Independence*, Delhi: Oxford University Press, 1986.

The construction of communalism in colonial North India (Delhi: Oxford University Press, 1990), and (editor) *The Indian nation in 1942* (Calcutta: K.P. Bagchi, 1988); and Sumit Sarkar (2): *A critique of colonial India* (Calcutta: Papyrus, 1985).

Timperlake, Edward & William Triplett II, *Red Dragon Raising Communist China'a military threat to America*.

Ukhul, B.D., Clouds over Understanding of the Vedas.

Uris, Leon, *Exodus*.

Virmani, Arvind, *Global Power from the 18th to the 21st Century: Power Potential* (VIP2), *Strategic Assets and Actual Power* (VIP).

www.defencejournal.com Pakistan Defense Journal.

Yergin, Daniel, *The Prize: The Epic Quest for Oil, Money and Power.*

Zakaria, Fareed, *The Future of Freedom: Illiberal Democracy at Home.*

Select Bibiliography (History)

Aurobindo, *The Secret of the Veda*, Pondicherry, India, Ed.7, 5. 1993.

Davis, Mike, *Late Victorian Holocausts*, Verso 2002.

Dayanand Saraswati, *Satyartha Prakash.*

Elst, K., *Indigenous Indians* (Agastya to Ambedkar), New Delhi, 1993.

Frawley, David, *Gods, Sages and Kings*, Utah, USA, 1991.

Hodivala S.K., *Zarathustra and His Contemporaries in the Rg Veda*, 1913.

Kak, S., "*On the decipherment of the Indus Script - A preliminary Study of its Connection with Brahmi*," Indian J. of History and Science, V.22.1, p.51-62, 1987.

Kulkarni, S.D., Ed., *Beginnings of Life History and Culture*, The Study of Indian History and Culture, Thane, India, 1993.

Kulkarni, S.D., Ed., *Glorious Epoch*, The Study of Indian History and Culture, Thane, India, 1993.

Kulkarni, S.D., *Aadi Shankara*, Bombay, India, 1987.

Maxmuller F., *History of Ancient Sanskrit Literature*, 1968.

Mittal, S.C., *India Distorted*, ISBN 8185880646, 1995, 3 Volumes.

Narayana Shastri, T.S., *Age of Shankara*, Madras, 1916.

Oak, P.N., *World Vedic Heritage*, New Delhi, 1984.

Pargiter, F. E., *Ancient Indian Historical Tradition*, OUP, London, 1922.

Patnaik, K.N.S, "*The Mahabharata Chronology*", Annual Research J. of the Institute of Rewriting Indian History, Pune, India, 1990.

Pococke, E., *India in Greece.*

Rajagopalachari, C., *Indian Philosophy.*

Ramachandran, V.G., *A Peep into the Past History*, Madras, 1982.

Rao, S.R., *Lothal and the Indus Valley Civilization*, Bombay, India, 1973.

Sathe, S., *Dates of the Buddha*, Hyderabad, India, 1987.

Sathe, Sriram, *Search for the Bharata War*, 1983.

Sengupta, P. C., (1947) Ancient Indian Chronology, University of Calcutta, Calcutta.

Sengupta, P. C., (1927) *Aryabhattiyum.*

Sethna, K.D., *The Problem of Aryan Origins*, New Delhi, 1992.

Spencer, H.S., *Are the Gathas pre-Vedic?,* 1965.

Talageri, S., *The Aryan Invasion and Indian Nationalism*, New Delhi, 1993.

The Aryan Pages, The Vedic institute Of Aryan Studies.

Tilak, B.G., *The Arctic Home in the Vedas*, Pune, India, 1987.

Tilak, B.G., *The Orion or Researches into the antiquity of the Vedas*, Pune, 1994.

Vallency, C., *Collectania De Rebus Hibernicus*, Dublin, 1804.

Vartak, P.V., *Swayambhu*, Pune, Bharat, 1988.

Vartak, P.V., *Vastav Ramayana (in Marathi),* Pune, Bharat, 1993.

Venkatachalam, K., *The Age of Buddha, Milinda and Amtiyoka and Yuga Purana*, Vijaywada, India, 1956.

Wheeler, M., *Civilization of the Indus Valley and Beyond.*

Yukteshwar, Sri, *The Holy Science*, Los Angeles, 1984.

References on Indic History

General

R.C. Majumdar: *The History and Culture of the Indian People* (HCIP) by is a comprehensive multivolume series that covers the entire history pretty well too but then he is also called "saffron" though what he wrote is not substantially distinguishable from that of the Islamic historians.

K.A. Nilakanta Sastri et al (editors.), *A comprehensive History of India,* Calcutta, 1957.

K.A. Nilakanta Sastri, *A History of South India from Prehistoric Times to the fall of Vijayanagar*, Madras, 1955.

Arun Shourie, *Eminent Historians, their technology, their line and their fraud*, ASA, New Delhi,1998.

A Brief Bibliography of Military History (University of Illinois), Contains a decent collection of titles on Indian History from Ancient to Post Independence, the era of the Ancients and the beginning of River valley Civilizations (7000 BCE to 4000 BCE).

Pande, G C., *The Dawn of Indian Civilization up to 600 BCE*,, PHISPC, Centre for the study of Civilizations,1999.

Raj Mohanka, *Royal Chronology of India* (an excellent start to unraveling the detailed chronology of ancient India and rescue it from the hopeless inconsistencies that it has been driven to by the initial mistakes of Sir William Jones and the cavalier treatment meted out by Friedrich Maximillian Müller.

R L Bhargava, *India in the Vedic age*.

Talageri, Shrikant G., *The RIG-VEDA:A Historical Analysis*, Aditya Prakashan, New Delhi,2000. There is an on line copy.

Dowson, John ,1820-1881, *A classical dictionary of Hindu mythology and religion, geography, history, and literature*. -- London, Truebner, 1879.

Danielou, Alain, "*The Myths and Gods of India*", Princeton Bollinger Series Somadeva,11. Jhdt. n. Chr.: Kathasaritsagara : der Ozean der Erzählungsströme : ausgewählte Erzählungen / übersetzt und erläutert von Alois Payer. -- 2. Buch I, Welle 1. -- 4. Vers 27 - 46: Rahmenerzählung I: Die Kurzgeschichte, Parvatis fruehere Geburt. -- Fassung vom 2006-11-16. -- *http://www.payer.de/somadeva/soma024.htm*.

David, Frawley (Vamadeva Shastri), *Rig Veda sand the History of India* (Rig Veda Bharata Itihaasa) Aditya Prakashan, 2001, New Delhi, ISBN 81-7742-039-9. American Institute of Vedic Studies, PO Box 8357, Santa Fe NM 87504-8357, www.vedanet.com.

Vedic Aryans and the Origins of Civilization,Navratna S. Rajaram & David Frawley, (with a Foreword by Klaus K. Klostermaier) New Delhi, Voice Of India, 2001, 3rd Edition.

Rajaram, N. S., and N. Jha, *The deciphered Indus script*, Aditya Prakashan, Delhi, 2005, ISBN 8177420151.

Chronologv of Ancient India : From the Times of the Rigvedic King Divodasa to Chandragupta Maurya, with Glimpses into the Political History of the Period/Sita Nath Pradhan. Reprint.. 1996, 291 p.

Contents: 1. Divodasa and Dasaratha. 2. Kings of other dynasties contemporary of Divodasa. 3. The descendants of the king Satvant of the Yadus. 4. The lineal descendants of Bhargava Vitahavya. 5. The Magadha dynasty. 6. The Hastinapur line. 7. The Northern Pancalas. 8. The Southern Pancala line. 9. The Anga dynasty. 10. The descendants of Dasaratha Aiksvaka. 11. The Janaka dynasty. 12. The Southern Kosala line. 13. The Kasi dynasty. 14. A series of Vedic teachers. 15. Distinguished Rsis belonging to the period. 16. Chronology. 17. Chronology developed in 'Rigvedic India' untenable. 18. Chronology developed in 'the Orion' untenable. 19. Aryan settlement of India during the Rgvedic period. 20. From Bimbisara to Chandragupta Maurya. 21. The Pradyota dynasty. 22. Important dates. 23. The date of the Mahabharata war. Index.

This book provides an interesting foray into the undated history of ancient Vedic, Brahmanic and Puranic India. Based upon the author's research into ancient Indian literature like the Puranas, Mahabharata, Ramayana, Aranyakas, Upanishads etc, along with Buddhist, Pali and Jain evidences; this work provides the only attempt at historically authenticating what has generally been relegated to the folk or mythical level. This includes providing the correct genealogies of the ancient Indian dynasties and putting events in a proper chronological order and to provide sequential dating to important events, such as the Mahabharata war. This work of remarkable scholarship has provided a critique of all existing works on the era and made reference to every known historical explanation." (from the jacket)

The Aryan Problem, A linguistic Approach, by Satya Swaroop Misra, Munshiram Manoharlal Publishers P. Ltd.

Bryant, Edwin and Laurie Patton, *The Indo Aryan Controversy* - Evidence and Inference in Indian History, Routledge, London, 2005.

Sethna, K D., *The Problem of Aryan Origins, from an Indian Point of View*, Aditya Prakashan, 1980

Sethna, K D., *Problems of Ancient India*, Delhi, Aditya, 2000, 306 p., ISBN 81-7742-026-7.

Dilip K Chakrabarti, *Colonial Indology, Socio-Politics of the Ancient Indian Past*, Munshiram Manoharlal Publishers P. Ltd., 1997.

B. P. Radhakrishna and S. S. Merh ,*Vedic Saraswati, Evolutionary History of a Lost River in North Western India* (Memoir 42) ,Geological Society of India, P.B. No. 1922, Govipuram, Bangalore-560019.

Pratapaditya Pal, *Art from the Indian Subcontinent*, Yale University Press, In association with the Norton Simon Art Foundation.

David Frawley, *The Rig Veda and the History of India*, AdityaPrakashan, Delhi, 2003.

Krishna Dvaipayana Vyasa, *The Srimad Bhagavatam*, Eng. Translation by J M Sanyal, Oriental Publishing Co. Calcutta, 1932.

Veda Vyas, *Astronomical Dating of the Mahabharata War*, ISBN 817460019,Hyderrabad, 1993.

The Era of Geographical Expansion and consolidation of Civilizational values (from the ancients up to 1000 CE)

Alberuni's India: An account of the Religion, Philosophy, Literature, Geography, Chronology, Astronomy, Customs, Laws, and Astrology of India about 1030 CE translated by Dr. Edward Sachau, published by Rupa and Co., New Delhi 2002.

Nilakanta Sastri, K A, Editor, *A comprehensive History of India*, Vol. II, The Mauryas and the Satavahanaas, ISBN 8170070597, Peoples Publishing House,New Delhi, 1987.

Jeanne L Trebold, *A Chronology of Indian Sculpture*;The Satavahana Chronology at Nasik, Artibus Asiae, Institute of Fine Arts, New York University, Volume XXXXII, 1970.

Sir Vepa Ramesam, *Andhra Chronology*, K Mahadevan, Madras, 1940.

The Era of conflicting Paradigms (1000 CE to 17th Century)

Mahomed Kasim Ferishta, translated by John Briggs, *History of the Rise and fall of the Mohamedan Power in India.*

Travels of Ibn Batuta, translated by H A R Gibb gives first hand account of the Sultanate rulers of India as observed by a Muslim traveller -- he can hardly be called "saffron".

Elliot and Dawson, *History of India as told by its own historians.*

Jadunath Sarkar is a well respected historian and his books on Aurangzeb and other Muslim rulers are also a good source. His book on Aurangzeb is not easily available since reprint rights are not granted. Some libraries might have old prints. It is worth reading though. Sarkar does have his bias against the Marathas, for whatever reason.

Abul Fazl, *Akbarnama*.

Jehangir, *Intikhab I Jahangiri*.

Lal, K.S., *Legacy of Muslim Rule in India*, New Delhi, Aditya Prakashan, 1992, 406 pp., ISBN 81 85179 03 04.

Other books by K.S. Lal:

History of the Khaljis (1950, 1967, 1980);

Twilight of the Sultanate (1963, 1980);

Studies in Asian History (edited - 1969);

Growth of Muslim Population in Medieval India (1973);

Early Muslims in India (1984);

The Mughal Harem (1988);

Indian Muslims: Who Are They? (1990);

Muslim Slave System in Medieval India (1994);

Growth of Scheduled Tribes and Castes in Medieval India, Aditya Prakashan (1995);

Theory and practice of the Muslim state in India, (1999);

The following is not a book on Indian History but describes the concept of Jihad:

Jihad in the West : Muslim Conquests from the 7th to the 21st Centuries by Paul Fregosi, Hardcover, 442 pp. (October 1998) Prometheus Books; ISBN:1573922471.

Sita Ram Goel, *Hindu Temples what happened to them*, Vol.2, the Islamic Evidence, Voice of india, ISBN 8185990034, Delhi, 1993.

Slavery and the Indian Slave trade during the middle ages, by Scot Levi.

2002, November: '*Hindus Beyond the Hindu Kush: Indians in the Central Asian Slave Trade,*' Journal of the Royal Asiatic Society, 3d ser. (12, 3), pp. 277-88.

Some British writers of Indian History from whom we have learnt Indian History

James Mills, *History of India*.

Major General John Malcolm, *A Memoir of the Central India* (1824).

Captain Grant Duff, *History of the Marathas* (1826).

Gen. John Briggs, *History of the Rise of Mohammedan Power in India* (1829), (translation of Tarikh i Farishta by Farishta).

Lt. Colonel James Todd, *Annals and Antiquities of Rajasthan* (1829-32).

Montstuart Elphinstone, (Resident at Peshwa Court, later Governor of Bombay), History of India (1841).

Joseph Davey, Cunningham (brother of Gen.A.Cunningham), *History of Sikhs*, (1849).

Lt. R.F. Burton, *History of Sindh* (1851).

Hunter, William Wilson, *The Indian Empire*, Asian Educational Services, Originally published 1886.

Thomas Babington Macaulay, *Critical and Historical Essays*

Sir H M Elliot & John Dowson, *The History of India as told by its own Historians*,The Mohammadan Period, First Published 1867, Reprinted 1990, 8 volumes, ISBN 8175360518.

Francis Younghusband, *Kashmir*.

British Colonial Period

Peter Hopkirk "*The Great Game*, The struggle for empire in Central Asia",Kodansha International, first published 1990.

Sir Penderel Moon, *The British Conquest and Dominion of India*", Published in two volumes by India Research Press, 1999, pp. 1264.

Independence Movement and Post Independence Period

R C Majumdar, '*History of the freedom movement in India*',1962, 2nd revised edition, Firma KL Mukhopadhyay, Calcutta, 1971.

Sir C Y Chintamani, *Indian Politics since the Mutiny*, Rupa and Co.,Delhi, 2002.

C Y Chintamani, The Liberal Editor, politician by Sunil Raman, Rupa and Co.,2002, describes the life of a genuine liberal, during an era when the word was used for those who were under suspicion of harboring seditious ideas against British Rule.

M Visvesvaraya, Engineer and Nation Builder, by Dilip Salvi, Rupa and Co., Delhi, 2003, ISBN 8129102269. Describes the life of one of India preeminent engineers during the British era.

V. L.N. Row, *Witness to a Saga*,[77] a memoir of my father describes many anecdotes during the British era from the point of view of a middleclass Indian.

V.P. Menon, *The Transfer of Power in India*, Bombay, 1957.

V.P. Menon, *The story of the Integration of the Indian states*, Bombay, 1956.

Claude Arpi, *The Fate of Tibet*, When big insects eat small insects,with a Foreword by His Holiness the Dalai Lama, New Delhi, Har-Anand, 1999.

Eminent Orientalists, an Anthology, First Published, Madras 1922, ISBN 81 20606973, AES reprint 1991.

S. Gurbachan Singh Talib, *Muslim League Attack on Sikhs and Hindus in the Punjab 1947,* Compiled for the SGPC, Introduction to the reprint by Ram Swarup, Voice of India, New Delhi.

Kosla Vepa, The South Asia file.[78]

Mittal, S.C., *India Distorted*, ISBN 8185880646, 1995, 3 Volumes.

Nicholas Dirks, *Castes of Mind*, Colonialism and the making of Modern India, Princeton U press, Princeton, 2001, ISBN 0891088950.

Nicholas Dirks, *The Scandal of Empire*, Belknap Harvard, Harvard, 2006, ISBN 0674021665.

Bernard Cohn, *Colonialism and its form of knowledge*, Oxford U Press, Delhi, 1997, ISBN 019564167.

Sarilla, Narendra Singh, *The Shadow of the Great game*, the untold story of India's Partition, Caroll and Graf Publishers, New York, NY, 10011, ISBN 978-0-78671-912-9.

The following are available as digitized editions

The links are given below:

http://www.indicethos.org/History/Digitallibrary.html

Early history of Kausambi, from the sixth century B.C. to the eleventh century A.D., by Nagendra Nath Ghosh.

Ancient India as described by Megasthenes and Arrian by J McCrindle.

---

77. http://vepa.us/dir5/Book/index.htm

78. http://indicethos.org/The%20South%20Asia%20File.html

Arrians History of Alexander by Henry Rooke (this version of the book has been altered and corrected by J Davis in 1812 and so this is not the original version of the book that was first published in 1729.

The History of India by Montstuart Elphinstone.

India in Greece: Or, Truth in Mythology: Containing the Source (Pocock)

Ancient and Medieval India by Manning.

Elementary Algebra with brief notices of History contains a good discussion of Indic mathematics.

Supplementary Catalog of Sanskrit, Pali and Prakrit Books.

Appendix J The Fundamental Postulates Behind The Colonial Paradigm of Indian History

Key Axioms

The key assumption is that the Indic[79] civilization that remains extant has been brought into the area by migrating races such as the Aryans, and in fact some would argue, that such a statement holds also for the so called Dravidians of India.

The second assumption implicit in all the assertions made by Occidentals about India is that no date for any significant scientific advance should be attributed to the Indics prior to the Golden age of Greece beginning in 600 BCE.

According to such a narrative everything that was worth preserving has been handed down to us over the centuries by migrations, within the last 3 1/2 millennia, into the subcontinent, from somewhere else. Such a viewpoint was first expressed by Hegel who took the view, subsequently internalized by Indics after being told ad nauseum by a whole slew of British historians from James Mills to the latest Oxford and Cambridge Histories that India was always a derivative civilization. It is not our contention that all historians have taken such a jaundiced view of the Indic past. There has been a school of historians and philosophers who have taken a Civilizational view of the Indic past, among whom we count Arnold Toynbee, Will Durant, Karl Potter,

79. We will define the adjective Indic (as in Indic civilization) to be inclusive of all the people who derived their civilization from the Dhaarmic traditions of the Indian subcontinent. For the most part we will restrict ourselves to the subset of those residing in the subcontinent including most of present day Afghanistan and some eastern regions of present day Iran.

Fernand Braudel and Samuel Huntington, who while they may agree with the chronology of the Occidental Historians of India, disagree profoundly with the notion that India is a derivative civilization.

It is also true that the history that is taught the children of India today is vastly at variance with the puranic accounts handed down to us over several millennia. It is to state it without any embellishments, a revised history that is completely at odds with the traditional history of India. Such a state of affairs persists even today, and most schoolchildren everywhere in the world are taught the erroneous chronology and that India lacks historical agency.

> The premise of this monograph is that the current narration of the History of the Indic people is seriously and fatally flawedboth with respect to the chronology as well as in content.

Meaning of History & Itihaasa

Historians and philosophers have been contemplating the meaning of history since, well, since the beginning of history! A simple definition of history is" remembering the past "or Knowledge of what has happened from the start until the present. It is also the knowledge of the past since record keeping was initiated. The purpose of studying history in school is to teach the student understanding of what has taken place so that we may build upon and understand how a nation functions and how it came to be. We also study the history of other nations and how their histories interact with our history. A greater awareness of history results in a more enlightened and educated citizenry. Knowledge of our past helps us understand the present and prepare for the future. Knowing the history of the world helps the individual respect and appreciate one's own form of government and society as well as become better informed about differences in the Civilizational ethos of other peoples of the world

"The word history comes from *Greek* (*istoria*), from the *Proto-Indo-European* **wid-tor-*, from the *root* **weid-*, "to know, to see"(this is a hypothesis). This root is also present in the English word wit, in the Latin words vision and video, in the *Sanskrit* word *veda*, and in the *Slavic* word *videti* and *vedati*, as well as others (The asterisk before a word indicates that it is a hypothetical construction, not an attested form.)

The *Ancient Greek* word, *istorîa*, means "knowledge acquired by investigation, inquiry". It was in that sense that *Aristotle* used the word in his, *Peri Ta Zoa Istória* or, in Latinized form, *Historia Animalium*. The term is derived from *hîstor* meaning *wise man*, *witness*, or *judge*.

We can see early attestations of in *Homeric Hymns, Heraclitus*, the *Athenian ephebes*' oath, and in *Boiotic* inscriptions (in a legal sense, either "judge" or "witness," or similar). The *form historeïn*, "to inquire", is an *Ionic* derivation, which spread first in *Classical Greece* and ultimately over all of *Hellenistic civilization*. The Ionic origin indicates a cognate meaning with its Indo Iranian predecessor. It was still in the Greek sense that *Francis Bacon* used the term in the late 16th century, when he wrote about "*Natural History*". For him, historia was "the knowledge of objects determined by space and time", that sort of knowledge provided by *memory* (while *science* was provided by *reason*, and *poetry* was provided by *fantasy*).The word entered the *English language* in *1390* with the meaning of "relation of incidents, story". In *Middle English*, the meaning was "story" in general. The restriction tó the meaning "record of past events" arises in the late *15th century*. In German, French, and most Germanic and Romance languages the same word is still used to mean both "history" and "story". The adjective *historical* is attested from *1561*, and *historic* from *1669*. *Historian* in the sense of a "researcher of history" is attested from *1531*. In all *European languages*, the substantive "history" is still used to mean both "what happened with men", and "the scholarly study of the happened", the latter sense sometimes distinguished with a capital letter, "History", or the word *historiography* (*more commonly in use in India*)".[80]

The original meaning of Itihaasa had a more precise sense than the word History. The etymology attested to by Panini indicates itiha to mean 'thus indeed, in this tradition'.[81]

One of the earliest references to Itihaasa in the literature of antiquity is in Chanakyas's Arthashastra. Our investigations lead us to believe that the Maurya empire for which he was the preceptor began in 1534 BCE. He defines Itihaasa, in the context of the syllabus prescribed for training of a Prince, with the following words:

पुराणमितिवृत्तमाख्यायिकोदाहरणं
धर्मार्थशास्त्रं चेतीतिहासः ।।

---

80. *Wikipedia*.

81. Katre, S.M., '*Dictionary of Panini*', Published by Deccan Collge, Part I, 1968.

Puraana (the chronicles of the ancients), Itivrtta (history), Akhyayika (tales), Udaaharana (illustrative stories), Dharmashastra (the canon of Righteous conduct), and Arthashastra (the science of Government) are known by (comprise the corpus of Itihaasa) History Kautilya's Arthashastra, Book 1, Chapter 5

Thus, History (Itihaasa) in this definition takes on the meaning more akin to the sense of Historiography and is perhaps even more eclectic and appears to indicate a superset of political science and History as we use them today. We feel vindicated therefore in calling this a conference on Indian History, since we seem to ascribe the same broad meaning that Kautilya did 3 millennia ago.

In the MB, which is itself considered Itihaasa, is the following verse in Adi Parva 1.267,268, that a knowledge of the Itihaasa and Purana is essential to the proper understanding the Veda.

tathA hi mahAbhArate mAnavIye ca - itihAsa-purANAbhyAM vedaM samupabRMhayetbibhety alpasrutAd vedo mAm aya? pratari?yati iti, pUranAt purANam iti cAnyatra. na cAvedena vedasya bRMhaNaM sambhavati nah y aparipUrNasya kanaka-valayasya trapuNA pUraNaM yujyate

तथ् हि महाभारते मानवीयेच "इतिहासपुराणाभ्यां वेदो समुपब्रिंयेत बिभेत्य अल्पश्रुतादं वेदो मामयं प्रहरिष्यति" इति पूरणात् पुराणम इति चन्यत्र। न च वेदेन वेदस्य ब्रमणं सम्भवति न ह्यपरिपूर्नस्य कनक वलयस्य त्रपुणा पुराणमुपयुज्यतो।

This is why the Mahabharata (Adi-Parva 1.267,268) and Manu-Samhita state, "One should complement one's understanding of the Vedas with the help of the Itihasas and the Puranas." And elsewhere it is stated, "The Puranas are called by that name because they are complete."

The quintessential quote is that of Kalhana in the Rajatarangini, who is regarded as a modern in Indian parlance

धर्मार्थकाममोक्षाणामुपदेशसमान्वितं।
पुरावृत्तं कथायुत्तमितिहासं प्रचक्षते।।

"Dharmaartha-kaama-moskshanaam upadesa-samanvitam |

Puraa-vrttam, kathaa-yuttarupam Ithihaasah prachakshate ||"

History will be the narration of events as they happened, in the form of a story, which will be an advice to the reader to be followed in life, to gain the purusaarthas namely Kama the satiation of desires through Artha the tool, by following the path of Dharma the human code of conduct to gain Moksha or liberation.

Clearly there is an emphasis on the traditions and on the utilitarian aspect of History, embedded in the etymology of Itihaasa. The reason we draw emphasis to the ambiguity in the use of the word History is that, in our usage in this conference, while we adhere to the broader usage of the word History, we have separated the Civilizational aspects in distinct sessions.

Appendix K The Debate Over the Origin of the Vedics

If one were to ask an average Indic whether he had any comments on the debate regarding the origin of the Vedics, his first reaction might be that he was not aware there was a debate and as far as he could recall the Vedics had since the beginning of recorded history, populated an area roughly contiguous with present day Haryana and Uttaranchal. In other words (it is my suspicion that) this topic is not exactly one that occupies center stage in the streets and living rooms of Mumbai and Kolkatta. However, this remains a subject with far reaching implications for the future of India. One example being the dialog that is taking place in India over the perceived inequalities among various classes of Indic society today, their causes and how they should be handled. One other point should be made regarding the consequences of such a hypothesis. The colonial overlord thereby made the implication very clearly that they were just the latest in a long line of conquerors and had as much right to be present as the descendants of the Vedics, who would after all be now be regarded as conqueror much as the Normans conquered England.

Ever since Friedrich Max Müller first postulated this hypothesis, it has been a major preoccupation of a fairly large section of linguists, historians, philologists, religious clergy and other academic scholars in Europe and now even in America. The reasons for this are not difficult to fathom. It was Sir William Jones who first noticed that there appeared to be a common origin of some commonly used words like father (Pater, Latin, pitr, Sanskrit), mother and brother. Soon it became apparent that even well known names of Gods in Greek and Roman Mythology such as Zeus (Dyaus, Sanskrit) and Jupiter (Dyaus Pitr, Sanskrit) had their origin in Sanskrit. This was a major revelation especially to the linguistic and historian community in Europe at that time, because it was a paradigm change in the manner in which they viewed the Indian subcontinent and the origins of their own language. How did this commonality in literally hundreds of words come about ? The simplest explanation at that time (and even today) was that there was a significant migration of people accompanied by invasions that was the primary engine for the spread of language. Even though Sanskrit was palpably the more ancient language in this group of languages, they immediately dismissed the notion that there was any kind of migration from the Indian subcontinent. Thus was born the Aryan Invasion Theory (AIT). The main flaw in the theory and there are many more described for example in the many links and books in this section the main flaw is that there is absolutely no record of such an invasion or even a migration in any of the vast literature of the Vedics.

This theory and its far reaching implications has escaped the notice of the Indic population in general, preoccupied as they were with the more mundane necessities of making a living and the more immediate task of nation building.

The invasion theory of Indian History was first postulated by Hegel (1831) that India lacked historical agency and that India was a cultural cul de sac from which nothing worthwhile ever emanated. The Aryan Invasion Theory (which has now morphed into Aryan Immigration or Influx Theory), based largely on linguistic conjectures and postulates is a narrative that was force fitted to Hegel's postulate. In one brilliant master stroke, the British killed several birds with one stone.

What were the Basic Postulates of AIT—that a race of nomadic Aryans came thundering across the passes of the Hindu Kush mountain range on horse drawn chariots and overcame the sedentary urban civilization of the Indus river valleys who happened to belong to the Dravidian race and then shortly thereafter in short order decided to compose the entire gamut of Vedic Literature from the Vedas, puranas, the smritis, the Brahmanas the Upanishads and the Itihaas of India. If this is was what really happened, the transformation from Central Asian Nomads to the intellectual speculations inherent in the Vedic literature must surely rank as one of the most rapid transformations in human history.

See for instance *http://www.boloji.com/architecture/00002.htm*

What did the postulation of AIT accomplish

Postulated a discontinuity between the Vedics and the Saraswathi Sindhu Civilization, and assigned a much more recent date to the Vedics and hopelessly confused the issue of the precedence of the Vedics.

Postulated the presence of two new races, Aryan and Dravidian, a racial nomenclature that was custom fitted to the Indian peninsula to suit the need of the colonial overlord for emphasizing the diversity of ethnic and linguistic communities in the subcontinent. When it became unfashionable to be Aryan, especially when the Germans, courtesy of Nietzsche and others elevated the category to the status of a master race, the nomenclature was changed to Indo-European and this has since morphed into various other names. Despite the lack of a proper definition both terms continue to be used ad nauseum when referring to certain ethnic groups in the Indian subcontinent and also as the defining word in the 'AIT' acronym. I may be forgiven for avoiding use of the word as much as possible, as I remain ignorant of the defining characteristics of the Aryan people.

Ergo, the Vedics became aliens to the subcontinent and became associated with the mythical Aryans, a noun which is never used in the Vedas, with all its 20th century fascist connotations. The communists in India have now latched on to this notion of the mythical Aryans and have decided that henceforth they will refer to any Hindu who does not conform to their jaundiced view of Indian history, as not only Aryan but also as a fascist. Such a notion was (and is) of course lapped up very willingly by the western press, as the irony of a fascist Brahmana priest performing a puja clad only in a loin cloth was too delicious to pass up and thus was born the nirvana, the piece de resistance of the clichê kingdom, the ad hominem of choice, the Hindutva[1] fascist. So lavishly is this appellation now applied to the millions of inhabitants of the Indian subcontinent, creating thereby the spectacle of the first instance of an impoverished fascist in the known galaxy and so widespread is this outlandish and absurd notion of the fascist Hindutva, that it has spawned at least one PhD thesis[2], more than a half a dozen books, excoriating the straw man of a Hindu nationalist' and is a major contributor to the bandwidth of the internet discussions on the sociology of India.

To top it off, the caste system was now associated with these marauding but anthropologically non-existent Aryan people.

The conclusion was inescapable -the British were simply a latter version of the Aryans to have conquered India and had as much legitimacy to remain and rule India as did the original Vedics.

Meanwhile back at the ranch, the defeated and displaced Dravidians allegedly retreated to the south and formed the bulk of the downtrodden castes (the castes were now delineated and created very conveniently and fortuitously by the colonial overlord who was never at a loss to miss such a golden opportunity as this) of modern India—gave rise to the plethora of Dravidian parties in the state of Tamilnadu. So much so that today no party can get elected in the southern state of Tamil Nadu without the appellation of Dravidian tacked on to its name.

To this day many Indians remain oblivious to the glaring fact that there is not a shred of evidence for this set of egregious hypotheses masquerading as a theory and the reasons for this sad state of affairs with the resulting disastrous effects on the body politic of the Indian Republic are too obvious to recount here. We trust we will have the opportunity to elaborate on these consequences in a later section, should there be need to do so.

[1] Please see glossary in the linguistics section for meanings of words of Indic or Sanskritic origin.

[2] Incidentally this thesis and the accompanying books by Dr. Koenraad Elst are definitely a landmark in the sense that he has marshaled a compelling narrative of why such an appellation in the Indian subcontinent is without relevance and in fact without any meaning whatsoever.

So what was once purely a preoccupation of the Europeans over their roots has now been transformed into a debate on the origin of the Vedics with large scale implications on the history of India. It is important to note that the writing or more precisely the rewriting or revising of Indian History was largely in the hand of the English since they were the colonial overlords and they retained control of the language of command and control, namely English ,by making it the official language of India. The engineering of this paradigm shift, was a major coup for the British administrators of colonial India. That it was a ploy to justify the colonial rule by the British 'descendants' of the Aryans of an earlier era was as much as admitted by the British Prime Minister himself ..We will let Navaratna Rajaram describe the situation in his own pithy style, as only he can do.

"The British, however, put it to more creative use for imperial purposes, especially as a tool in making their rule acceptable to Indians. A recent BBC report admitted (October 6, 2005). 'It [the Aryan invasion theory] gave a historical precedent to justify the role and status of the British Raj, who could argue that they were transforming India for the better in the same way that the Aryans had done thousands of years earlier.' That is to say, the British presented themselves as a 'new and improved brand of Aryans' who were only completing the work left undone by their ancestors in the hoary past. This is how the British Prime Minister Stanley Baldwin put it in the House of Commons.

> Now, after ages, the two branches of the great Aryan ancestry have again been brought together by providence- By establishing British rule in India, God said to the British, "I have brought you and the Indians together after a long separation, Mit is your duty to raise them to their own level as quickly as possible Mbrothers as you are..."

This leaves little to the imagination.". The BBC show also lists the adverse effects of the AIT as follows;

Dangers of the theory

Opponents of the Aryan invasion theory claim that it denies the Indian origin of India's predominant culture, and gives the credit for Indian culture to invaders from elsewhere. They say that it even teaches that some of the most revered books of Hindu scripture are not actually Indian, and it devalues India's culture by portraying it as less ancient than it actually is. The theory was not just wrong, some say, but included unacceptably racist ideas:

> it suggested that Indian culture was not a culture in its own right, but a synthesis of elements from other cultures.
>
> it implied that Hinduism was not an authentically Indian religion but the result of cultural imperialism.
>
> it suggested that Indian culture was static, and only changed under outside influences.
>
> it suggested that the dark-skinned Dravidian people of the South of India had got their faith from light-skinned Aryan invaders.

it implied that indigenous people were incapable of creatively developing their faith.

it suggested that indigenous peoples could only acquire new religious and cultural ideas from other races, by invasion or other processes.

it accepted that race was a biologically based concept (rather than, at least in part, a social construct) that provided a sensible way of ranking people in a hierarchy, which provided a partial basis for the caste system.

it provided a basis for racism in the Imperial context by suggesting that the peoples of Northern India were descended from invaders from Europe and so racially closer to the British Raj.

it gave a historical precedent to justify the role and status of the British Raj, who could argue that they were transforming India for the better in the same way that the Aryans had done thousands of years earlier.

it downgraded the intellectual status of India and its people by giving a falsely late date to elements of Indian science and culture.

So successful was this endeavor of postulating the AIT, that today most of the prescribed English language textbooks in India mention the AIT as fact and not as an unproven hypothesis. What is even sadder is that a significant proportion of the population in India have internalized this version of history and are vociferous in debating in favor of it. The debate has been documented by Edwin Bryant (2005),within the context of the framework established by the European Indologists, while pronouncing himself an agnostic on the issue. We will touch upon several aspects of the debate in this section.

Appendix L Glossary

A

Abda - Year (as in Yugabda 5109 (2007).

Abhijit - Abhijit Nakshatra: Abhijit Nakshatra is called the intercalary(IC) Nakshatra as it appear as a small (smaller duration as compared to normal duration of Nakshatra 13d 20m) Nakshatra between Uttarashadha and Sravana. The duration of Uttarashadha is divided into four parts and the first three paadas are assigned to Uttarashadha, which makes the duration of Uttarashadha to be 10deg with each paada to be 2d 30m. The remaining one paada of Uttarashadha is assigned to Abhijit, the intercalary Nakshatra. Similarly beginning 1/15th part of Sravana is given to Abhijit, making its total length to be 253.33 min, i.e., 4d 13m 20s. The remaining 14/15th part of Sravana is assigned to the four padas of Sravana, making the total duration of Sravana to be 12d 26m 40s.

Acharya - a spiritual guide or teacher. See Sankaracharya.

Adharma - absence of righteousness, disorder, evil, immorality.

Adhikamaasa or intercalary month - Leap month or intercalary month introduced to account for the lack of synchronization between a lunar period and a solar period, i.e., the solar period (or year) is not an exact multiple of a lunar month. Literally means additional month. An intercalation takes place when 2 lunar months begin in the same solar month, the former of the 2 is called the intercalary month or adhikamaasa.

Adi - first, primordial as in Adi Sankara.

Aditi - In Hinduism, Aditi (Sanskrit - limitless) is a goddess of the sky, consciousness, the past, the future and fertility. She is an ancient goddess, mother of Agni and the Adityas with Kashyapa. She is associated with cows, a very holy animal in Hindu beliefs. Aditi is the daughter of Daksha and Veerni. She gave birth to the Devas who were beautiful, intelligent and pious to the Almighty. Although the goddess Aditi is mentioned nearly eighty times in the rg-veda, it is difficult to get a clear picture of her nature. She is usually mentioned along with other gods and goddesses, there is no one hymn addressed exclusively to her, and unlike many other vedic deities, she is not obviously related to some natural phenomenon. compared to Usha and Prithvi, her character seems ill defined. She is virtually featureless physically. perhaps the most outstanding attribute of Aditi is her motherhood. She is preeminently the mother of the Adityas, a group of 7 or 8 gods which include Mitra, Aryaman, Bhaga, Varuna, Daksha and Ansa. (2.27.1) Aditi is also said to be the mother of the great god Indra, the mother of kings (2.27), and the mother of gods (1.113.19). Unlike Prithvi, however, whose motherhood is also central to her nature, Aditi does not have a male consort in the Rig Veda. as a mothering presence, Aditi is often asked to guard the one who petitions her (1.106.7 ; 8.18.6) or to provide him or her with wealth, safety, and abundance (10.100; 1.94.15).

Aditya - In Hinduism, the Adityas are a group of solar deities, sons of Aditi and Kashyapa. In the Rigveda, they are seven deities of the heavens, chief of these being Varuna, followed by Mitra, Aryaman, Bhaga, Daksha, and Ansa, the seventh Aditya was probably the Sun, Surya or Savitar. As a class of gods, the Rigvedic Adityas were distinct from the Visvedevas. In the Yajurveda (Taittiriya Samhita), their number is given as eight. In the Brahmanas, their number is expanded to twelve, corresponding to the twelve months:Ansa ,Aryaman, Bhaga ,Daksha ,Dhatri, Indra, Mitra, Ravi, Savitar, Surya , Varuna, Yama Aditya in the (Chandogya-Upanishad) is also a name of Vishnu, in his Vamana (dwarf) Avatar. Dictionary of Hindu Lore and Legend (ISBN 0500510881) by Anna Dhallapiccola.

Adhyasa - used to refer to the 'mistake' that we make when we 'superimpose' a false appearance upon the reality or mix up the real and the unreal.

Adrishta - opposite of drishta or Unseen,a metaphor for the consequences of past actions,which may be unanticipated.

Advaita - not two (dvaita).

Agama - Ancient Sanskrit religious text.

Detail of an analemma, on a globe by Gilman Joslin, Boston, 1890, in the collection of the Library of Congress. (By Lawrence W. Jackson Jr./wp.com)

Plate 19: Detail of an analemma *(facing pg. 164 (i))*

"Winter", depicted on an atlas by John Blaeu, Amsterdam, 1662-1665, in the collection of the Library of Congress. (By Lawrence W. Jackson Jr./wp.com)

Plate 20: Winter *(facing pg. 164 (ii))*

Ahimsa - abstention from injury to all life forms.

Amaavasya - new moon.

Analemma - Detail of an analemma, on a globe by Gilman Joslin, Boston, 1890, in the collection of the Library of Congress. (By Lawrence W. Jackson Jr./wp.com).

At noon in a perfect world, the sun would always be positioned 93 million miles directly over the equator, and the Earth, an unblemished sphere, would rotate evenly on a precisely vertical axis. The seasons would never change. Every day would last as long as every other. And we'd never have the equinoxes and solstices that mark the four quarters of the year.

As it happens, however, the Earth's axis is tilted and, according to Ruth Freitag, a senior science specialist at the Library of Congress, the "slightly eccentric ellipse" of the Earth's orbit around the sun led astronomers to come up with a consistent way to determine mean time, the time by which we all set our clocks. "The natural system is full of variables, and that's without even considering the irregularities of the Earth's rotation, which came to light in the late 19th century," says Freitag.

Thus we have the analemma, the somewhat mysterious looking figure-eight diagram on many globes and maps. The analemma charts where and when the sun will appear directly overhead in the "torrid zone," between the Tropic of Cancer and the Tropic of Capricorn. The curves of the analemma also mark the solstices and equinoxes. The winter solstice, occurring when the sun is at its southernmost position in the torrid zone, is shown on the most extreme point of an analemma's lower arc.

"In the days before the radio, the analemma was also useful for correcting clocks," says author David Greenhood in his book "Mapping."

The days may be dark now but the horizon looks bright: Since the winter solstice marks the shortest day and the longest night of the year, the days will begin to stretch out from now until the summer solstice. Come February and March, when cold temperatures have you fearing that winter will never end, at least the sun will hang a little longer in the evening sky.

AnumAna - anumaana or inference is one of the most important contributions of the system of metaknowledge known as Nyaya (which translates as Logic).

Anushtup chandas - A meter in prosody with 32 syllables.

Aparapaska - full moon to new moon period.

Apastambha - Apastambha was an ancient Vedic savant ,who composed the Sulvasutra named after him, credited with approximation for square root of two. His goal was among others to design ritual altars and to conform to the rules of Vastu Sastra,circa 2500 BCE. Apastambha predates Aryabhatta since Aryabhatta refers to the Sulvasutras in his magnum opus Aryabhattium.

Artha - Object, purpose, aim, significance, import. Attainment of worldly riches, prosperity, wealth, one of the goals of life prescribed by the Vedics in the Brahma Vidya.

Aranyakas - The third part of each of the Vedas (after Samhitas, and Brahmanas) elaborating various spiritualistic practices for forest dwelling initiates into spirituality. The Aranyakas (Sanskrit ara?yaka) are part of the Hindu sruti; these religious scriptures are sometimes argued to be part of either the Brahmanas or Upanishads. The name translates to "the forest books", meaning, treatises for hermits or sadhus living in the wilderness. This contrasts with the grhyasutras, treatises intended for domestic life. Their language is early Classical Sanskrit, and together with the bulk of the Upanishads, the Aranyakas form the basis of Vedanta.

Arati - A ritual in which a plate or thali with a deepa(oil lamp) and other items of ritual purification such ahs flowers, incense,kumkum and turmeric, are waved at lelast 3 times clockwise around a venerated person or object. Sometimes the plate may contain just water with kumkum dissolved in it.

Arjava - straightforwardness at all times.

Arjuna - The third of the five pandava princes, whose expertise lies in Archery . He is the protagonist in the Bhagvad Gita, the disciple of his friend and mentor Sri Krishna, the avatar of the Lord Himself.

Aryabhatta - ancient Indian mathematician the astronomer laureate of India, who lived in the Post Vedic period. His dating is controversial but could be as early as 2500 BCE and if so is contemporaneous or even predates Babylonian mathematicians, see Aryabhata I.

Arya - is an adjective, meaning noble such as in Arya Putr, noble son or noble prince.

Aryan - A term connoting the fictitious Aryan race, see also Vedics, should not be used synonymously with Aryan which has a racial connotation. Arya is purely a behavioral adjective and nothing more.

Aryan Race - A fictitious classification without any scientific basis used by the Europeans to distinguish themselves from the Semitic speaking people of the world. A word that has been foisted upon the Vedics who used the adjective Arya meaning of noble behavior. there was no racial connotation as there is now in Europe.

Ashvamedha - A part of Rajasuya ritual performed by emperors to establish their sway over allies and neighboring kingdoms.

Asuras - Demons of the Vedic Hindus, linguistically cognate with Ahura (e.g. Ahura Mazda) in Zoroastrianism. Thus, while in Vedic religion the Asuras are demonic, in Zoroastrianism, the Ahura are benign. This inversion also applies to the other class of immortals: where the Vedic devas are benevolent, the Zoroastrian daevas are malevolent. It is believed that this resulted in the Great schism between the Vedic Hindus and the followers of Zoroaster(Dhrutarashtra) who migrated west into what is Iran today.

Avidya - The state of ignorance which needs to be dispelled at the outset, before one can begin the journey in earnest towards self fulfillment and Moksha. 'Ignorance is bliss' or so the satire goes. Ignorance most certainly is not bliss. It is one of the greatest sins a Hindu can commit. Avidya (Para or Apara) is an unpardonable excuse and as soon as a person determines he/she is in a state of Avidya, they should take steps to remedy the situation.

Ayana - Course or journey; refers to the apparent direction of the suns course through the sky, uttarayana (north), dakshinaayana (south); cited in Sankalpam. Going, walking; road, path, way. Used in astronomy for advancing, precession; the sun's progress northward or southward, from one solstice to the other, is an ayana or half-year, two ayanas making one year. Also the equinoctial and solstitial points, the term for the solstice being ayananta. Finally, ayana signifies circulatory courses or circulations, as of the universe.

Ayanamsa - Ayanamsa is the Sanskrit term for the longitudinal difference between the tropical or Sayana and sidereal or Nirayana zodiacs. It is defined as the angle by which the sidereal ecliptic longitude of a celestial body is less than its tropical ecliptic longitude.

The sidereal ecliptic longitude of a celestial body is its longitude on the ecliptic defined with respect to the "fixed" stars.

The tropical ecliptic longitude of a celestial body is its longitude on the ecliptic defined with respect to the vernal equinox point.

Since the vernal equinox point precesses westwards at a rate of 50".29 per year with respect to the fixed stars, the longitude of a fixed body defined with respect to it will increase slowly. On the other hand, since the stars "do not move" (this ignores the effect of proper motion) the longitude of a fixed body defined with respect to them will never change.

Ayanachalana - See Precession of the equinoxes (synonym kraantipaatagati).

Ayanaantha - Solstice.

Ayanabhaaga - Amount of precession. i.e. arc of the ecliptic lying between the vernal equinox and the Indian zero point, synonym Ayanaaamsa.

B

Bhakti Yoga - An approach to worship and spiritual practice in the Hindu tradition characterized by personal devotion to a divinity , often mediated by a holy person or teacher somewhat akin to the relationship with Christ among certain sects and adherents of Christianity.

Bhartrihari - Bhartrihari along with Panini and Patanjali who preceded him by several centuries is regarded as one of the main contrbutors to the field of linguistics in ancient India. He introduced the notion of shabda tattwa or shabda pramaanam, namely "the notion of the originary word (shabda) as transcending the bounds of spoken and written language and meaning. Understood as shabda tattva-the "word principle," this complex idea explains the nature of consciousness, the awareness of all forms of phenomenal appearances, and posits an identity obtains between these, which is none other than Brahman. It is thus language as a fundamentally ontological principle that accounts for how we are able to conceptualize and communicate the awareness of objects. The metaphysical notion of shabda Brahman posits the unity of all existence as the foundation for all linguistically designated individual phenomena.

Bhashya - Commentary on a celebrated or scriptural work (e.g. Adi Sankara's Bhashya on the Bhagavad Gita).

Bhoodivas - A terrestrial day.

Bhoogola - The sphere of the earth.

Brahm-acharya - Or student life, when a boy lives with his teacher (Guru) and receives both religious and secular instruction. The youth is trained in self control, and acquires such virtues as chastity, truthfulness, faith, and self surrender.

Brahmana - the correct pronunciation includes a short 'a' vowel at the end, the first 'a' is a long vowel while the second is a short one. The literal meaning is one who attains Brahman is a Brahmana - Brahavit Brahaiva bhavati - is the sruti and is the strict definition of a Brahmana. In this day and age it is difficult to fathom in a short period of time whether a particular person has realized Brahman or not. In such a circumstance one looks for adherence to the ethical values of the Hindu and whether the person has the qualities mentioned therein. One of the 4 varnas of society possessing a predominantly static guan amongst the three gunas (Traigunya) rajas, tamas and satva. The Sanaatana Dharma strove to inculcate a meritocracy and recognizes everybody is not capable of meeting the same challenges. It is not a one size fits all ideology. The Dharma also recognizes there is diversity in the human species that not everybody can become a doctor or a star football player and that the person by reason of his gunas may not have the inclination, fortitude and desire to put in the long years of training necessary to become a doctor. These differences are not necessarily related to ones appearance or even heredity but have to do with whether a person has the discipline, the single minded focus and fortitude to undertake the arduous task of becoming a doctor or a Vedic priest or a star football player. Every fetus has the potential for fulfillment and Moksha but whether every single person rises to the demands of the tradition is a different matter, despite the fact that it is within the reach of each and every individual. In the modern era the Brahmana has adapted himself to the rigors and demands of a predominantly technological milieu and has filled many roles such as Doctor, Engineer, lawyer, Journalist, politician, think tank adviser, Professor, corporate executive, in addition to being a priest. Even so, the priestly Brahmana community remains one of the poorest in India today.

Brahmana - texts associated with each Veda.

Brahmavidya - Brahmavidya or Paravidya (metaphysics metaknowledge or higher knowledge) is the vehicle for attaining Moksha in the path known as Jnana Yoga and Yogasastra(the means to attain the same) is the practical discipline needed to attain Brahmavidya.

Brahmanism - Brahmanism is an ersatz terminology used to describe Sanatana Dharma that has become popular in certain circles in the west. It is clear that the Dharma is a whole family of beliefs and darshanas. It has been thus since a very long time. The Vedic texts have survived several millennia of wars and natural disasters, but it is quite possible other texts have been lost. It has never been the contention of Hindus that the Vedas are the only canon to have originated in the Indian subcontinent. But it is clear that they are among the few to survive over the millennia. Furthermore the implication that Brahmanas had exclusive control over the content and practice of the faith is demeaning and insulting to the Sanatana Dharma which has had a longline of Rishis and Sages who have expounded on the faith few of whom have been Brahmanas. Belief systems that did not subscribe to the Vedic canon have been extant for a very long time and have been known as Nastik Dharmas and include among others Charvaka, Jainism and Buddhism. It is therefore unnecessary to invent a new word Brahmanism to descrioe an ancient faith which has a perfectly good name namely Sanatana Dharma. It is just as misleading, if one were to use the word Rabbi-ism to describe the faith taught in Synagogues simply because the issue is not who teaches the faith but the content.

Brahmi script - Brahmi is a "syllabic alphabet", meaning that each sign can be either a simple consonant or a syllable with the consonant and the inherent vowel /a/. Other syllabic alphabets outside of South Asia include Old Persian and Meroðtic. However, unlike these two systems, Brahmi (and all subsequent Brahmi-derived scripts) indicates the same consonant with a different vowel by drawing extra strokes, called matras, attached to the character. Ligatures are used to indicate consonant clusters. The Brahmi script was first deciphered by James Princep although I find it difficult to believe that they could not find a single Indian who was capable of deciphering the Brahmi script.

C

Caste - Derived from Portuguese Casta, Caste has a meaning quite distinct from Varna which has been accepted as being part of the tradition. Caste according to the Portuguese means a race or a breed. Varna makes no such distinction and to ascribe racial motivations for a system based on division of labor depending on individual inclinations and which is a meritocracy to boot, is totally unconscionable, but that is exactly what the colonial power did with great success . The Sanatana Dharma makes no apologies for being a meritocracy based on competency and character and it is only after the advent of colonial rule that it took on the character of a racial and ethnic division based on birth. It is a tribute to the tenacity and persistence of the British that their viewpoint has prevailed and has been internalized by the Indic population for the most part. Yet it behooves those of us who know better to keep reminding everybody that the colonial viewpoint reflects a conjured up reality that has no relation to a core value nor is it derived from core beliefs held since antiquity. see also Varnashrama dharma.

Celestial (Equatorial) Coordinate System - the most commonly used astronomical coordinate system for indicating the positions of stars or other celestial objects on the celestial sphere . The celestial sphere is an imaginary sphere with the observer at its center. It represents the entire sky; all celestial objects other than the earth are imagined as being located on its inside surface. If the earth's axis is extended, the points where it intersects the celestial sphere are called the celestial poles; the north celestial pole is directly above the earth's North Pole, and the south celestial pole directly above the earth's South Pole. The great circle on the celestial sphere halfway between the celestial poles is called the celestial equator; it can be thought of as the earth's equator projected onto the celestial sphere. It divides the celestial sphere into the northern and southern skies. An important reference point on the celestial equator is the vernal equinox , the point at which the sun crosses the celestial equator in March. To designate the position of a star, the astronomer considers an imaginary great circle passing through the celestial poles and through the star in question. This is the star's hour circle , analogous to a meridian of longitude on earth. The astronomer then measures the angle between the vernal equinox and the point where the hour circle intersects the celestial equator. This angle is called the star's right ascension and is measured in hours, minutes, and seconds rather than in the more familiar degrees, minutes, and seconds. (There are 360 degrees or 24 hours in a full circle.) The right ascension is always measured eastward from the vernal equinox. Next the observer measures along the star's hour circle the angle between the celestial equator and the position of the star. This angle is called the declination of the star and is measured in degrees, minutes, and seconds north or south of the celestial equator, analogous to latitude on the earth. Right ascension and declination together determine the location of a star on the celestial sphere. The right ascensions and declinations of many stars are listed in various reference tables published for astronomers and navigators. Because a star's position may change slightly (see proper motion and precession of the equinoxes), such tables must be revised at regular intervals. By definition, the vernal equinox is located at right ascension 0 h and declination 0°.

Celestial equator Nadivruth, Nadivalaya - The great circle on the celestial sphere halfway between the celestial poles is called the celestial equator.

D

Dakshinayana - The southward journey of the Sun towards the Winter solstice, from its northernmost point during the Summer solstice usually identified as Dakshinayana Punyakala on July 16.

Dasha - Ten as in Dashaavatara, the ten Avatars of Vishnu.

Decimal system - see also place value system, decimal system [Latin= of tenths], numeration system based on powers of 10. A number is written as a row of digits, with each position in the row corresponding to a certain power of 10. A decimal point in the row divides it into those powers of 10 equal to or greater than 0 and those less than 0, i.e., negative powers of 10. Positions farther to the left of the decimal point correspond to increasing positive powers of 10 and those farther to the right to increasing negative powers, i.e., to division by higher positive powers of 10. For example:

4,309=(4x10**3)+(3x10**2)+(0x10**1)+(9x10**0)=4,000+300+0+9, and 4.309=(4x10**0)+(3x10**-1)+(0x10**-'2)+(9x10**-'3)=4+3/10+0/100+9/1000.

It is believed that the decimal system is based on 10 because humans have 10 fingers and so became used to counting by 10s early in the course of civilization. The decimal system was introduced into Europe c.1300. It greatly simplified arithmetic and was a much-needed improvement over the Roman numerals, which did not use a positional system. A number written in the decimal system is called a decimal, although sometimes this term is used to refer only to a proper fraction written in this system and not to a mixed number. Decimals are added and subtracted in the same way as are integers (whole numbers) except that when these operations are written in columnar form the decimal points in the column entries and in the answer must all be placed one under another. In multiplying two decimals the operation is the same as for integers except that the number of decimal places in the product, i.e., digits to the right of the decimal point, is equal to the sum of the decimal places in the factors; e.g., the factor 7.24 to two decimal places and the factor 6.3 to one decimal place have the product 45.612 to three decimal places. In division, e.g., 4.32 /12.8 where there is a decimal point in the divisor (4.32), the point is shifted to the extreme right (i.e., to 432.) and the decimal point in the dividend (12.8) is shifted the same number of places to the right (to 1280), with one or more zeros added before the decimal to make this possible. The decimal point in the quotient is then placed above that in the dividend, i.e.,

432|1280.0 zeros are added to the right of the decimal point in the dividend as needed, and the division proceeds the same as for integers. The decimal system is widely used in various systems employing numbers. The metric system of weights and measures, used in most of the world, is based on the decimal system, as are most systems of national currency.

Dharma - one of the four kinds of human aspirations, which are dharma, artha, kama and moksha. dharma: "Righteous living." The fulfillment of virtue, good works, duties and responsibilities, restraints and observances - performing one's part in the service of society. This includes pursuit of truth under a guru of a particular Parampara and sAmpradaya. Dharma is of four primary forms. It is the steady guide for artha and kama.

Dharma (Baudhik) - A central notion of Buddhism, used in various contexts;

1. The cosmic law, the great norm, underlying our world; above all the law of karmically determined rebirth.
2. The teaching of the Buddha, who recognized and formulated this law; thus the teaching exdpresses the universal truth. The Dharma in this sense existed before the birth of the historical Buddha, who is no more than a manifestation of it. This is the Dharma in which the Buddhist takes refuge.
3. Norms of behavior and ethical rules.
4. Manifestation of reality, of the general state of affairs.

Dravidian languages - An unverifiable hypothesis made to distinguish the languages of the south of India (Dravida) from those of the north. In reality, a Telugu speaking person , ostensibly a Dravidian language, can understand Sanskrit far more readily than even an accomplished scholar in sanskrit in the west. This despite the putative similarity between the European languages and Sanskrit.

Drkchaya - Parallax.

Druhyu - One of 5 clans namely Anus, Druhyus, Turvashas, Puru, Yadu, the sons of Yayati. Druhyu is the 3rd son of Yayati. His dynasty is listed in Chapter 23 of the Bhagavata Puraana.The descendants of Druhyu eventually went on to become Zarathushtrans, followers of Zarathushtra (Dhrutashtra) and subsequently formed the Aryamanush (Greek corruption Achaemenid) empire, e.g. Darius = Druhyu (Sanskrit) Daryavahyu (Persian). Some of the ancient parsian kings belonging to the Aryamanush Dynasty

Haxamanish or ACHAEMENES, first King of Persia, was mythical.

Teispes c. 7th century BC. (this is the Greek version of the name)

Kurash I (or CYRUS I) c. late 7th Century BC, son of Teispes.

Ariaramnes c. late 7th century BC, son of Teispes.

Kambujia I (or CAMBYSES I) ? - 559 BC, son of Kurash I.

Kurash II (or CYRUS II) 559 - c. 550 BC when he became King of Kings, son of Kambuyia I.

For other Old Persian Sanskrit names see for instance,

http:/indicstudies.us/Archives/Linguistics/Persian names. I recommend all the readers of Indic origin (and others) use Sanskrit names for Iranian kings. That will force us into a thought process that they were all a part of the Vedic civilization.

E

Ecliptic-kraanthivruth - the great circle on the celestial sphere that lies in the plane of the earth's orbit (called the plane of the ecliptic). Because of the earth's yearly revolution around the sun, the sun appears to move in an annual journey through the heavens with the ecliptic as its path. The ecliptic is the principal axis in the ecliptic coordinate system. The two points at which the ecliptic crosses the celestial equator are the equinoxes. The obliquity of the ecliptic is the inclination of the plane of the ecliptic to the plane of the celestial equator, an angle of about 23 1/2 °. The constellations through which the ecliptic passes are the constellations of the zodiac.

Ekadasi - Ekadasi is the eleventh lunar day (Tithi) of the Shukla (bright) or Krishna (dark) Paksha (fortnight) respectively ,of every lunar month in the Hindu calendar (Panchanga). In Hinduism and Jainism, it is considered spiritually beneficial day. Scriptures recommend observing an (ideally waterless) fast from sunset on the day prior to Ekadasi until 48 minutes after sunrise on the day following Ekadasi. Ekadasi is a Sanskrit word, which means 'the eleventh'. It refers to the eleventh day of a fortnight belonging to a lunar month. There are two fortnights in a lunar month-the bright and the dark. So, Ekadasi occurs twice in a month, in the bright fortnight and the dark fortnight. The special feature of Ekadasi, as most people know it, is a fast, abstinence from food. This is how it is usually understood. In fact, the fast is only a practical expression and a symbol of something else that we are expected to do, which is of special significance to our personality.

Epicycles - In the Ptolemaic system of astronomy, the epicycle (literally: on the circle in Greek) was a geometric model to explain the variations in speed and direction of the apparent motion of the Moon, Sun, and planets. It was designed by Apollonius of Perga at the end of the 3rd century BC. In particular it explained retrograde motion. Secondarily, it also explained changes in the distance of the planet from Earth.

Epistemology - The Theory of Knowledge is concerned with the means of acquiring knowledge. The root of the English word is the Greek word episteme meaning knowledge. This includes logical argument or reasoning, inference, testimony, and perception. All these words have precise equivalents in Sanskrit and the word for epistemology in Sanskrit is Praamanya, the theory of knowledge. The systematic study of the theory of knowledge goes back to great antiquity and the names associated with these disciplines include among others Pannini, Patanjali. Yajnavalkya and Bhartrihari. It is our contention that most if not all of these savants lived in the millennium prior to the Christian era.

Equinox, vernal equinox (Vasanth Sampat), autumnal equinox - either of two points on the celestial sphere where the ecliptic and the celestial equator intersect. The vernal equinox, also known as "the first point of Aries," is the point at which the sun appears to cross the celestial equator from south to north. This occurs about Mar. 21, marking the beginning of spring in the Northern Hemisphere. At the autumnal equinox, about Sept. 23, the sun again appears to cross the celestial equator, this time from north to south; this marks the beginning of autumn in the Northern Hemisphere. On the date of either equinox, night and day are of equal length (12 hr each) in all parts of the world; the word equinox is often used to refer to either of these dates. The equinoxes are not fixed points on the celestial sphere but move westward along the ecliptic, passing through all the constellations of the zodiac in 26,000 years. This motion is called the precession of the equinoxes. The vernal equinox is a reference point in the equatorial coordinate system.

Equator - See Vishuvat.

F

Four noble truths - (Baudhika).

There is suffering (dukkha) in the world.

Suffering arises out of desire

It is possible to end suffering.

The way to end suffering is to adopt the eightfold path (ashtaangika marga).

G

Gaudapada - Proponent of Advaita Vedanta and well versed in Buddhism. His most celebrated work is the Kaarika (Gloss) on the Mandukya Upanishad.

Gotra - A term applied to a clan, a group of families, or a lineage - exogamous and patrilineal - whose members trace their descent to a common ancestor, usually a Rishi of the Vedic era. Atreya, Bharadvaja Dhananjaya, Gautam, Haritasa, Kaushika, Kashyapa, Kaundinya, Kutsasa, Lomash, Mandvya, Mouna Bhargava, Mudgala Maudgalya, Moudgil, Modgil, Parashara, Sangar, Sankyanasa, Shandilya, Somnasser, Srivatsa, Upamanyu, Vadula, Vashishta, Vatsa, Veetahavya, Viswamitra, Yaska.

Gregorian Calendar Reform

When Julius Caesar took power in Rome, the Roman calendar had ceased to reflect the year accurately. The provision of adding an intercalary month to the year when needed had not been applied consistently, because it affected the length of terms of office. The Julian reform lengthened the months (except February, owing to its religious significance) and provided for an intercalary day to be added every four years to February, creating a leap year. This produced a noticeably more accurate calendar, but it was based on the calculation of a year as 365 days and 6 hours (365.25 d). In fact, the year is 11 minutes and 14 seconds less than that. This had the effect of adding three-quarters of an hour to a year, and the effect accumulated. By the sixteenth century, the vernal equinox fell on March 10.

Under Pope Gregory XIII the leap rule was altered: century years, which are divisible by four, would not be leap years unless they are also divisible by 400. This makes the mean year 365.2425 days (365 d, 5 h, 49 min, 12 s) long. While this does not synchronize the years

The Reform of the Calendar
Pope Gregory XIII Meets with His Calendar Commission, c. 1581

Plate 21: The Reform of the Calendar *(facing pg. 176)*

entirely, it would require 35 centuries to accumulate a day. This new calendar was synchronized with the traditional seasons again and was not applied to dates in the past, which caused a leap of at least ten days from the final day the Julian calendar was in effect. Thus the day after October 4 1582 was named October 15, 1582 and the 11 days in between are completely missing. This reform slowly spread through the nations that used the Julian calendar, although the Russian church year still uses the Julian calendar. The times varied so widely that some countries had to drop more than ten days: Great Britain, for instance, dropped eleven because the new Gregorian calendar was adopted only in.

Reformers cite several problems with the Gregorian calendar:

It is not perpetual. Each year starts on a different day of the week and calendars expire every year.

It is difficult to determine the weekday of any given day of the year or month.

Months are not equal in length nor regularly distributed across the year, requiring mnemonics (e.g. "Thirty days hath SeptemberṀ") to remember which month is 28, 29, 30 or 31 days long.

The year's four quarters (of three full months each) are not equal. Business quarters that are equal would make accounting easier.

Its epoch (origin) is not religiously neutral. The same applies to month and weekday names in many languages.

Each month has no connection with the lunar phases.

It is impossible to solve all these issues in just one calendar.

360 ÷ 7 = 51-3/7 360 ÷ 12 = 30

364 ÷ 7 = 52 = 4 x 13 364 ÷ 12 = 30-1/3

365 ÷ 7 = 52-1/7 365 ÷ 12 = 30-5/12

366 ÷ 7 = 52-2/7 366 ÷ 12 = 30-1/2

Most plans evolve around the solar year of little more than 365 days. This number does not divide well by seven or twelve, which are the traditional numbers of days per week and months per year respectively. The nearby numbers 360, 364 and 366 are divisible in better ways. There are also lunar centric proposals.

Grihastya - The second stage of the varna ashrama system, namely that of a householder ormarried man or woman.

Gunas - There are 3 Gunas, Sattwa, Rajas and Tamas and these three Gunas occur in each and every individual in varying degrees. The relative proportion of each in the total determines the essential nature of the individual. It follows that at any given time a individual, may exhibit different modes of behavior as his personality matures and develops. The son of a Brahmana may choose not to follow the priestly vocation and may elect to go into law. As a general rule of thumb one elects to be in a profession which utilizes his Gunas fully. For example Brahmanas tend to cluster around intellectual pursuits (teaching, legal, corporate management, administration etc. In the past the choice of professions available to Brahmanas were limited to priestly duties and the services he could render as a Minister to the Maharaja including mundane tasks such as accounting and cooking. In recent years substantial numbers of Brahmanas faced with increasing discrimination from their own government have elected to go into Business, so that his Varna is that of a Vaisya, unless he maintains his competency and knowledge of the Vedic scripture and adheres to the injunctions of a Brahmana. Most Indian philosophers accept the view of the Samkhya philosophy when it refers to the definition of the Gunas and their relationship to Prakriti and Purusha.

Guna Varna Vyavastha - The Varna system, namely Guna Varna Vyavastha, that produced the Varnashrama Dharma was conscious of the fact that this was the world's early attempt at a meritocracy. That the system was eminently successful in its own way , I have no doubt because the resulting civilization flourished for well over 5 millennia, until its very foundations were attacked by barbarians from both within and without; by barbarians, whose notion of entertainment was to build a pyramid of skulls, in order to terrorize the local population to capitulate. The current system in place after the colonial power was done reinventing and reshaping it to its own specifications, and which goes by the name Caste, is so utterly different in all significant ways, that we can safely say it has little to do with the Hindu faith or Hindu traditions such as the Guna Varna Vyavastha. The vedic division of people into 4 Varnas (Brahmana, Rajanya, Vaisya and Shudra) is by Guna and Guna only and is known as the Guna Varna Vyavastha. The Asrama system refers to the four stages of one's life, namely Brahmacharya (life of an unmarried student), Grihasthya (life of a householder), Vanaprasthaya (life of a retired householder), sannyasa (life of a monk).

H

Hinduism - Also known as Sanaatana Dharma, the eternal faith; there are roughly 900 million Hindus in the world as of 2008 (see Dharma)

I

Indo-Aryan languages - A family of languages spoken over a large area of the Eurasian land mass; see Indo-European Languages.

Indo-European languages - A family of languages spoken over a vast geographical area from India to most parts of Europe.

Indo-Iranian languages - the Indo Iranian branch of the Indo Europrean language family, spoken in central asia,iran and the Indian subcontinent.

Indology - Indology is a name given by Indologists to the academic study of the history, languages, and cultures of the Indian subcontinent. Strictly speaking it encompasses the study of the languages, scripts of all of Asia that was influenced by Indic culture It may be surprising to learn that the first pioneer in Indology was the 12th Century Pope, Honorius IV. The Holy Father encouraged the learning of oriental languages in order to preach Christianity amongst the pagans. Soon after this in 1312, the Ecumenical Council of the Vatican decided that- "The Holy Church should have an abundant number of Catholics well versed in the languages, especially in those of the infidels, so as to be able to instruct them in the sacred doctrine." The result of this was the creation of the chairs of Hebrew, Arabic and Chaldean at the Universities of Bologna, Oxford, Paris and Salamanca. A century later in 1434, the General Council of Basel returned to this theme and decreed that -"All Bishops must sometimes each year send men well-grounded in the divine word to those parts where Jews and other infidels live, to preach and explain the truth of the Catholic faith in such a way that the infidels who hear them may come to recognize their errors. Let them compel them to hear their preaching." 1. Centuries later in 1870, during the First Vatican Council, Hinduism was condemned in the "five anathemas against pantheism" according to the Jesuit priest John Hardon in the Church-authorized book, The Catholic Catechism. However, interests in Indology only took shape and concrete direction after the British came to India, with the advent of the discovery of Sanskrit by Sir William Jones in the 1770's. Other names for Indology are Indic studies or Indian studies or South Asian studies. Political motivations have been always dominant in the pursuit of Indological studies right from the outset since the time of Sir William Jones, when he discovered the existence of Sanskrit. In fact the British presence in India was steadily increasing long before the Battle of Plassey in 1757 CE, but so great was the insularity of the colonial overlord that it took almost almost three hundred years for a scholar like Sir William to show up in India after Vasco da Gama landed of the cost of Goa in 1492 CE, and notice the similarities between Sanskrit and the european languages.

Indus script - While several decipherments have been proposed including the recent work by Rajaram and Jha,[1] it is possible the problem may never achieve a solution satisfactory to both the Indics and the Western indologists. Most Indics believe that this was the forerunner of the Brahmi script. The Brahmi script is the progenitor of almost all of the languages and scripts of India and most of the rest of South East Asia. The Brahmi script has all of the phonetic characteristics to be found in all the successor scripts of Asia. To suggest a semitic origin for a Brahmi script is highly problematical since semitic scripts (including all the Roman scripts of Europe) do not have the characteristic Vowel strokes that Brahmi scripts have whenever a vowel is appended to a consonant such as in - (the long 'a' vowel is represented by a vertical stroke). The name Brahmi suggests that the script was developed along the banks of the Sarasvati river, since Brahmi is synonymous with Sarasvati.

Indus Valley Civilization or Harappan Civilization - AKA Sarasvati Sindhu Civilization (SSC), the civilization that endured for several millennia in the Sarasvati and Sindhu (Indus) river valleys the people who inhabited these valleys are also referred to as the Vedic Harappans by Bhagwan Singh. Most of the recent excavations indicate a heavy preponderance of settlements, about 400 in number on the banks of the dried up Sarasvatii river. Mohenjo Daro and Harappa represent a late phase of the civilization. European Indologists go to extraordinary lengths to make a distinction between the Vedic civilization and the SSC despite the fact they are located spatially and temporally in the same place and time. That they got away with this subterfuge for such a long time (it is still the official version of History in Indian text books) is a tribute to the farsightedness and tenacity of successive British administrators and scholars who always put British national interest before every other criterion including the truth. Their reasons for engaging in such intellectual dishonesty are chronicled in the South Asia File.[2]

---

1. Rajaram, N.S., and N Jha, 'The Deciphered Indus Script', Aditay Prakashan, Delhi, 2005, ISBN 8177420151.

2. The South Asia File.

"Jantar Mantar", a series of astronomical observatories built by Maharaja Jai Singh of Jaipur, the most well known of which is the one in Delhi
See for instance http://www.crystalinks.com/indiastronomy.html

Plate 22; Jantar Mantar *(facing pg. 180)*

Iranian peoples - The ancient Iranians or Avestans, the people who composed the Avesta, have much in common with the Vedics. In fact it is believed by some that the Iranians are descended from the Druhyus. The language of the Avesta is easily discernible to those familiar with Sanskrit and the names of Persian Kings (the original names not the Greek version we learned in English history books) For instance the Sanskrit or Iranian version of Darius is Druhyu. It is surmised that a branch of the Bhrigu Rishi family, eventually composed the Avesta and that Dhritarashtra (Zoroaster) the founder of the Parsee religion, was a Bhrigu.

J

Jantar Mantar

A series of astronomical observatories built by Maharaja Jai Singh of Jaipur, the most well known of which is the one in Delhi. See for instance

http://www.crystalinks.com/indiastronomy.html

Jnana Yoga - the path of knowledge Jnana (also spelled "Gyana"; Devanagari) is the Sanskrit term for knowledge. In Hinduism it means true knowledge, Para Vidya, the knowledge that one's self atman is Ultimate Reality Brahman. In Buddhism, it refers to pure awareness that is free of conceptual encumbrances, and is contrasted with Vijnana, which is a moment of 'divided knowing'. Jnana yoga is one path (marga) towards moksha (liberation), while Yoga offers different paths for different temperaments such as Bhakti and Karma Yoga.

Jivanmukta - Adi Sankara gives the true definition of a Jivanmukta - The great souls he says, calm and tranquil, live, regenerating the world like the spring; and themselves having crossed the ocean of embodied existence, and death, help those who struggle, for the same end, without the least trace of personal motives or advantage.

Jyotisha - one of the 6 Vedangas, also known as the science of light. It includes the study of the motion of Celestial Objects or Astronomy and the effects of the forces arising from these bodies and their effects on the human mind. It is the hypothesis of Vedic Astrology that such effects can be predicted by studying the relative location of the planets and the stars. Jyotisha is often discussed as the instructional element of the Rig Veda, and as such is a Vedangas, or "body part" of the Vedas. Jyotisha is called the Eye of the Veda, for its believed ability to view both phenomenal reality and wisdom itself. Part of a larger Vedic curriculum including mathematics, architecture, medical and military applications. The author of this Vedanga is purported to be one Lagadha.

K

Kalidasa - The poet laureate of ancient India. The author of the most widely known text and play Shakuntala.

Kalpasutras - constitutes part of the Vedanga consists of Grhyasutras, Dharmasutras, Sulvasutras, Srautasutras.

Kama - "Pleasure,desire,wish, love; enjoyment." Earthly love, aesthetic and cultural fulfillment, pleasures of the world (often used in the sense of sexual desire, but not necessarily so), the joys of family, intellectual satisfaction. Enjoyment of happiness, security, creativity, usefulness and inspiration. An essential ingredient for the emotional health of an individual and recognized as such by the ancient Vedics. Kama is one of the four Purusharthas or goals of life, the others being dharma, artha and moksha.

Kaarika - Gloss or explanatory text of an original text, such as the Kaarika of the Mandukya Upanishad by Gaudapada.

Karma Yoga - Karma yoga, or the "discipline of action" is based on the teachings of the Bhagavad Gita, a holy scripture of Hinduism. One of the four pillars of yoga, Karma yoga focuses on the adherence to duty (dharma) while remaining detached from the reward. It states that one can attain Moksha (salvation) by doing ones duties in an unselfish manner. A great portion of the Bhagavad Gita is engaged in discussing the efficacy of various Yogas towards the goal of self realization or Moksha. Initially Arjuna is bewildered, when Bhagavan says that the Yoga of Knowledge is superior to the Yoga of action, even though desireless it may be. Why then do you ask me to fight asks an exasperated Arjuna of his friend and mentor, if such be the case. The answer by Bhagavan and elucidated by Adi Sankara in his Bhashya is one of the major insights of this lovely Celestial song. As explained by Adi Sankara, Karma Yoga consists of 4 principles 1. Giving up an egoistic attitude (BG 18-46), 2. Giving up the hankering for the fruits or results of one's action (BG 2-39), 3. Maintaining equanimity in the face of desirable andhappy circumstances as well as undesirable and not so pleasant situations (BG 2-48) 4. Surrendering of all actions as an offering to the Lord Ishwara) wholeheartedly (BG 3-33). It is possible to transcend Karma Yoga by the Yoga of Knowledge, which is in fact the superior approach, but such an alternative is not for every individual, and is best suited for those who have realized Brahman.

Khagola - Celestial sphere or armillary sphere, a term used for both the geometrical celestial sphere as well as the astronomical instrument called the armillary sphere.

Kshatriya - the varna identified in the classical Indic tradition as those entitled to exercise military power and perform sacrifices, the dominant Guna in the Kshatriya varna is one of Rajas, and a passion for action. It is your Dharma to engage in action protect the aged and infirm and the children and women in your protection. It is better to follow ones own Dharma (dictated by ones Gunas) admonished Sri Krishna to Arjuna than to try something, however beguiling, which is not so suited.

Kurgan - a region in Europe from where the putative emigration of the mythical Aryan race took place.

Kushana Empire

M

Madhavacharya - Celebrated religious teacher and scholar of the 14th century, one of the main teachers of the Dvaita-Vedanta school of pronounced dualism. It teaches the existence or permanent reality of two fundamental principles in universal nature: spirit and matter, or divinity and the universe. This dualism is in direct contrast with the unity doctrine taught in the Advaita-Vedanta or nondualistic system of Sankaracharya.

Mahavrata - winter solstice.

Mahaavaakya, - The 4 expressions that embody Vedanta, the essence of attaining Jivanmukta.

The Mahaavaakyas are the four "Great Sayings" of the Upanishads, foundational religious texts of Hinduism.

These four sayings encapsulate the central Truth of Hinduism.

The Mahaavaakya are:

1. *Prajnaanam Brahman* "Conscious is Brahman" (Aitareya Upanishad 3.3).
2. *Ayam Atma Brahman* "This Self (Atman) is Brahman" (Mandukya Upanishad 1.2)
3. *Tat Tvam Asi* - "That Thou art " (Chandogya Upanishad 6.8.7)
4. *Aham Brahmasmi* - "I am Brahman" (Brihadaranyaka Upanishad 1.4.10)

All four of these, in one way or another, indicate the unity of the individual human being with Brahman. Brahman is Absolute Reality, Cosmic Consciousness, the fundamental Primordial essence from which all divinities and all worlds arise and the Dharma asserts that each human being, in her or his innermost self, is this ultimate transcendent God-Reality. It is through practices like yoga, and meditation that the individual can realize her or his unity with the Divine and escape bonds of this world. The most forthright statement of the above proposition is to be found in texts propounding Advaita Vedanta. The Bhagavad Gita is one of the texts that enumerate the various paths one may take to attain Jivanmukta.

Mananam - part of the process of gathering of knowledge using techniques such as sravanam,mananam and nididhyasanam. Mananam means to ponder over the material that one has read or heard.

Metonic cycle (see also Adhikamaasa) - a cycle whereby every three years a lunar month is added to bring the lunar cycle in synchronization with the solar cycle. It turns out that it takes nineteen years to bring the two cycles in synchronization, so that a new moon occurs exactly on the same solar day that it did 19 years ago. When combined with the 4 year cycle used in the Julian calendar, yields a total cyclic time of 7*4*19 = 532 years, This is the time in years, that has to elapse in order for the same weekday to occur on the same date, for every month of th eyear. It is attributed to Meton, the Greek astronomer and now is credited to Babylonian astronomers, in the 5th century BCE, but should properly be credited to Yajnavalkya in the Satapatha Brahmana, who first postulated the 95 year old synchronization cycle. The higher number was necessitated by the greater accuracy of the observations and the greater accuracy that the Ancient Indics demanded in the final result.

Mitanni - when the Hittite and the Mitanni (2 neighboring kingdoms in Anatolia, present day Turkey signed a treaty they invoked the blessings of their Gods . The invocation is addressed to the Nasatyas, Mitra and Varuna, Hindu Vedic deities from a distant past.

Moksha - "Liberation." Is synonymous with Freedom from rebirth through the ultimate attainment, realization of the Self God, PArasiva. The spiritual attainments and superconscious joys, attending renunciation and yoga leading to Self Realization. Moksha comes through the fulfillment of dharma, artha and kAma (known in Tamil as aram, porul and inbam, and explained by Tiruvalluvar in Tirukural) in the current or past lives, so that one is no longer attached to worldly joys or sorrows. It is the supreme goal of life, called paramartha. This is a distinction between the DhArmic traditions originating in the Indian subcontinent from the very earliest time periods in history and other religious belief systems. The propensity to cater to the higher needs (in the Maslow hierarchy) from the very inception of the tradition is a uniquely Indic development. Merely to emphasize this as a spiritual characteristic is to mnimize the pragmatic and psychological needs of the human species. Paying special attention to the fulfillment of these needs is a distinctive characteristic of Indic dharma.

Mumukshutwa - An intense thirst for Brahmavidya or higher knowledge (Paara Vidya).

N

Nakshatras - The concept of positing 27 Nakshatras in the sidereal zodiac goes back to antiquity at least in India. The ancients divided the sky in 27 or 28 lunar mansions or Nakshatras, characterized by asterisms (apparent groups of stars), one for each day that the Moon follows its track among the stars.

Naksatra-vidya - The astronomical aspect of Jyotisha (which includes Astrology.

Nididhyasanam - the final step of the 3 step process of sravanam, mananam, nididhyasanam, involves deep meditation and requires mumukshutwa and titiksha.

Nirukta - this treatise was authored by Yaska and deals with Etymology, a branch of Linguistics, the study of the roots of all words, made simpler by the intentional highlighting of Dhaatu in sanskrit. Yaska is one of the bright galaxy among the plethora of broad spectrum philosophers in the ancient Vedic era, who counted numerous skills in their repertoire linguistics being just one of their many fields of expertise.

Nighantu - Yaska's Vedic Glossary,Nirukta is a commentary on the Nighantu.

Nirvana - blown out or extinguished as in the case of a lamp. Nirvana is generally used to refer to a material life that has been extinguished, i.e. for one who has achieved freedom from rebirth. The term Nirvana is commonly used in Buddhism as the final stage a practitioner strives for. The word does not mean heaven and is analogous to Moksha in the Sanaatana dharma

Nischitaaartham - Engagement ceremony prior to a wedding. Literally means 'firming up' of the relationship and is usually commemorated with a Puja and an exchange of rings, gifts and invitations to the wedding ceremony.

P

Pancha - sanskrit term for five e.g. Panchabana, Panchatantra.

Parampara - tradition,as in likhita Parampara (written tradition), srauta Parampara (oral tradition), guru Parampara, (the guru-disciple tradition).

Place Value System - the most common Sanskrit word for this is sthana which literally means place, and refers to the decimal system of numbers where the value of a number is determined by its location with respect to other numbers to the right, e.g. 3 followed by a 0, means the number is thirty.

Poornima - full moon.

Pope Gregory XIII (Ugo Bioncompagni,1502 - 1585) - sent missionaries to India (and China) mainly to learn from the Namputhiris of Kerala. He suppressed knowledge that did not agree with thre church dogma and also issued a proclamation that no knowledge, regardless of its source, be attributed to other than Catholics. In other words he flouted the concept of intellectual property with impunity. The Gregorian Calendar was fixed shortly thereafter (the return of the Jesuits from Malabar.

Prasthanatrayi - Prasthanatrayi, literally, three points of departure, (IAST Prasthanatrayi) refers to the three canonical texts of Hindu philosophy, especially the Vedanta schools. It consists of: the anishads, known as Upadesha prasthana (injunctive texts),the Brahma Sutras, known as Nyaya prasthana (logical text), the Bhagavad Gita, known as Sadhana prasthana (practical text).

Pratyaksha - Prathyaksha pramaana: This is called direct proof, as it is perceived by the sense organs. These organs are only instruments. The mind enters them and helps them to function. There are some limitations on the senses like disease and imperfection, that make proof obtained by this method to be infirm. For example, a normal eye can see all colors, a jaundiced eye sees everything as yellow. Though the laddu is sweet, the tongue of a malaria patient classifies it as bitter. Here, there are two points of view. From the point of view of the matter it is sweet. But from the point of view of the senses it is bitter. It can be concluded, therefore, direct proof is not complete evidence for real justice.

Precession of the Equinoxes (see also Ayanachalana) see also equinox - The earth revolves around the Sun once in 365 days 5 hours 48 minutes and 46 seconds. Considered from the earth, the Sun appears to complete one round of the ecliptic during this period. This is called a tropical year. In the span of a tropical year, the earth regains its original angular position with the Sun. It is also called the year of seasons since on this Earth-Sun cycle depends the occurrence, and timing, of seasons. If we consider the revolution of the Sun around the earth from one vernal equinox (around 21st March, when the day and night all over the globe are equal) to the next vernal equinox, it takes one tropical year to do so. However, if at the end of a tropical year from one vernal equinox to the next, we consider the position of the earth with reference to a fixed star of the zodiac, the earth appears to lie some 50.26 seconds of celestial longitude to the west of its original position. In order for the earth to attain the same position with respect to a fixed star after one revolution, it takes a time span of 365 days 6 hours 9 minutes and some 9.5 seconds. This duration of time is called a sidereal year .The sidereal year is just over 20 minutes longer than the tropical year. Each year, the Vernal equinox will fall short by 50.26 seconds along the zodiac reckoned along the fixed stars. This continuous receding of the Vernal equinox along the zodiac is called the Precession of the equinoxes.

Proto-Indo-European - PIE for short is a constructed language for which there is no existence theorem . It is based on unproven hypothesis.

Proto Dravidian - the alleged hypothetical ancestor language to the modern languages of Telugu, Tamil, Kannada, Tulu and Malayalam. Again there is no proof that a single human ever spoke the language. There is no reference to such a language in any of the vast literary works of India south or north.

Purana - literally means the ancients. Traditional sanskrit texts dealing with diverse topics such as the creation of the world, legends, genealogy of sovereigns, In the Indic context, puranas have special significance both from a temporal stand point and from a historical perspective.

Purusha, Paurusheya, Apaurusheya - In Hinduism, Purusha ("Cosmic Man") is the "self" which pervades the universe. The Vedic divinities are considered to be the human mind's interpretation of the many facets of Purusha. According to the Rigvedic Purusha sukta, Purusha was dismembered by the devas -- his mind is the moon, his eyes are the sun, and his breath is the wind. In Samkhya, a school of Hindu philosophy, Purusha is pure consciousness. It is thought to be our true identity, to be contrasted with Prakrti, or the material world, which contains all of our organs, senses, and intellectual faculties.Amore restrcted meaning of purusha is youth or human (paurusheya). Hinduism in that sense is an Apaurusheya belief system as opposed to the revealed or prophetic faiths such as Judaism,Christianity or Islam which would therefore come under the category of paurusheya religions.

Purushartha - Purushartha or Manushyartheha is the pursuit of the four kinds of human aspirations, which are dharma, artha, kama and moksha. The four pursuits in which humans may legitimately engage, also called chaturvarga, "four-fold good", is a basic principle of Hindu ethics.

Purvapaksha - new moon to full moon period.

Pramanam, Epistemology - the process of gaining knowledge, sometimes used to express the goal as well as the means to attain knowledge, as in Apaurusheya Pramaanam.

R

Rajas - Raajasik individuals are filled with a desire and passion to undertake new projects and goad others into action. Many leaders exhibit a Raajasik temperament.

Raja Yoga - Raja Yoga, as outlined by Patanjali, describes eight "limbs" of spiritual practices, half of which might be classified as meditation. Underlying them is the assumption that a yogi should still the fluctuations of his or her mind: Yoga cittavrrti nirodha.

Ramayana - a Hindu epic in which Rama, avatar of Vishnu vanquishes Ravana and is reunited with his spouse Seetha.

Rig Veda - The earliest and the most prominent of the Vedas, the compositions of the Ancient Indics who we will refer to also as the Vedics,held to be sacred and termed Sruti by many Hindus, the chief characteristic was their oral tradition.

Roma people - The name that the Gypsies are known by in Europe, reflecting their large numbers in Romania.

S

Sampradaya - In Hinduism, a Sampradaya is a tradition encompassing a common philosophy but embracing many different schools, groups, or guru lineages (called parampara). By becoming initiated (diksha) into a parampara one automatically belongs to its proper sampradaya.

Sankaracharya - The great proponent of Advaita Vedanta. Bhagavatpada Acharya Sankara was a veritable institution masquerading as an individual. There is controversy over the date of his birth, ranging from 509 BCE to 788 CE.

Saankhya - Saamkhya is considered to be the oldest among the philosophical systems dating back to about 7c BC. Kapila, the author of 'Saamkhya Sutra", is considered to be the originator of this system. The "Saamkhya Karika" of Ishwarakrishna is the earliest available text on Saamkhya dating to about 3c AD. Saamkhya's name is derived from root word Saamkhya (enumeration) and is reflective than authoritative. Well-known commentaries are Gaudapada's bhasya, Vacaspati Misra's Tattwa-kaumudi, Vijnanabhiksu's Saamkhya-pravacanbhasya, and Mathara's Matharavrtti.

The Saamkhya system proposes the theory of evolution (prakriti-purusha) that is accepted by all other systems. The purusha (soul) of this system is unchanging and is a witness to the changes of prakriti. Hence the Saamkhya system is based on dualism wherein nature (prakriti) and conscious spirit (purusha) are separate entities not derived from one another. There can be many purushas since one man can attain enlightenment while the rest do not, whereas prakriti is one. It is identified with pure objectivity, phenomenal reality, which is non-conscious.

Prakriti possess three fundamental natures; (1) The pure and fine Sattva (2) the active Rajas and (3) the coarse and heavy Tamas. Sattva accounts for thought and intelligibility, experienced psychologically as pleasure, thinking, clarity, understanding and detachment. Rajas accounts for motion, energy and activity and it is experienced psychologically as suffering, craving and attachment. Tamas accounts for restraint and inertia. It is experienced psychologically as delusion, depression and dullness.

The conscious Purusha excites the unconscious Prakriti and in this process upsets the equilibrium of the various gunas. According to Saamkhya there are twenty-five tatvas which arise due to the union of purusha and prakriti. Their union is often described as the ride of a lame man with perfect sight (purusha) on the shoulders of a blind person of sure foot (prakriti). Their process of evolution is as given below and it accounts for the different tatvas. In Saamkhya creation is the development of the different effects from mulaprakriti and destruction their dissolution into mulaprakriti.

Saamkhya is essentially atheistic because it believes that the existence of god cannot be proved. Prakriti, the cause of evolution of world, does not evolve for itself but for Purusha-the ultimate consciousness. The self is immortal but due to ignorance (avidya) it confuses itself with the body, mind and senses. If avidya is replaced by vidya the self is free from suffering and this state of liberation is called kaivalya. Yoga is the practical side of Saamkhya.

Sanskrit, Samskrtam - Sanskrit (sañskṛtam).The adjective sañskṛtam-means "refined, consecrated, sanctified". The language referred to as sañskṛtam vak "the refined language" has by definition always been a 'high' language, used for religious and scientific discourse and contrasted with the languages spoken by the people.

Saptarishi - The Ursa Major constellation. The Saptarishi play a major role in Hindu astronomy. A number of yugas in Hindu philosophy, the cycle of creation is divided into four Yugas (ages.): Satya Yuga or Krita Yuga, Treta Yuga, Dwapara Yuga, Kali Yuga make a manvantara Each manvantara has a set of seven rishis who help in preserving order and propagating knowledge in that manavantra. Bharadwaja is one of the seven rishis of the Vaivasvata Manavantra. The other six rishis of the Vaivasvata manavantra are Atri, Vasistha, Jamadagni, Gauthama, Visvāmitra and Agastya. Atri is a legendary bard and scholar, and a son of Brahma. Jamadagni, is the father of Parashurama, one of the avatars of Vishnu. King Kaartaveerya Arjuna and his army visited Jamadagni, who fed his guest and the whole army with his divine cow; the king demanded the cow and Jamadagni refused because he needed the cow for his religious ceremonies. King Kaartaveerya Arjuna sent his soldiers to take the cow and Parashurama killed the entire army and the king with his axe (given to him by Shiva). In return, the princes beheaded Jamadagni. In revenge, Parashurama destroys large numbers of the Kshatriyas.

Brahmarishi Viswamitra is one of the seven venerated sages of Hindu mythology. He is a kshatriya (Warrior caste) by birth, but has transcended into the brahmin priestly caste with his tough penance.

Vasishta, in Hindu mythology was chief of the seven venerated sages (or Saptharishi) and the Rajaguru of the Solar Dynasty. He was famous for subduing the armies of Viswamitra. He had in his possession the divine cow Nandini who could grant anything to her owner.

Gauthama and Kashyapa: Kashyapa ("tortoise") is an ancient god (one of the rishis), father of the devas, asuras, nagas and all of humanity. He is married to Aditi, with whom he is the father of Agni and the Adityas. He received the spoils of Parashurama's conquest of King Kaartaveerya Arjuna.

Sapta Saindhava - Land of the seven rivers has been generally identified as Punjab by the modern scholars. Rulers of the western lands, the

Druhyus and the Anus, preserved the Rig Veda and helped the Puru Bharats in building a Dhaarmic empire.

Sattva - Individuals who are predominantly Sattvic are attached to happiness and to knowledge.

Satya - truthfulness in thought and speech.

Shaastra or Shastra or sastra - Shastra is a Sanskrit word used to denote education/knowledge in a general sense. The word is generally used as a suffix in the context of technical or specialised knowledge in a defined area of practice. For example, Astra shastra means, knowledge about "Handling of weapons", Astra means weapons, and Shastra is their knowledge.Extending this meaning, the shastra is commonly used to mean a treatise or text written in explanation of some idea, especially in matters involving religion. In Buddhism, a shastra is often a commentary written at a later date to explain an earlier scripture or sutra.In the Indonesian language, 'sastra' is a word meaning 'literature'.

Shabda pramaanam (Bhartrihari) See Bhartrihari

Shatapatha Brahmana

Shatapatha Brahmana Brahmana of one-hundred paths) - is one of the prose texts describing the Vedic ritual. It belongs to the vajasaneyi madhyandina shakha of the White Yajurveda. It survives in two recensions, Madhyandina and Kanva, with the former having the eponymous 100 brahmanas in 14 books, and the latter 104 brahmanas in 17 books. Linguistically, it belongs to the Brahmana period of Vedic Sanskrit, dated by Western Indologists to the first half of the 1st millennium BC. Hindu scholars have dated it to around 1800 BC, based on the reference in it of migration from the Sarasvati river area to east India, because the river is said to have dried up around 1900 BC. The 14 books of the Madhyandina recension can be divided into two major parts. The first 9 books have close textual commentaries, often line by line, of the first 18 books, of the corresponding Samhita of the Yajurveda. The following 5 books cover supplementary and ritualistically newer material, besides including the celebrated Brihataaranyaka Upanishad as most of the 14th and last book. The celebrated author of the Shatapatha brahmana is reputed to be Yajnyavalkya himself. He is also reputed to have made the observation that the the 95 year synchronization cycle provides an accurate measure of the repeatability of lunar phenomena. The Shatapatha Brahmana was translated into English by Prof. Julius Eggeling, in the late 19th century, in 5 volumes published as part of the *Sacred Books of the East series*. Retrieved from:

"http://en.wikipedia.org/wiki/Shatapatha_Brahmana"

Shakti,????? - the female energy principle, in the Indic tradition ,the primordial icon of strength and energy is associated with the feminine gender.

Shaanti - peace of mind attained through the disciplines of Raja Yoga.

Shaucha - cleanliness.

Sidereal Day - Nakshatra divas, a mean sidereal day is about 23h56m in length. Due to variations in the rotation rate of the Earth, however, the rate of an ideal sidereal clock deviates from any simple multiple of a

Sidereal Month - Sidereal month The actual period of the Moon's orbit as measured in a fixed frame of reference is known as a sidereal month, because it is the time it takes the Moon to return to the same position on the celestial sphere among the fixed stars (Latin: sidus): 27.321 661 days (27 d 7 h 43 min 11.5 s) or about 27 ? days. This type of month has appeared among cultures in the Middle East, India, and China in the following way: they divided the sky in 27 or 28 lunar mansions, characterized by asterisms (apparent groups of stars), one for each day that the Moon follows its track among the stars.

Sidereal Time - During the course of one day, the earth has moved a short distance along its orbit around the sun, and so must rotate a small extra angular distance before the sun reaches its highest point. The stars, however, are so far away that the earth's movement along its orbit makes a generally negligible difference to their apparent direction (see, however parallax), and so they return to their highest point in slightly less than 24 hours. A mean sidereal day is about 23h56m in length. Due to variations in the rotation rate of the Earth, however, the rate of an ideal sidereal clock deviates from any simple multiple of a civil clock.

Sidereal Year - In order for the earth to attain the same position with respect to a fixed star after one revolution, it takes a time span of 365 days 6 hours 9 minutes and some 9.5 seconds. This duration of time is called a sidereal year .The sidereal year is just over 20 minutes longer than the tropical year; this time difference is equivalent to 50.26 seconds of celestial longitude.Each year, the Vernal equinox will fall short by 50.26 seconds along the zodiac reckoned along the fixed stars.

Smrti - that which is remembered. There are a number of texts that are specifically classed as smrti and are mostly named after the name of the rshi expounded on the smrti such as Parashara smrti, Manu smrti and Yajnavalkya smrti.

Solar Day - Solar time is measured by the apparent diurnal motion of the sun, and local noon in solar time is defined as the moment when the sun is at its highest point in the sky (exactly due south in the northern hemisphere and due north in the southern hemisphere). The time taken for the sun to return to its highest point is exactly 24 hours, or a solar day.

Sramaña tradition - A srama? a is one who performs acts of mortification or austerity. According to the definition, a being is himself responsible for his own deeds. Salvation, therefore, can be achieved by anybody irrespective of caste, creed, color or culture. The cycle of rebirth to which every individual is subject is viewed as the cause and substratum of misery. The goal of every person is to evolve a way to escape from the cycle of rebirth, namely by discounting ritual as a means of an emancipation and establishing from the misery of Sañsara, through pious religious activities. The term has been used in the past as a synonym for the Baudhik tradition.

Srautasutras - Srauta is the adjectival form of Sruti (that which is heard)and is one of the 4 constituent sutras in the Kalpasutra (see also Sulvasutra).

Sravanam - Comes from the same root as shruti. Essentially means learning by listening. Sravanam, mananam, nididhyasanam is the 3 step process towards Brahma vidya and self realization. In reality it is the approach generally adopted to the study of most subjects especially those with complex concepts.

Sruti - that which is heard as opposed to that which is remembered (smrti). The smrtis were composed by famous rishis.

Sulvasutras - The Sulvasutras (or Sulbasutras) or aphorisms of the cord (measurements were made using a string stretched between 2 pegs). The resulting mathematical manipulations needed to solve the problems of finding areas and volumes of reasonably complex shapes formed the subject matter of the Sulvasutras. The Sulvasutras were part of the KalpaSutra appendices to the Veda. KalpaSutra consisted of Grhyasutras, Srautasutras, Dharmasuturas and Sulvasutras. The KalpaSutras in turn are part of the Vedanga (limbs of the Veda) comprising of Chandas (meter), Nirukta(etymology), Vyakarana Grammar, Jyotisha (Astronomy and astrology) and Kalpasutras. One set of such Sutras are the Kalpa Sutras which consisted of Srauta Sutras, Dharma Sutras, Grihya Sutras and Sulva Sutras. The Srauta Sutras give elaborate rules for the performance of Vedic sacrifices; the Grihya Sutras deal with domestic religious ceremonies; the Dharmasutras contain the rudiments of Hindu Law and the Sulva Sutras form the earliest source of Hindu Mathematics.

Suryaprajnapati - A Jaina astronomical treatise, which uses a 5 year lunisolar cycle. One of the great contributions of the Jainas to Astronomy and Mathematics in Ancient India. The Jaina tradition exhibited a very superior knowledge of the exact sciences when compared to similar civilizations of that period.

T

Tamas - Tamas is inertia born of ignorance. It enshrouds the discrimination of man and inclines him to indolence, sleep and renders him inert. By nature it is destructive.

Tithi/ Lunar Day - The area covered by the Moon in its transit away from the Sun, computed for the moment of its conjunction with Sun to its true longitude at the moment of the epoch. It is obtained by subtracting the Longitude of the Sun from the longitude of the Moon. A tithi is completed when the longitude of Moon gains exactly 12 degrees or its multiple on that of Sun and therefore there are 30 tithis in a lunar month. Is the root of the word atithi which means Guest in sanskritam (meaning one who may show up at any time or day but should be welcomed regardless.

http://en.wikipedia.org/wiki/Tithi

Titiksha (Sanskrit) - [from the verbal root tij to urge, incite to action, be active in endurance or patience].Patience, resignation, endurance; not mere passive resignation, but an active attitude of patience in supporting the events of life. Mystically, the fifth state of raja yoga - "one of supreme indifference; submission, if necessary, to what is called 'pleasures and pains for all,' but deriving neither pleasure nor pain from such submission - in short, 'the becoming physically, mentally, and morally indifferent and insensible to either pleasure or pain" (VS 93). The meaning however is not of a cold, heartless, impassive attitude towards the sufferings of others, but an active positive attitude, so far as one's individual pleasures or pains are considered, but likewise involving an active attitude of compassion for the tribulations and sufferings of others. The same thought is involved in the title Diamond-heart, given to adepts: as hard and indifferent to one's own sorrows as the diamond is hard and enduring, yet like the diamond reflecting in its facets as in mirrors the sufferings and sorrows of all around.

Also personified as a goddess, the wife of Dharma (divine law) and daughter of Daksha.

Tocharia - A people who lived in the Tarim basin of current day China, and who spoke a Indo European language.

U

Upanishads - Of the one hundred and eight extant Upanishads sixteen were recognized by Adi Sankara as authentic and authoritative. In his commentary on the Vedanta Aphorisms he included quotations from six. On the other ten he wrote elaborate commentaries. It is these ten which...have come to be regarded as the principal Upanishads: Isa, Kena, Katha, Prasna, Mundaka, Mandukya, Chandogya, Brhadaranyaka, Aitareya, and Taittiriya."

Urheimat - A postulate that the Proto Indo European people (another postulate) originally lived in a common homeland or Urheimat at some distant past. While this is a very beguiling assumption, there is absolutely no evidence in Archaeology of such a Urheimat. It is purely a hypothetical construct only of academic interest. See the translations of the passages from the Rg quoted in the section on AIT, in the context of the discussion on the debate of the origin of the Vedic people.

Uttarayana - The Sun's northward journey, as viewed from the earth) from winter solstice (shortest daylight hours) to summer solstice (the longest day in the calendar). Usually celebrated throughout India as Makara Sankranti and Pongal.

V

Vaisya - One who benefits humanity by his efforts and specialization in trade, commerce and agriculture. The commercial sector of society.

Varna asrama dharma - The system, namely Guna Varna Vyavastha, that produced the Varnashrama Dharma was conscious of the fact that this was the worlds early attempt at a meritocracy. That the sytem was eminently successful in its own way, I have no doubt because the resulting civilization flourished for well over 5 millennia, until its very foundations were attacked by barbarians from both within and without by Barbarians, whose notion of entertainment was to build a pyramid of skulls, in order to terrorize the local population to capitulate. The current system in place after the colonial power was done reinventing and reshaping it to its own specifications, and which goes by the name Caste, is so utterly different in all significant ways that we can safely say it has little to do with the Hindu faith or Hindu traditions such as the Guna Varna Vyavastha.

Vedanga Jyotisha (VJ) - the earliest codified texts of ancient India, and consists of the Rig Jyotisha,(RJ) the Atharva Jyotisha(AJ) and the Yajusa Jyotisha(YJ) . The RJ consists of 36 verses and the YJ consists of 44 verses and the authorship of these two is ascribed to Lagadha.

Vedic civilization - the civilization of the people who composed the Vedas and the vast literature of cosmic proportions associated with the SanAtana Dharma.

Vedics or the Vedic people - the people who composed the Vedas and their Universe of allies and adversaries.

Vedic Saraswati River - The Saraswati river is mentioned in several verses in the Rg at least 50 times as a river flowing from the mountains to the sea. Satellite data has shown evidence of a dried up river bed. Some examples of these quotations are given in the AIT page, *http://www.indicethos.org/AIT/*. All the AIT and their progeny ignore this significant fact. It is as if the relevance of the reference to the Saraswati is of no significance at all and if they do deign to acknowledge the reference to the Sarasvati they claim it is small stream in Afghanistan that never reaches the sea. Reminds one of Oliver Goldsmiths Village Schoolmaster, where even though vanquished he could argue still.

Vernal Equinox - see equinox.

Vikshepa, kshepa - Celestial latitude, the angle between the celestial equator and the position of the star, measured in the plane of the great circle. This angle is called the declination of the star and is measured in degrees, minutes, and seconds north or south of the celestial equator, analogous to latitude on the earth.

Vishnu - sustainer of the Universe, whose Avatars came down to earth from time to time to reestablish order in the universe. The Srimad Bhaagavatam is a chronicle of the avatars of Vishnu.

Visuva - spring equinox.

Visuvant - summer solstice.

Vishuvat - Equator.

Vivaaha - marriage ceremony.

Y

Yogasastra - The means to attain Moksha or Self Realization, a knowledge of Metaphysical aspects of the human consciousness.

Yuezhi - the Chinese name for the Kushans who invaded India.

Yuga - an era of the world.

Plate 23: The Author, Dr. Kosla Vepa *(facing pg. 196)*

About the Author

KOSLA VEPA Ph.D

Kosla Vepa is a member of the Global Indic Diaspora, originally a native of Andhra Pradesh state in India and has had the good fortune to have been brought up and have had his education in various parts of India including, Bihar, Maharashtra, and Karnataka. He matriculated from Andhra University in 1955. Among the schools which he has attended are St.Xaviers College, Bombay, Karnatak University, Indian Institute of Science, Bangalore, and the University Of Waterloo, Ontario, Canada. His highest degree is a PhD in the area of Engineering Mechanics. His professional and technical interests include successful research and development engineering experience in the Information technology, aero-engine and energy industries across the globe and an abiding interest in the history of the Mathematical sciences in antiquity.

Currently Dr. Vepa has significant interests in a wide variety of subjects including ontological principles in science and philosophy, Ancient Indian history, Vedas and Vedanta, Mathematical Sciences in India during antiquity, the growth and evolution of civilizations to name a few. His major activity is to further the aims and objectives of the Indic Studies Foundation, stated in the link below and to further the progress towards an accurate rendering of the narrative of the Story of the Civilization of the Indic peoples.

When he finds time he pursues his hobbies of photography and astronomy, Dr. Vepa resides in the San Francisco Bay Area.

Publications and Essays of General Interest

Indic Studies Foundation, *http://indicstudies.us/*

Book Astronomical Dating of Events & Select Vignettes from Indian history, *http://tinyurl.com/3wglhv*

The Societal Stockholm Syndrome

http://vepa.us/dir6/SSS1.htm

India and the Great Game

http://vepa.us/dir00/GreatGame.htm

Secularism and the Hindu

What's in a name (chapter 4 of this book)

Debate on the origin of the Vedics (appendix K of this book)

India and US Missile defense cited in *The Evolution of U.S.-Indian Ties: Missile Defense in an Emerging Strategic Relationship* Ashley Tellis, International Security - Volume 30, Number 4, Spring 2006, pp. 113-151.

Indo-US relations (circa 1999) (Appendix F of this book)

A prolegomena to A History of the Indic Civilization

Vedic Mathematicians in ancient India Part I

Vedic Mathematicians in ancient India Part II

Vedic Mathematicians in ancient India Part III

The South Asia File (monograph to be published)

Book *The Dhaarmik Traditions* (monograph to be published)

Book *Indology and Indologists* - a study of people and their motives

Ancient Indic contributions to the Exact Sciences - manuscript in preparation.

PhD Thesis

The Indic Mathematical tradition, The Hindu Renaissance, Vol.IV no. IV, pp 19-24, Paper presented at the HEC 2006 in Los Angeles, Ca, and Nov.2006.

Source Book (Anthology) of Mathematics and Astronomy from Indic Antiquity (under construction).

More at websites *www.indicstudies.us*, *www.vepa.us/dir00*, *www.kaushal42.blogspot.com*

Indic Studies Foundation

The Indic Studies Foundation, seeks to propagate a more accurate and rational approach to the study and dissemination of the Indian

Civilizational ethos in the world, particularly in the United States and India. While India regards herself as a Civilizational Power, the image that India evokes is far removed from that of the Indics as they see themselves.

Vision

We will be guided by the vision of an Indic Civilization that regains the relative stature that it had attained during the millennia between 5000 BCE and 1200 CE and establishes a more competitive posture as it scales new heights.

Indic Studies Foundation is committed to devising and executing plans that will focus awareness on the antiquity, diversity, intellectual vibrancy, the logical rigor and ontological scope of Indic civilization, the profound contributions it has made to many spheres of activity of humanity.

Comprehend the nature and breadth of adversarial theologies which seek to malign the Indic ethos, dispel lacunae and misconceptions in the understanding of Indic traditions in India and the Western hemisphere, as exemplified by the case of the California Text Book Misrepresentation of Ancient India in 2005/2006.

Explore the progress in realizing the unfulfilled promise and potential of this nation and its talented populace.

The Foundation will undertake a series of seminars annually with an exclusive focus on Indic history—to specifically research the distorted history, ,assess its consequences, and remedy the situation by facilitating impartial/professional research into Indic history, and in addition will conduct programs to correct the history in the academia, media and in public perception.

In furtherance of these goals we have

Delivered lectures and presentations on the following topics

The South Asia File

The Indic Mathematical Tradition

India's Contributions to the sciences during Antiquity

Organized a seminar on Distorted History, Causes, Consequences and Remedies

We are planning a series of seminars in India and the US on the distortions in Indian History and increase awareness of the need for an accurate history of India and the process by which we may arrive at the same. We have prepared educational materials and calendars for dissemination to schools in India and the US. The first of these seminars in India titled the International conference on Indian History, ICIH 2009 and will be held in Delhi on January 9-11, 2009 at the India International Centre in Delhi, India.

Index

D

J

M

S

T

U

Z